WALES

AND THE WARS OF THE ROSES

Engraving of Owen Glyndwr taken from his seal.

WALES
AND THE WARS OF THE ROSES

H.T. EVANS

WITH AN INTRODUCTION BY R.A. GRIFFITHS

ALAN SUTTON PUBLISHING LIMITED

First published in the United Kingdom in 1915
Cambridge University Press

First published in this edition in the United Kingdom in 1995
Alan Sutton Publishing Limited
Phoenix Mill · Far Thrupp · Stroud · Gloucestershire

British Library Cataloguing in Publication Data

Evans, H.T.
  Wales and the Wars of the Roses. – New ed
  I. Title
  924.04

ISBN 0-7509-0922-6

Typeset in 11/12pt Erhardt.
Typesetting and origination by
Alan Sutton Publishing Limited.
Printed in Great Britain by
Butler & Tanner, Frome, Somerset.

Contents

Preface to the First Edition

As its title suggests, the present volume is an attempt to examine the struggle between Lancaster and York from the standpoint of Wales and the Marches. Contemporary chroniclers give us vague and fragmentary reports of what happened there, though supplementary sources of information enable us to piece together a fairly consecutive and intelligible story.

From the first battle of St Albans to the accession of Edward IV, the centre of gravity of the military situation was in the Marches: Ludlow was the chief seat of the duke of York, and the vast Mortimer estates in mid-Wales his favourite recruiting ground. It was here that he experienced his first serious reverse – at Ludford Bridge; it was here, too, that his son Edward, earl of March, won his way to the throne – at Mortimer's Cross. Further, Henry Tudor landed at Milford Haven, and with a predominantly Welsh army defeated Richard III at Bosworth. For these reasons alone unique interest attaches to Wales and the Marches in this thirty years' war; and it is to be hoped that the investigation will throw some light on much that has hitherto remained obscure.

I have ventured to use contemporary Welsh poets as authorities; this has made it necessary to include a chapter on their value as historical evidence. It was thought necessary, also, to give some account of the state of things in Wales during the first half of the fifteenth century, and of the part played by Welshmen in the last phases of the Hundred Years War with France.

I am deeply indebted to Prof. J.E. Lloyd, MA, of Bangor University, for revising the proofs and for much salutary criticism; and to Mr J. Alban Morris of Cardiff for placing at my disposal his transcript of the manuscript *History of Wales*, by Ellis Griffith, in the Mostyn Library.

H.T.E.
10 January 1915

Acknowledgements

H.T. Evans's text has been reproduced as originally published. Welsh place names and personal names are retained in the form the author used.

The publishers wish to record their appreciation of the cooperation of Mr Leslie Evans of Cardiff in this new edition of his father's book; and to Geoffrey Wheeler for his work on the illustrations.

Introduction

Rarely does a monograph written by a grammar-school teacher retain substantial value for historians eighty years after its publication. Yet that is the fate of H.T. Evans's *Wales and the Wars of the Roses*, which first appeared in 1915. This is a tribute to the author and to the importance of his subject.

Howell Thomas Evans was born in 1877 into a working-class industrial community on the fringes of Swansea. As a callow youth of nineteen, he went to the new university college at Aberystwyth, which was not much older than Evans himself, and spent four years studying the arts there.[1] Within a few months of securing his University of Wales degree in 1900, he successfully completed examinations for an external degree in history from the University of London. Of his teachers, it appears to have been Edward Edwards, the younger brother of the distinguished historian, man of letters and educationalist, O.M. Edwards, who decisively encouraged Evans's intellectual development, especially towards the study of history. Edward Edwards, securely embedded in Aberystwyth as professor of history from 1895 until 1930, was an inspiring teacher, though otherwise of negligible academic accomplishments.[2] He probably eased Evans's path to his own college, St John's, Cambridge, in 1902, and for two years the young Welshman was supervised by the eminent historian and constitutional authority, J.R. Tanner. Evans's studies at Aberystwyth, his abiding interest in his own country, and Tanner's expert tuition resulted in a MA thesis on the subject of Wales during the age of the Wars of the Roses.

A post as schoolmaster at Cardiff Intermediate School for Boys (later Cardiff High School) (1905–17) placed him within reach of Cardiff's Free Library, which in 1895 had acquired much of the Celtic library of the noted bibliophile, Sir Thomas Phillipps; there, too, Evans was able to consort with Welsh literary scholars and historians from the local university college, among them Ernest Hughes, subsequently the first professor of history at the University College of Swansea. This lively intellectual environment stimulated Evans to complete a number of history books and articles and, in 1909, a prize-winning essay entitled 'Welshmen in the Wars of the Roses' for the National Eisteddfod held in London. In the following year he travelled to London again (and, he noted in his diary, 'saw an airship on the journey') to address the Cymmrodorion Society on the subject of 'William Herbert, Earl of Pembroke', one of Edward IV's closest and staunchest supporters in England and Wales during the king's first reign.[3] At last, in 1915, Cambridge University Press published Evans's most scholarly work, *Wales and the Wars of the Roses*, which has remained for three-quarters of a century the only comprehensive study of its subject.

The book provided a solid foundation for a reassessment of Wales's history between Owain Glyndŵr's rebellion and the accession of Henry Tudor, and of the part which Wales played in wider developments. Although mainly a political and military history, one of its most significant virtues was that it recognized the value of the mass of contemporary Welsh poetry as an historical source (see ch. 1), and Evans's own researches coincided with a revival of interest in the fifteenth-century poets, several of whose *œuvres* had recently been published. Indeed, Evans himself had earlier written another prize-winning essay for the 1910 National Eisteddfod on probably the most notable of these poets, 'A critical examination of the works of Lewis Glyn Cothi'. His book also referred more than once to the chronicle – still unpublished today – written by 'the soldier of Calais', Elis Gruffudd (died 1552), who incorporated information and tradition from English, French and Welsh sources, as well as from his own experience.[4]

The career and antecedents of Sir Rhys ap Thomas were correctly regarded by Evans as central to any assessment of the Wars of the Roses, especially but not exclusively in south and west Wales. Until Evans wrote, the seventeenth-century 'Life of Sir Rhys,' penned by his descendant, Henry Rice (died *c.* 1651), and amounting to a history of this most prominent family of the fifteenth and early sixteenth centuries, was generally accepted as an account reliable in all particulars: of the rise of the family in Carmarthenshire, its role in the civil wars, and Sir Rhys's part in Henry Tudor's march to victory at Bosworth Field and in the successes – especially military successes – of the reign that followed. When the 'Life' became widely known after its publication in 1796, it appeared to support the common view that Welshmen had yearned for Henry Tudor's return and that the battle of Bosworth was a Welsh triumph. Indeed, it offered stirring material with which to reinforce the tradition of Welsh approval of the Tudor monarchs, and to extend this approval to their Hanoverian and Victorian successors.[5] Sir Rhys's reputation accordingly blossomed during the nineteenth century. Even the great archivist and biographer of Richard III and Henry VII, James Gairdner (1828–1912), enthused about its historical value. The sounder and less imaginative researches of H.T. Evans poured cold water on much of this. He made pertinent comments on the 'Life', yet the severity of his judgments had the effect of deterring practically all twentieth-century historians from using this fascinating and major source. Whereas he rightly noted that it had been 'the favourite resort of generations of less responsible writers' than Gairdner, his austere criticisms were not entirely warranted: 'a vein of unreality runs through the whole biography and its details cannot stand the limelight of historical criticism'; and 'there is so much deliberate fabrication in that document that it would be dangerous to place any reliance whatever upon it.'[6] The result was that the 'Life' remained inaccessible, let alone edited, until 1993, and students of the fifteenth century were uncertain of the amount of confidence to be placed in its stories, assertions and assessments.[7]

During the past thirty years, serious efforts have resumed to advance our understanding of Wales during the fifteenth century and its place in the era of civil war. The principality shires of the west and north that were the patrimony of the kings of England (and, from time to time, of their eldest sons as princes of Wales) have attracted attention in their governmental, political and social aspects.[8] Several of the marcher lordships have been studied, most notably Glamorgan, Gower, Newport, Ruthin, and the estates (mostly in the south-east) of the Stafford dukes of Buckingham, and of Jasper Tudor, earl of Pembroke and lord of even wider Welsh and English estates during an eventful career.[9] Attention has also been drawn to Edward IV's policies towards the government of a principality that retained strong Lancastrian loyalties after Edward IV's accession in 1461, and of a Welsh march that was divided in its allegiance.[10] The fortunes of a few outstanding families of knights and esquires in fifteenth-century Wales have been chronicled, including their often critical role in the dynastic struggles in both England and Wales: as examples, from southern Wales, the Herberts of Raglan, the Perrots of Pembrokeshire, and the family of Gruffydd ap Nicholas, grandfather of Sir Rhys ap Thomas.[11] Each of these themes was identified by H.T. Evans.

Evans also appreciated the consequences of Glyndŵr's uprising and the ways in which it affected royal and aristocratic attitudes to Wales in the decades that followed (ch. 2). His discussion of 'Wales and the French Wars' (ch. 3), which had 'not hitherto received even a cursory examnination', suggests that he was aware of the impact of the military disasters in France on the Lancastrian monarchy at home. Indeed, J.E. Lloyd, Wales's foremost historian of the Middle Ages, judged the book's pages on Matthew Gough, the Welsh soldier who played a leading part in resisting John Cade's rebellion in London in 1450, to be among its most interesting and novel. And Evans took the careers of the earlier Tudors – Edmund, earl of Richmond, and Jasper, earl of Pembroke, and their father Owen – beyond the romantic tales of poets and Victorian writers and placed them securely in the political context of the Lancastrian and Yorkist age.

Some of these themes have of course been developed since Evans's day; others have not. Relatively little progress has been made in evaluating contemporary Welsh poetry as a source for social and political attitudes in Wales and towards kings and lords outside it, while Elis Gruffudd's chronicle remains unedited, unpublished and little studied.[12] For all the attention that has been lavished on Henry Tudor's antecedents and forebears, and the chords they struck among Welsh people before and after 1485, there has been no over-arching study made of Welsh society during the fifteenth century. And few of the major studies of the civil wars assigned more than a minor role to events and developments in Wales – rather, a castle besieged here or a battle fought there, a recalcitrant tenantry slow to pay its dues to an English lord like Richard, duke of York (died 1460), or an English magnate like Richard, duke of Gloucester, cutting his teeth in Welsh government before mounting to greater things.[13] *Wales and the Wars of the Roses* is still the only coherent narrative of events.

An anonymous reviewer of the book in the *Times Literary Review* commented in 1915 that 'No student of the Wars of the Roses would be able to neglect it, for the

Welsh aspect of the wars had been unjustifiably neglected hitherto by our historians'. This verdict received an echo nine years later in the striking phrases of G.M. Trevelyan: 'The Wars of the Roses were to a large extent a quarrel between Welsh Marcher Lords, who were also great English nobles, closely related to the English throne'.[14] More than fifty years after its publication, as forthright a critic as S.B. Chrimes could still acknowledge the importance of Evans's book and regret that it had long ceased to be available in print.

H.T. Evans was a significant figure in the academic and popular intellectual renaissance in turn-of-the-century Wales. He was a prolific writer, especially of textbooks for the young people of Wales who had been given an opportunity to study the history of their own country following the reform of the school syllabus in the first decade of the twentieth century. No less compelling was his conviction that the history of Britain would be more accurately understood if Wales and Welsh people were assigned their due place in it. In this he was regarded at the time as something of a pioneer – two generations before those who now claim to have founded 'the new British history'. In response to criticisms of one of his earlier – and popular – books, *A History of England and Wales, 1485–1910*, Evans wrote:

> It is a commonplace that in current histories of England, Wales is a blank except perhaps for a passing reference to the death of Llywelyn the Great and a somewhat more elaborate digression on the end of Welsh independence, or for a notice of questionable accuracy and unquestionable hostility to Owen Glyndwr, who not infrequently is described as a ruthless robber who stole the lands of Lord Grey of Ruthin and refused to give them back! (*Western Mail*, 20 December 1910)

Despite assuming the heavier duties of headmaster of Aberaeron County School in Cardiganshire in 1917 (a post he held until his retirement in 1944), H.T. Evans continued to write school textbooks and radio scripts on the history of Wales and its place in British developments. And when *The Dictionary of Welsh Biography* was planned by his old patron, J.E. (now Sir John) Lloyd, and his successor as history teacher at Cardiff Intermediate School, Professor R.T. Jenkins, no one was more appropriate than H.T. Evans to contribute authoritative articles on Matthew Gough, William Herbert, earl of Pembroke, his son, the second earl, and on Dafydd ab Ifan ab Einion, the defender of Harlech Castle, the last Lancastrian outpost to fall to the Yorkists (1468). H.T. Evans died in 1950, before *The Dictionary* was published. *Wales and the Wars of the Roses* was his greatest scholarly achievement and it is an enduring one that deserves to be reissued.

Ralph A. Griffiths
University of Wales, Swansea

Notes

1 Leslie Evans, *Portrait of a Pioneer* (Llandybïe, Dyfed, 1982), is an engaging biography of H.T. Evans by one of his sons. A number of details in the Introduction are taken from it.

2 E.I. Ellis, *The University College of Wales, Aberystwyth, 1872–1972* (Cardiff, 1972), pp. 129, 233.

3 Subsequently published in *Transactions of the Honourable Society of Cymmrodorion*, 1909–10.

4 Attention had been drawn to the chronicle, now in two parts, National Library of Wales MS.

5276 and, the latter part, NLW, Mostyn MS. 158, in *Historical Manuscripts Commission: Reports on Manuscripts in the Welsh Language* (London, 1898–1900); *Dictionary of Welsh Biography to 1940* (London, 1959), p. 319. For the poetry available in 1915, see I. Williams (ed.), *Casgliad o Waith Ieuan Deulwyn* (Bangor, 1909); J.C. Morrice (ed.), *Gwaith Hywel Swrdwal a'i Fab Ieuan* (Bangor, 1908); and G. Mechain and I. Tegid (eds), *Gwaith Lewys Glyn Cothi* (2 vols, Oxford, 1837), with an English transalation ed. J. Jones and W. Davies, *The Poetical Works of Lewis Glyn Cothi* (2 vols. in 1, Oxford, 1837).

5 John Davies, 'Victoria and Victorian Wales', in G.H. Jenkins and J.B. Smith (eds), *Politics and Society in Wales, 1840–1922* (Cardiff, 1988), pp. 13ff.

6 Below pp. 6, 129; and cf. pp. 12–14, 23, 93, 220 n.1. The 'Life' first appeared in *The Cambrian Register*, I (1796), 49–144.

7 R.A. Griffiths, *Sir Rhys ap Thomas and his Family: A Study in the Wars of the Roses and Early Tudor Politics* (Cardiff, 1993), with a new edition of the 'Life' on pp. 133–293.

8 Idem, 'Royal Government in the Southern Counties of the Principality of Wales, 1422–1485' (unpublished University of Bristol PhD thesis, 1962); idem, *The Principality of Wales in the Later Middle Ages*, Vol. I: *South Wales, 1277–1536* (Cardiff, 1971); A.D. Carr, *Medieval Anglesey* (Llangefni, 1982).

9 T.B. Pugh (ed.), *The Glamorgan County History*, Vol. III: *The Middle Ages* (Cardiff, 1971 (for Glamorgan and Gower)) idem, *The Marcher Lordships of South Wales, 1415–1536* (Cardiff, 1963) (the Stafford lordships); A.C. Reeves, *Newport Lordship, 1317–1536* (Ann Arbor, Michigan, 1979); R.I. Jack, 'The Lords Grey of Ruthin, 1325–1490: A Study in the Lesser Baronage' (unpublished University of London PhD thesis, 1961); C. Rawcliffe, *The Staffords, Earls of Stafford and Dukes of Buckingham, 1394–1521* (Cambridge, 1978); R.S. Thomas, 'The Political Career, Estates and "Connection" of Jasper Tudor, Earl of Pembroke and Duke of Bedford (d. 1495)' (unpublished University of Wales PhD thesis, 1971).

10 D.E. Lowe, 'The Council of the Prince of Wales and the Decline of the Herbert Family during the Reign of Edward IV', *Bulletin of the Board of Celtic Studies*, XXVII (1977–8), 278–96; idem, 'Patronage and Politics: Edward IV, the Wydevilles and the Council of the Prince of Wales, 1471–83', ibid., XXIX (1980–2), 545–73; and, in general, R.A. Griffiths, 'Wales and the Marches', in S.B. Chrimes, C.D. Ross and R.A. Griffiths (eds), *Fifteenth Century England, 1399–1509* (Manchester, 1972; 2nd edn, Stroud, 1995), pp. 145–72, reprinted in R.A. Griffiths, *King and Country: England and Wales in the Fifteenth Century* (London, 1991), ch. 4.

11 D.H. Thomas, 'The Herberts of Raglan as Supporters of the House of York in the second half of the Fifteenth Century' (unpublished University of Wales MA thesis, 1968); G.H.R. Kent, 'The Estates of the Herbert Family in the Mid-Fifteenth Century' (unpublished University of Keele PhD thesis, 1973); R.K. Turvey, 'The Perrot Family and their Circle in South-west Wales in the Later Middle Ages' (unpublished University of Wales PhD thesis, 1988); J.M. Lloyd, 'The Rise and Fall of the House of Dinefwr (the Rhys Family), 1430–1530' (unpublished University of Wales MA thesis, 1963); Griffiths, *Sir Rhys ap Thomas*.

12 The surviving *œuvres* of most major poets of the fifteenth century have been published: see Glanmor Williams, *Recovery, Reorientation and Reform: Wales, c. 1415–1642* (Oxford, 1987), pp. 492–5. For the relatively sparse historical commentary, see A.O.H. Jarman and G.R. Hughes (eds), *A Guide to Welsh Literature*, Vol. 2 (Swansea, 1979); Pugh, *Glamorgan County History*, III, ch.X; E.D. Jones, *Beirdd y Bymthegfed Ganrif a'u Cefndir* (Aberystwyth, 1982); E. Roberts, *Dafydd ap Gwilym o Fathafarn* (Caernarfon, 1981); and works noted in Williams, *Wales, c. 1415–1642*, pp. 508–11. On Elis Gruffudd see Thomas Jones, 'A Welsh Chronicler in Tudor England', *Welsh History Review*, I (1960), 1–17; P.T.J. Morgan, 'Elis Gruffudd of Gronant – Tudor Chronicler Extraordinary', *Flintshire Historical Society Journal*, XXV (1971–2), 9–20.

13 For example, C.D. Ross, *Edward IV* (London, 1974), and *Richard III* (London, 1981); A.E. Goodman, *The Wars of the Roses* (London, 1981); P.A. Johnson, *Duke Richard of York, 1411–1460* (Oxford, 1988); Rosemary Horrox, *Richard III: A Study of Service* (Cambridge, 1989).

14 G.M. Trevelyan, *History of England* (3rd edn, London, 1945), p. 259.

Wales and the Marches, c. 1455.

CHAPTER ONE

The Historical Value of Contemporary Welsh Literature

In the course of the present narrative, an endeavour will be made to show that Wales and the border counties exercised a more formidable and decisive influence than is generally believed upon the course of the struggle between Lancaster and York. The history of the period has been thickly overgrown with the moss of tradition, romance, and myth, most of which accumulated during the sixteenth and seventeenth centuries. A great deal of the fiction was clearly invented to inflate family pride; some was due to a literal interpretation of purely rhetorical passages in the panegyrics of the poets. It is needless to say that such material, except what can be shown to have a foundation of truth, or at least of strong probability, is worthless as historical evidence. Yet, it has held sway for many centuries, and has given rise to considerable confusion. It will be essential to our purpose to rely exclusively upon original documents and contemporary sources of information. Among these will be included certain Welsh records which have been hitherto, and are still to a large extent, unexplored fields of historical research. The greater part of this material is in manuscript, scattered broadcast in public and private libraries. Some of it is already in print, but in many different publications, and consequently most inaccessible to the average student.

In so far as events were recorded at all in Wales during the second half of the fifteenth century, that function was performed by the poets. Their chief interest, admittedly, is literary and linguistic. Nevertheless, the student of history may reasonably inquire what may be their title to credence, what reliance can be placed upon them, and with what abatements their presentation of persons and events should be accepted as truth.

Let it at once be granted that these men did not profess to write down facts, dry and ungarnished. History would have gained much, and literature lost little, if the bards, instead of writing historical poems, had recorded their information in the form of annals or chronicles. But they were primarily poets, not chroniclers. As poets, they necessarily employ the artifices of their craft. They exaggerate; they invent; they draw upon their armoury of rhetoric. They colour, and frequently distort, facts to suit the exigencies of the occasion, and in the interests of those whose patronage they solicited. Their information is often garbled.

Further, those portions of their writings which have any value for the historian are not poems descriptive of events and actions. They are odes and elegies for the glorification of individuals, and only incidentally admit descriptive narrative. The fabrications of rhetoric, therefore, are not absent. There is little minuteness of detail; rarely any chronology or geography. Genealogies are plentiful, but of family rather than of general interest. There is an amplitude of vague, hazy allusions, which were doubtless perfectly intelligible to that generation; to us they are shades of a vanished past.

Lastly, they are prejudiced, especially against the Saxon. Many of their poems were written under the sting of humiliation, when the wounds of defeat were still open and sore. Invective not infrequently descends to vilification. In this respect the poetry of the period cannot be paralleled at any epoch in the history of the literature of Wales.

This feature in the poets, however, has its value for the historian; for it reveals the deep chasm which separated the two nations. Its most outspoken exponent was Lewis Glyn Cothi, who could rarely hide his invincible repugnance to the name of Saxon. It detracts considerably from the historical value of his testimony that he was himself a victim of persecution at the hands of English residents in Wales. He tells us that, having made preparations for taking up his abode in Chester, he was unceremoniously expelled from the city, and his belongings looted by the inhabitants. His fiercest attacks were delivered when his feelings were thus embittered by personal affront, or by such a national disaster as that at Edgecote. The same applies, though in a lesser degree, to the lambent sarcasm of Guto'r Glyn. He had occasion to journey through many parts of England, visiting among other places Warwick, Stafford and Coventry. When he reached the north of England, he experienced a very hostile disposition towards his language and country. However, his weapons are not poisoned, though his threats are generally well directed.

These two are not the only poets that bear witness to the estrangement between the nations. Ieuan Deulwyn, smarting beneath the exclusion of his countrymen from civil rights, implores Sir Richard Herbert 'to lock the door of privilege against the Saxon'.

Chwi a ellwch â'ch allwydd
Roi clo ar sais rhag cael swydd.

Dafydd Llwyd appeals to Jasper Tudor to bring to an end the days of official intolerance, and warns his countrymen against 'putting their faith in the signet of the Saxon'. But we are not surprised to find such bitterness in the poet when we know that he was the friend of Griffith Vaughan, who was brutally murdered by

Lord Grey of Powys in 1447. Some of Tudur Penllyn's lines are equally acrid, and were also largely the outcome of personal injury. The poets' invective was thus sharpened on a whetstone of disappointment, injustice, oppression, and cruelty; their anger burned fiercely; yet the dregs of passion are of little value, for serious history cannot be built on diatribes.

Whatever pretensions to historical verity these poets may have must rest mainly on their close acquaintanceship with some of the chief politicians of the day. This enabled them to obtain information at first hand from the actors themselves. This is the most that can be said on behalf of chroniclers in general, few of whom were actual eye-witnesses of the events they describe. The majority can claim no more than that they were contemporary. The Welsh poet, on the other hand, was a welcome guest at the homes of the gentry, whom he visited at regular intervals.

Lewis Glyn Cothi's home was situated in the valley of the Cothi, in Carmarthenshire. Close by lay Newton, the home of his patron, Griffith ap Nicholas, who dominated West Wales in the middle of the century. He was intimate with the Herberts of Raglan, and with the Vaughans of Bredwardine and Tretower. At times we catch glimpses of him in Chester, Flint, and Anglesey. His list of patrons, in fact, includes every contemporary Welshman of note. Ieuan Deulwyn, another Carmarthenshire poet, was a native of Kidwelly. He also dedicated several odes to the Herberts. Guto'r Glyn came from the neighbourhood of Llangollen, in the valley of the Dee. He was as ubiquitous as Lewis Glyn Cothi, and not less in demand as a household bard. Dafydd Llwyd and Tudur Penllyn lived in Merionethshire, on terms of friendship with the garrison at Harlech. There are strong grounds for the belief that Robin Ddu, the swarthy bard of Anglesey, met Owen Tudor when the latter withdrew to Wales after his escape from Newgate.

It is to be observed, moreover, that the poets may have obtained access to the chief English politicians. Humphrey, duke of Gloucester, as earl of Pembroke, and for many years chief justice either of North Wales or of the South, had occasion to pay several visits to the country. He was an ardent patron of letters. But though there appears to be no evidence in his voluminous correspondence with men of letters that he ever came into close touch with Welsh literary circles, Lewis Glyn Cothi alludes to him in terms of sympathy and admiration. The early promotion of Reginald Pecock, apparently a native of West Wales, was due to the influence and patronage of Humphrey. Griffith ap Nicholas, the patron and neighbour of Lewis Glyn Cothi, together with a large number of other Welshmen, was in the duke's retinue when he appeared at the parliament of Bury in 1447.

In their writings these poets show abundant traces that they were alive to the march of events. It was an essential part of their business to get information, and turn it to account. It is impossible to avoid the conviction that Lewis Glyn Cothi derived the raw material for his vivid description of the battle of Edgecote directly from some of the Herberts or the Vaughans, or their associates in that murderous fight. In his ode to Thomas ap Roger, who was among the slain, it is not difficult to discern what is intrinsically improbable, or what is palpably the product of the poet's imagination. When the poet asserts that the greatest carnage on that day took place under his hero's standard, we are inclined to ascribe it to a natural

Humphrey, duke of Gloucester, from a sixteenth-century drawing, possibly based on a work of c. 1424, in the Bibliothèque d'Arras.

anxiety to magnify and applaud. Even the professed historian cannot always avoid the artifices of eloquence; and fifteenth-century chroniclers are rarely impartial. But in this ode there are undoubted germs of truth. A basis of fact underlies the amplifications and excesses of rhetoric. The statements that part of the Welsh army cut its way through the ranks of the northerners, that Thomas ap Roger fought against desperate odds with a broken lance, that the combatants amid the clash and clangour of battle shouted, some for Edward, others for king Harry, some for Herbert, others for Warwick, have a note of probability and truth. Facts are hard to hide; fabrication is not always easy. It is not strange, therefore, that the above description is in many ways substantiated by Hall, the Tudor chronicler. Guto'r Glyn's realistic version of the campaign against Harlech Castle by the Herberts in 1468 is also a valuable piece of historical evidence which it would be fastidious to ignore. Briefly, and divested of its trappings, it amounts to this. One division of the attacking army advanced along the coast of North Wales, leaving a trail of devastation and ruin; another advanced from the south; Harlech offered but a feeble resistance – 'By a Herbert it could be obtained for the asking'; and the army numbered about nine thousand, an estimate which, as we shall see, is corroborated by Hall, and roughly by the Issue Rolls.

It has always been assumed that William Herbert, earl of Pembroke, was a steady Yorkist. Lewis Glyn Cothi implies the contrary, and further research has proved conclusively that he was correct. The editor of the only edition of the poet failed to appreciate this fact, and consequently became enmeshed in a tangle of contradictions. The same poet observes that the sons of Griffith ap Nicholas were on the side of Lancaster, and William of Worcester agrees with him. We must therefore dismiss as worthless the idle story of the family biographer in the *Cambrian Register*, though that document has been credited by so distinguished an authority as James Gairdner, and has been the favourite resort of generations of less responsible writers.

One important function of the fifteenth-century Welsh poet should not be overlooked. He was an instrument in the hands of the leader of the moment to advertise prospective political movements, sometimes openly, at other times in enigma.

Prophecies there are in plenty, the pardonable effervescence of a seething nationalism. But it would be a mistake to regard these futurist proclamations as the forecasts of partisans, destitute of foundation, and unwarranted in fact. In one of his poems Lewis Glyn Cothi, apprehensive for the cause of Margaret and her son Edward, alludes to Jasper Tudor's search for assistance in France and Brittany, his forthcoming return to Wales by sea, and his probable landing at Milford Haven about the Feast of St John. No date is given; but the facts coincide with the movements of Jasper Tudor during the few months which immediately preceded the battle of Mortimer's Cross. For Jasper actually obtained help abroad; he came by sea; the battle took place in the first week in February. Now the Feast of St John the Evangelist would be 27 December, and the few intervening weeks would enable Jasper to gather his forces and reach Mortimer's Cross, in Herefordshire, by February.

Similarly, there are copious references to the prospective invasion of Henry of Richmond in 1485, which we cannot entirely ignore as vague and unreliable prophecy. It is a curious coincidence that the cherished belief of the medieval Welsh sage, that a Welshman would one day ascend the throne of Britain, found its fulfilment in the person of Henry Tudor.

It has been said – and this is the prevailing modern view – that 'during the civil war there was but one rose, the white rose of York, there was no Lancastrian rose: the red rose of the House of Tudor first appeared on Bosworth Field.' This may be true of England; it is not true of Wales. The red rose of the Tudors had appeared in Wales long before it blossomed in splendour on Bosworth field. From the very beginning of the war the Tudors made Wales their special sphere of action. Edmund, earl of Richmond, came here early in 1456, and made Pembroke and Tenby his headquarters. On his death the same year, his place was taken by his brother Jasper, earl of Pembroke. From then till 1485 the history of the war in Wales is largely a record of the movements and the schemes, the failures and the successes of Jasper.

It is not surprising, therefore, that contemporary Welsh literature should contain frequent allusions to the family device. One or two instances shall suffice. In an ode to Owen Tudor, written soon after the battle of Mortimer's Cross, Robin Ddu, the Anglesey poet, while bewailing his hero's death, transfers his hopes to Jasper, and prophesies 'the victory of the red dragon over the dishonoured white'.

> Draig wen ddibarch yn gwarchae
> A draig goch a dyr y cae.

Although in this couplet the play between 'red' and 'white' is unmistakable, the 'dragon' as a substitute for 'rose ' may not seem convincing. However, the same poet in a poem written during the exile of the Tudors, looks forward hopefully to the time when 'red roses will rule in splendour':

> Rhos cochion mewn rhwysg uchel.

Guto'r Glyn, in an ode to Roger Kynaston, composed shortly after the return of Edward IV, plays upon the conflict between a 'rose of silver' and 'a rose of gold'. The rose is also a favourite emblem with Dafydd Llwyd, a warm associate of Jasper. The white rose of York, too, had its adherents. Lewis Glyn Cothi, exultant in praise of Sir William Herbert's prowess in the north of England, describes how 'he triumphed with white roses':

> A oresgynodd â'i ros gwynion.

But as the white rose is acknowledged to have been a device of the Yorkists, it is unnecessary to enlarge on this point.

The poets, moreover, were not ill-informed on events in France, in which hosts of Welshmen took an active share; but their information is largely of local interest only. How they obtained their knowledge is not altogether a matter of conjecture. A constant stream of warriors passed to and fro between the two countries. Scores of French prisoners were at various times lodged in the royal castles of North Wales. On the conclusion of the war, although a few like John

Edward, who had married a French wife, became subjects of the king of France, the majority returned to their native land with tales of plunder and adventure.

Guto'r Glyn voices the consternation with which the news of Mathew Gough's capture was received in Wales, and urges the collection of a ransom to redeem him. Lewis Glyn Cothi hints at the same warrior's exploit at the battle of Formigny in 1450, when, at the head of his men, he cut his way through the French lines to safety; and we see no reason to reject the same writer's statement that Gough's life on that occasion was saved by Gwilym Gwent. His death on London Bridge, while endeavouring to save the city from Cade's rebels, sent the nation into mourning, a fact which is curiously corroborated by William of Worcester in a quaint Latin couplet.[1]

Crowned Tudor Rose symbol of Henry VII.

The Anglesey poet already referred to appears to be our earliest authority for the romance of Owen Tudor and Catherine, the widowed queen of Henry V. Robin Ddu was in close touch with the Tudors and the chief families of North Wales. It is possible, probable even, that he got his information from Owen Tudor himself. The version in Stowe, which is the one generally accepted, is substantially the same, but of a later date.

Enough has now been said to show at least that these writers cannot altogether be ignored by the student of the history of the latter half of the fifteenth century. But after all, the supreme importance of the poets lies in another direction. It is not theirs to record facts. It is theirs to give expression to the debates and the promptings of the nation's soul. And if we are to seek in them an accurate interpretation of popular feeling, the dynastic question as such had no meaning in Wales. Not one of them holds a brief to buttress either Lancaster or York. They sing the glory of a Tudor or a Herbert according as each rises to eminence, and bids fair to become a national leader. Nor can it be said that they exposed themselves to a charge of apostasy if their panegyrics thus alternated between the one and the other. They were consistent in their nationalism. To them Herbert and Tudor were nationalists, not party leaders. Lewis Glyn Cothi saw in Edward IV a descendant of Gwladys the Dark, daughter of Llewelyn the Great; and he appeals to him, 'a royal Welshman', to rid them of oppression, and ameliorate the condition of the peasant. Similarly, Henry of Richmond found enthusiastic support in Wales not because he represented the claims of Lancaster, but because he was the grandson of Owen Tudor.

No leader of dazzling pre-eminence had arisen in Wales since Owen Glyndwr. 'Those who are awake know that Wales has long since fallen into a deep sleep, and awaits an embraving champion.'

Cysgu 'roedd Cymru medd sawl a'i gwyl
Yn hir heb flaenawr fau ragorawl.

These are the words of Lewis Glyn Cothi who knew the nation's pulse better than any of his contemporaries. The wars of Owen Glyndwr had left the country bruised, and shackled by an oppressive penal code. The people were restive, and in the second half of the century became animated by a profound, sustained passion to rid themselves of the incubus of alien officials. They were no longer inspired by false hopes of an independent nationality. That ideal had perished. Yet Wales a nation was as virile a principle as in the days of the last Llywelyn; and to advocate it was the touchstone of true worth in her leaders. The poets tuned their harps to blazon the nation's name, and to proclaim the chieftain best fitted to deliver them from bondage.

The first of such men was Griffith ap Nicholas. He died about the time that Jasper Tudor came to Wales. In Jasper the poet saw two important qualifications for leadership: he was related by birth to the reigning sovereign, Henry VI; and he was the son of Owen Tudor. Accordingly, all were urged to unite beneath his standard. Not in vain; a fact which is forcibly exemplified by the campaign of Ludford. When Jasper's cause waned, the mantle of leadership was transferred to William Herbert, whose star rose rapidly above the horizon after the battle of Mortimer's Cross. After the death of Herbert at Edgecote in 1469, the poets centre their hopes once more in Jasper and his young nephew, Henry of Richmond.

In some poems the prospective saviour of his country is designated 'Owen the Deliverer'. That this belief in 'Owen' was not a delusion finds curious illustration in the Welsh Tudor chronicler, Ellis Griffith, whose 'History of Wales' is still in manuscript only in the library of Lord Mostyn. For the general history of the period under consideration this history must be consulted with caution. In many respects it is worthless. The following story, however, is interesting and suggestive.

King Henry VI.

William ap Griffith was a chieftain of North Wales. Deeply disappointed by the death of Edmund Tudor, earl of Richmond, before a son had been born to him, he threw his bard, Robin Ddu, into prison, exclaiming angrily: 'You made me believe that a scion of the House of Owen would one day restore us the crown of Britain. You now perceive that your prophecy was false, for Edmund has left no son to succeed him.' Soon it became known that the duchess was about to give birth to a child. Robin Ddu was immediately set free and despatched to Pembroke. A son was born, and they called his name Owen, by which name young Henry Tudor was for many years known among the Welsh.[2]

On the social life of Wales at this period the poets are invaluable. They throw interesting light also on ecclesiastical affairs. Lewis Glyn Cothi is trenchant in his satire upon the friars and the travelling minstrels, though his lampoon is often less robust than that of Guto'r Glyn. The sale of indulgences, and even the papacy itself, come beneath their scourge. 'The Church is as impotent as the Government,' says Tudur Penllyn, 'and armies have become the instrument of the devil.' Dice, chess, carol-singing, cards, and dancing relieved the monotony of everyday life.

The 'Life of Sir Rhys ap Thomas' in the *Cambrian Register* (1795) is a work which has enjoyed much popularity, and has formed the basis of almost everything that has been written on Wales during the second half of the fifteenth century. The original manuscript appears to have been written in the early part of the seventeenth century by one who claimed some relationship to Rhys ap Thomas, in order, as he states, to dash in pieces some false, forged traditions respecting him. The writer traces the history of the family from the time of Griffith ap Nicholas, the grandfather of Rhys.

The style is attractive, and characterized by unusual dramatic power. The writer was familiar with the chronicles of Hall and Holinshed; in fact his account, when it deals with the general events of history, is largely a reproduction of Hall. He has also perused some of the fifteenth-century Welsh poets, but not critically; for he presumes that they give the literal truth and translates them accordingly. He states, for example, that Griffith ap Nicholas possessed seven strong castles, and that three great dukes with two other great judges of the realm attempted and failed 'to crush and tread him under foot'. These statements are a translation of an ode to Griffith by Gwilym ap Ieuan Hen.[3]

The writer then proceeds to amplify. The three dukes were 'Richard, duke of York, Humphrey, duke of Buckingham, and Henry, duke of Warwick, or rather Jasper, earl of Pembroke, to whom he had just cause of quarrel because Jasper took a liking to Griffith's castle of Cilgerran.' It is no doubt true that these lords had large interests in Wales; and further, that Griffith was actually engaged in strife with Jasper's brother, Edmund. But Jasper's relations with the family were friendly, and Griffith's sons fought with him against the Yorkists at Mortimer's Cross; while it is certain that Cilgerran did not belong to Griffith ap Nicholas.

Moreover, the account given here of the attitude of Griffith towards the rival houses of York and Lancaster is seriously at variance with that given by Lewis Glyn Cothi; for it states that Griffith, having been found guilty of felony, offered his services to the duke of York, and fought and died at Mortimer's Cross. To this we shall return. There are many adventurous tales which we have no means of verifying, but they are of personal, rather than general interest. Some of them, indeed, bear a striking resemblance to those connected with other individuals at this period. Like Lord Stanley, Rhys ap Thomas is required by Richard III to give his son as a hostage; while the story that Rhys, having promised Richard that whoever, ill-affected to the state, should dare to land in Wales where he (Rhys) had any employments under his majesty 'he must resolve with himself to make his entrance and irruption over my bellie', and that, to verify his oath, he suffered Henry of Richmond, on landing at Dale, to pass over his body – this story also has its counterpart in the annals of Shrewsbury. The author asserts, further, that Rhys was absolute in the neighbourhood of Milford Haven where Henry landed, that he kept Carmarthen Castle, that Richard required him to safeguard Milford Haven against foreign invasion, and that he joined Henry at Dale, all of which are either contradicted by known facts or unsubstantiated by independent evidence. It would therefore be unsafe to take this work as a reliable guide.

The recognized contemporary chroniclers have very little to say of Wales. Their references are few and shadowy – the impressions of men who view things from afar. There is not a single continuous record. We have therefore to gather the sequence of events from a mass of material drawn from such official documents as the Rolls of Parliament, Rymer's *Foedera*, the Patent Rolls, *Acts and Proceedings of the Privy Council*, the Deputy Keeper's *Reports*, Inquisitiones post mortem, Statutes of the Realm, the *Paston Letters* and other correspondence, Municipal Records, and the original material to be found in the publications of various societies. Such material, though disconnected, is on the whole beyond suspicion, and it is possible to obtain from them a tolerably clear idea of the march of events.[4]

APPENDIX

Extract from the MS 'History of Wales', by Ellis Griffith, in the Mostyn Library.

Genedigaeth Henri ap yr Edmwnt a dreith ym mlaen hyn o lafur. Yn y pryd a'r amser yr ydoedd brudiwr a bardd mawr o vewn tir Gwynedd y neb a elwid Rhobin Ddu brydydd . . . yr hwn ynn hyn o amser ynny blaen a ddywedasai i Syr William Gruffuth yr hwn yn y cyfamser aoedd ben Siambyrlen o Wynedd i dygai Rishmwn goron tyrnas lloygyr am iben or achos yngydrym ac ir marchog gafel y gwirionedd o varwolaeth Iarll Ritsmwnt y vo a ddanvones i gyrchu y bardd wrth yr hwn y dywed ef drwy ymravaelion eiriau gwattwarus yn y modd yma. Aha Hrobin deg. Wele mor deg i mae ych brudiau chwi ynn dyvod tydi a wnaethost i mi ac i lawer dyn goelio i dygai Ritshmwnt goron y dyrnas. Megis ac i dangosais di imi yn fynnych o amseroedd or blaen. Neithyr yrowan ir wyf i ynn gweled yn amlwg nad oes onid ffuent a chelwydd oth ymddiddanau di. Or achos y dywed y prydydd drwy gythrudd a llid ynn y modd hwn. Serre pette iarll Richmwnt gwedi marw ag wedi llosgi i gorff ef ac wedi boddi y lludw etto i mae i wraig ef yn feichiog ar ettivedd mab, yr hwn a fydd brenin o loygyr or achos yma, megis ac y mae'r chwedyl yn sathredig ymysg y Cymru, y vo a gedwis y Siambyrlen y bardd megys ynn garcharor oni gavas ef wir wybodaeth fod yr iarlles yn feichiog ac yna y vo a ollyngodd Robin yn hrydd yr hwn o fewn ychydig o amser ynnol a gymerth i shiwrnai o Wynedd i ddeheubarth. Ac ir oedd ef ynghastell Penvro pan oedd yr Iarlles yn travaelio oi chlevyd ac wrth i gynghor ef i kymerth hi y Siambyr o fewn y twr a dreithir uchod yn y lle y ganned iddi vab. Megis y mae gwyr hen o Gymru yn dywedud a hennwyd ynni vedyddio Ywain. Neithyr pan ir goshibion ddangos ir iarlles i henw ef y hi a beris ir esgob droi i henw ef ai hennwi ef Henry neithyr val kynt gwyr Cymru ai galwai ef Ywain yn vynnych no henri yr hwn wedi ddyvod ef mewn oedran affoes allan or deyrnas i dir ffrainck rhag ofn brenin Edwart.

CHAPTER TWO

The Penal Laws

The rising of Owen Glyndwr in the first decade of the century was in some respects the greatest social calamity that the country ever experienced. The widespread ruin of monasteries and the relentless devastation of lands were the least among the evils which it brought in its train. In the first place, Wales was for many years afterwards regarded as an active volcano which might at any moment break out in violent eruption.

> Beware of Walys, Criste Jhesu mutt us kepe
> That it make not oure childeis childe to wepe,
> Ne us also, if it go his waye
> By unwarenesse; seth that many a day
> Men have beferde of here rebellioun.
> Loke wele aboute, for, God wote, we have nede.[1]

The English government considered it necessary to maintain a considerable force of archers and men-at-arms in the most disaffected districts. Apart from the castle garrisons at Carnarvon, Harlech, Carmarthen and other royal strongholds, a force of about a thousand men was stationed in the very heart of the country, at Cymmer and Bala in Merionethshire, and at Strata Florida in Carmarthenshire. Even when England was being drained of its fighting men for the French wars of Henry V, Wales could not be left without a guard of nearly a thousand men.[2] In the eyes of patriotic Welshmen this military occupation served as a mark of abiding captivity and national subjection.

Henry V, who had acquired an invaluable military training in Wales during his youth, was statesman enough to perceive that a disaffected Wales was a menace he could not afford to ignore, or treat with indifference. And so, being engrossed in plans of foreign conquest, he became anxious for a complete reconciliation. Owen Glyndwr himself was still, apparently, at large, and the possibility of a renewal of active hostilities not altogether remote. Thus, on the eve of the campaign of Agincourt in 1415, just before the army embarked from France, David Howel, a Welshman of note, was charged with complicity in the conspiracy of the earl of Cambridge. In his confession Cambridge stated that the earl of March, who was

Richard, earl of Cambridge. Drawing from a lost figure of him once in the glass at Canterbury Cathedral.

to replace Henry V on the throne, was to be taken to Wales, and there proclaimed king; that the royal castles in Wales were to be seized; and that David Howel was to engineer a rising in North Wales. David Howel's complicity in the affair could not be proved; for, in the following year, he complained in parliament that he had been indicted of treason by one John Eliot before the king's justices, and that Eliot did not appear to support the charge.[3]

Aware of the intractable temper of his Welsh enemies, the king sent repeated offers of pardon to Owen Glyndwr or his representative. A few weeks before his departure for France he sent Gilbert Talbot on a peaceful mission to Wales, with authority to pardon any rebels who might be disposed to submit. The following year Talbot went on a second embassy of a similar nature, armed with power to negotiate with Owen's son Meredith, as Owen himself could not be found.[4]

Moreover, it stands recorded that Henry gave instructions for the rebuilding of some of the monasteries that had been destroyed in the war. The abbey of Llanfaes in Anglesey was to be restored, and at least two of the monks were to be Welsh.[5]

The rising of Owen Glyndwr, in the second place, left a bitter heritage of feud among the Welsh families themselves. Many of them had been opposed to Owen's action from the beginning, and none more vehemently than David Gam, whose daughter Gwladys became the mother of the Herberts of Raglan. These loyalists were proscribed and ruthlessly persecuted by what may with propriety be called the patriots: their lands were devastated; many were imprisoned; not a few escaped vengeance by enlisting for the wars in France. For more than a generation frequent complaints were made to parliament that those who had been loyal to the government were the victims of ill-treatment by Owen's partisans and those of their blood.[6] Some, apparently, found refuge in the old Welsh custom of *rhaith*, according to which three hundred men were required to swear to the loyalty or innocence of the accused.[7] However, the feud between patriot and loyalist was fiercely active long after the accession of Henry VI.[8]

But blood-feuds and the establishment of a species of martial law throughout the land were not the only or the least of the evil results of Glyndwr's rising. It produced a code of penal laws which increased in severity until the cataclysm of

St Mary's Priory Church, Abergavenny. Tomb and effigies of Gwladys, daughter of David Gam, and her husband Sir William ap Thomas (d. 1446). The mother of Sir William Herbert, she died in 1451.

the Wars of the Roses swept away the old order of things, and ushered in a new era of coalition and prosperity. For many generations Welshmen were denied the ordinary privileges of citizenship: they could not acquire property in land within or near the boroughs; they could not serve on juries; intermarriage between them and the English was forbidden; they could not hold office under the Crown; no Englishman could be convicted on the oath of a Welshman.[9]

These protective walls, which sought to guard the interests of English residents in Wales, could not long withstand the assaults of social and political storms. The peasant fought for a path to freedom; his lord hungered for more land; the artisan was rising to a position of independence; the merchant opened up new avenues of trade; home and foreign wars created a demand for Welsh soldiers; in the midst of all came a prolonged strife which finally shattered the filigree of social distinctions between the two nations. But while these forces were gathering strength the average Welshman was grievously handicapped by the penal laws. It would have been inexpedient, if not difficult, to withhold citizenship from a Welshman of commanding local influence, whose power and interests could be enlisted on the side of order by granting him denizenship. This appears to have been the position of Rees ap Thomas, a Cardiganshire chieftain, who was admitted to the full rights of a citizen in 1413, and was the first thus to be favoured, unless we carry our history further back than the accession of Henry V. Rees subsequently held an official position of some moment in West Wales and received the alien priory of St Clear's.[10] Some years later, Griffith ap Nicholas was granted the privileges of Englishmen for similar reasons. To have made him the victim of a harsh penal code would have been unwise, perhaps dangerous. The same may be said of Griffith Dwnn to whom, in 1421, parliament granted the full liberties of a loyal subject.[11] His family played a conspicuous part in the politics of the second half of the century.

The penal laws, in that they forbade a Welshman to hold or purchase lands in England, affected, more by chance than by design, the civil rights of those who had migrated from Wales to England before the passing of the statutes, and had acquired a territorial interest there. But for their petitions to parliament, we might never have suspected their Welsh origin. Such was Lewis John, who is described as having been born of a Welsh father and mother. He had acquired a status in England as a freeman of the city of London; he possessed estates in Essex, and was Warden of the Mint in London and Calais.[12] John Montgomery[13] and John Steward were Welshmen who found themselves in the same difficulty. Both served with distinction at Agincourt, and afterwards in Normandy. The rights of such men were separately safeguarded by parliament on petition.

It is beyond the scope of the present inquiry to follow the careers of these men in detail, or investigate the extent to which the people of Wales sought and found a larger ambit of enterprise in the general affairs of the country. In the Church they are represented by Reginald Pecock, the most daring thinker of his age, and by the astute diplomatist Philip Morgan, who became Bishop of Worcester and Chancellor of Normandy. In war, no soldier of the day won greater fame than Mathew Gough; and but for his brilliance, a host of lesser lights from Wales would burn more brightly. Owen Tudor gave proof of courtly qualities by winning the affection of Queen Catherine. Few mastered the shifts of statecraft more successfully than William Herbert. Some of these, on account of the eminence they achieved in the Wars of the Roses, or the splendour in which they are wreathed in contemporary Welsh literature, will appear often in our story. Others, like Pecock and Philip Morgan, who do not directly affect the story of Wales, have no claims upon the present narrative.

To resume. Many obtained emancipation from civil thraldom by their eminent services in the French wars; for example, David ap Thomas of Cardiganshire, in 1427, for his unswerving loyalty to Henry V. In this instance the liberation was not made hereditary.[14] A few years later he was to suffer imprisonment for his adherence to Humphrey, duke of Gloucester. In 1430 Rhys ap Madoc 'born in Wales' received denizenship at the special request of the House of Commons for his sovereign heroism at Crevant and Verneuil. He appears to have been in personal attendance upon the duke of Bedford when the latter crossed from France to England to compose the differences between Cardinal Beaufort and the duke of Gloucester.[15] The yoke next fell from the shoulders of Morgan Meredith. He marked his deliverance by a prosperous trade in barley with the Netherlands, and later acquired some ascendancy in the local affairs of Kent.[16] In 1432 the franchise was bestowed upon Owen ap Meredith, who was probably the romantic Owen ap Meredith ap Tudor, better known as Owen Tudor.[17] There is a forbidding leanness about this grant which betokens flagrant insincerity or intriguing suspicion. He could not become a citizen or a burgess, nor hold a Crown office in any city, borough, or market town. By a process of elimination we infer that he could bear arms, acquire land, intermarry, and serve on a jury. He might hold a household appointment, a fact of outstanding significance in his particular case. As we shall see, he was already the husband of Queen Catherine, though the fact was not generally known.

Another illuminating case is that of William ap William ap Griffith, who described himself as 'English on his mother's side, being son to Joan, daughter of William Stanley, knight, and part English on his father's side.' His father, he declared, had been loyal to the Crown against Owen Glyndwr, and had been despoiled of his lands in consequence. Parliament gave a guarded assent to his request; for William was not to marry a Welsh wife, and he was not permitted to hold any royal office in Wales.[18] Three years later, however, these embarrassing restrictions were removed. The government became more liberal under Edward IV. In 1468 Morgan ap Meredith of Carnarvonshire, and one David Canons, were enabled to become burgesses of any Carnarvonshire boroughs, or of any other town in Wales and the Marches, with freedom to hold office and carry arms.[19]

But of those that were formally emancipated by parliament the most aggressive was Griffith ap Nicholas, a remarkable character who dominated West Wales in the middle of the fifteenth century. No reliable account of him is extant, for the spurious biographical sketch in the *Cambrian Register*, which was written more than a century and a half after his death, is a picturesque web of fancy woven to embellish a family pedigree.[20] His grandson was that Sir Rhys ap Thomas who is said to have deceived Richard III by an ingenious piece of sophistry, and who afterwards won a knighthood on Bosworth field.

Griffith was intensely national, and in his generous patronage of the bards faithfully mirrors the Welsh aristocracy of his day. He is the subject of many a panegyric in contemporary poetry where, with pardonable poetic licence, he is extolled as the autocrat of the south and the ruler of the west from Carmarthen to Anglesey.[21] His home was Newton, now Dynevor, near Llandilo, in Carmarthenshire. He held the position of approver for the king in Dynevor as early as 1425; so that he must have obtained release from civic servitude before that date, although the parliamentary recognition of it was only recorded twenty years afterwards. Moreover, he was farmer of the lordship of Dynevor in 1440.[22]

A curious instance of the abduction of a woman of property gives him a lurid ascendancy which is not substantiated by the little we know of him. Margaret, the widow of Sir Thomas Maliphant, was journeying from Pembrokeshire to London, when she was seized by an unscrupulous adventurer Lewis Leyshon, who speciously represented himself as her protector against the violence of Griffith ap Nicholas. Lewis escorted her in the guise of a friend as far as Twygeston, near Bridgend, the home of his accomplice, Gilbert Turberville. He then unmasked his dark purpose, which was to force her to become his wife. Margaret's honour, however, defied imprisonment, brutality, as well as the hypocritical pleadings of the parish vicar.[23] A similar case of abduction occurred in Lancashire about the same time, when Lady Butler was taken from her chamber at Bartonwood, and carried off in 'her kirtle and her smokke' by one William Pulle of Wirral, who compelled her to say the words of matrimony in the parish church of Bidstone.[24]

In 1443, by a royal grant, Griffith ap Nicholas was invested with the town of Tregaron, and the commote of Pennarth in which it was situated, a large district in the upper valley of the Teivy, during the minority of Maud, daughter and heiress of William Clement.[25] We shall probably not be far wrong in attributing this grant to the favourable influence of Humphrey, duke of Gloucester, who had been made Chief Justice of South Wales in 1440, and who spent some time in Carmarthenshire and Cardiganshire during these years, for Griffith soon became one of the duke's most devoted followers.

He continued to advance in power and position in subsequent years. In 1444 he was formally admitted as a fully privileged English subject.[26] The penal code was by this time tottering ominously: 'Welshmen in increasing numbers seek to be citizens and to have the same freedom as Englishmen, which will be to the utter destruction of all Englishmen.' Such were the words of the burgesses of North Wales who, becoming alarmed at the robust vitality of the Welsh, petitioned parliament to put an end to it. Parliament, in acquiescing, specifically exempted William Bulkley of Anglesey, 'an Englishman who had married a woman of half-blood Welsh', and Griffith ap Nicholas. This indirect allusion is our only official record of Griffith's denizenship, but it implies that he had received it some years previously. At a later period his name appears on a number of commissions. For example, in 1445 he was authorized with a few others to inquire into the felonies of one David ap Meredith of Aberystwyth.[27]

The number of those thus formally unfettered by parliament was comparatively few. Nevertheless, it should not be assumed that the laws against Welshmen were equally stringent throughout Wales. Their own selfish propensities, and the struggle for existence in the turbid pools of riot, compelled the lords-marcher to lean towards tolerance; for the greater the number of law-abiding burgesses, the greater the security in the towns on their demesnes, and the greater their revenues.

It may be asserted with a fair degree of probability that the early towns of Wales were not so exclusively foreign as they are sometimes represented to have been. It is certain that there was no general prohibition against the Welsh on the part of the lords-marcher, in whose demesnes most of the towns came into existence. Nor did the unfortunate results of Glyndwr's rebellion operate for any length of time so as to exclude Welshmen from the towns of the Marches. In 1406 Edward Charlton granted a charter to Welshpool, according to which only Welshmen 'who were with us in the rebellion shall be taken into the liberty'. There were Welsh bailiffs in Tenby in the first decade of the fifteenth century. A charter of the Mortimers to Usk about the same time declares that the corporation 'having obtained our licence may freely make any Welshman a burgess of our town'.[28] But if there was a less stringent regime in the Marches, it cannot be too strongly emphasized that the penal code perpetuated the cleavage between the two nations, discouraged the Welsh from peaceful enterprise, and produced considerable irritation, especially in the shires.

So far we have dealt mainly with those causes of unrest which might be traced directly to Owen Glyndwr's rising. There were others of a more remote origin. Since the conquest of the Principality by Edward I, Wales had been divided into shire-ground and the Marches. The shires were Anglesey, Merionethshire, Carnarvonshire, Carmarthenshire, Cardiganshire and Flintshire. There were two counties-palatine, namely, the earldom of Pembroke, and the lordship of Glamorgan. In all these the organization was in every respect similar to that of an English county. The rest of Wales was known as the Marches. Here every lord was a law unto himself.

Throughout the Marches Welsh and English customs existed side by side, but the tendency was for the latter to encroach upon the former. Thus, in 1415, the Welsh chieftains on the estates of the duchy of Lancaster in West Wales petitioned that they should hold their lands according to the custom of their forefathers, and that estates should not escheat to the Crown in default of heirs direct.[29] Sometimes dues exacted according to English law were superimposed upon those exacted by Welsh law. In 1417 Edward Stradling and the tenants of Bassaleg, in the seigniory of Newport, were distrained upon for a tallage; but the seizures were afterwards restored to them on the ground that the tallage had not been paid in ancient times except when the lord attained his majority.[30]

There were instances where the burden became intolerable, and many of the villeins were driven to seek elsewhere a more lenient rule, or a more adventurous existence. In 1446 the king's bondsmen of North Wales were absolved from the duty of executing felons, to which they were compelled by the sheriff, 'by reason whereof bondmen have gone from the counties to divers parts of England, so that many towns are desolate, and rents and services and pence are taken away'.[31] In some parts villeinage was rampant in its most hideous form. In 1449 a number of villeins were sold to William Griffith of North Wales 'with their successors procreated and to be procreated, and all their goods'.[32]

Of all the plagues that infested the stricken land the worst was that of official tyranny. This statement applies more especially to the royal shires. Here the officials from the 'Warnester,' or watcher at the town gate, to the constable of the castle, from the bailiff to the sheriff, were aliens whose sympathies were rudely antagonistic to Welsh sentiment. Only in the lower orders of the Church did the native element predominate. During the first half of the century all the sheriffs of the counties of North Wales were English. So also were the constables of the castles, the chamberlains and the justices. The same is true of South Wales. Whenever we meet with the constables of Cardigan, Aberystwyth, Dynevor, Dryslwyn, Carmarthen, Laugharne, or even with such minor officials as porters, they are invariably English. It is not until the accession of Edward IV that a change appears.

The cleavage between the two peoples, and especially the clash between the native element and their English officials, is faithfully mirrored in contemporary Welsh literature, one of the chief features of which, as we have already remarked, is its hostility towards the Saxon. The poet Lewis Glyn Cothi, for example, exults in the rise of Griffith ap Nicholas to official status because he views it as the opening of a new era, when 'the Saxon will no longer be found presiding over the Sessions or holding an official position amongst us'.[33] It is in the poets of the period, too, that we must seek a true expression of the temper of public opinion in face of the disabilities under which the people laboured. Although contemporary poetry was produced largely at the command of the rich, and to eulogize them, and thus savours of a fawning timidity in dealing with social evils, nevertheless, there are many suggestive references to a deep and widespread unrest. 'Life is sad and heavy, men who were formerly in bondage are gradually becoming more enslaved,' says Lewis Glyn Cothi.[34]

The same poet frequently calls upon his heroes to draw their swords in defence of the common people and the innocent.[35] Similarly Guto'r Glyn, in a glowing panegyric to Edward IV: 'Woe betide us who have been born in servitude, and are the prey of strong thieves. Restore order. Come thyself, valiant Edward, and check the oppressors.'[36]

Nor did the overbearing temper of the nobility, and the decline of Welsh law and custom escape the poets. Lewis Glyn Cothi implores Owen ap Griffith 'to mete out justice to the proud, and restore their ancient customs to the timid'.[37] Similarly he appeals to another patron to 'restore to Wales her own law'.[38] Guto'r Glyn bewails the social restrictions which debarred anyone not of baronial lineage from rising above his station, and vigorously assails the ineffectiveness of the ecclesiastical law to curb the immoderate licence of the clergy. One of the noblest features of Thomas ap Rosser, a chieftain slain at Edgecote, was that he evinced practical sympathy for the common people.[39]

Bearing these circumstances in mind, it is not difficult to realize that contempt of law, which was general throughout the country, found most congenial soil in the Marches, where every lord was responsible for the maintenance of order within his own territories, and was frequently not without reason to subvert it. It is a commonplace of history that the Marches experienced every species of lawlessness which national acerbities, official vindictiveness, and the negation of effective judicial administration, could engender in a land of pathless woods and inaccessible mountains.[40] The Marches were deluged by all the barbarous evils of a degenerate feudalism, countless in number and variety. Scientific atrocity had almost become an axiom of life. The savage licence and wolfish avarice of the strong were let loose upon the weak and the law-abiding. No recorded deed of romantic heroism relieves the abject brutality of a Lord Powys, the murderer of

Griffith Vaughan,[41] or the dexterous perfidy of a Grey of Ruthin. There is no splendid villainy even, such as is recorded in the annals of some of the Italian states during the century, unless it be the murder of Sir Christopher Talbot who was struck to the heart at his own castle of Caws.[42] Official records present nothing better than a frightful spectacle of barbarity, a catalogue of robberies and tragedies.

The chief sufferers were the inhabitants of Herefordshire, Gloucestershire and Shropshire, who frequently reported their grievances to parliament. Their cornfields were ruined, their stock reduced to ashes, their cattle driven to the mountains; and not infrequently they were themselves imprisoned until heavy ransoms were paid. Merchants who plied their trade in the west were the prey of a godless nobility and a brutalized peasantry. Security of transit was impossible where the king's writ did not run.[43] The estuary of the Severn swarmed with pirates, every creek giving shelter to its seadogs who had their accomplices in the towns.

They issued forth like an armed fleet in battle array.[44] The merchants of Bristol were not more immune than those of Ireland or Denmark.[45] Stolen cattle and stock were transferred recklessly by night from one side of the Severn to the other, and robbers were not to be deterred by legislation forbidding night-ferrying. The peasantry retaliated upon the insolence and ferocity of the municipal officials of North Wales with organized raids upon Conway, Dolgelly and Beaumaris on market days, which sometimes ended in bloodshed.[46] If the people were wronged they were not so servile as to return thanks for it.

It need hardly be stated that this bewildering lawlessness was not the work of irresponsible hordes of outlaws and hardened ruffians. Those who were not to be constrained to the mean duties of villeins, when villeinage was fast becoming an anachronism, simply became the retainers of a depraved nobility whose predatory habits they aped. John Talbot of Goodrich Castle was a valiant soldier. In 1424 his services were required in France to assist in rescuing Crotoy. He refused to go until he had indemnified himself for the arrears of his wages, as constable of Montgomery Castle, by a profitable raid upon the prosperous citizens and farmers of Herefordshire.[47] Sir Reginald Grey and Hugh Wenlok were also among his unfortunate victims.[48] William Fitzwarren levied a body of armed men in Wales and deprived Richard Hankford of Whittington of his castle. The Corbets were bold enough to abuse and rob the collectors of the fifteenth in Shrewsbury.[49] John ap Meredith, a cousin of Owen Tudor, fought out his feuds alternately with William Griffith, chamberlain of North Wales, and the Thelwalls of Dyffryn Clwyd.[50]

About the year 1442 the blaze of riot raged with amazing fury, private property and public finance being equally involved in the general ruin. It was found impossible to arrest miscreants. They passed from one lordship to another, and 'having no place certain to tarry' transferred their ill-gotten wealth to places of security, and themselves beyond the reach of law and justice.[51] There was no decent reverence for the monasteries. Some years previously a papal bull had empowered the abbot of Margam to excommunicate a number of people who had despoiled the abbey of Neath.[52] But the Pope's curse could not kill a fly, and his servants could be bought for a song.[53] The abbey of Strata Florida was placed under the care and government of the abbots of Whitland and Margam because the abbot could not guard it against strong thieves and robbers.[54] The abbot of Basingwerk, in Flintshire, complained of his losses through riots and robberies.[55] The abbot of Vale Royal in Cheshire lodges a similar complaint that

> whereas he is fiefed of Llanbadarn and other property in the counties of Cardigan and Carmarthen, and as in the said shires are some Welshmen to whom the said abbot has not given such rewards as they desired, they have indicted him at the sessions of divers felonies to compel him to give them rewards and fees; and when he came to appear to the indictment he could not pass through certain lordships without being assaulted and beaten.[56]

Moreover, 'Welshmen accused of treason have been found to come into the towns and markets and stay there for several days without being arrested, because the sheriff and his ministers oftentimes have no knowledge of their persons nor of their being within the said county, some for favour and amity, some for doubt of hurt.'[57] Such obliquity of conduct as these extracts reveal necessarily affected the royal revenues. The Exchequer suffered by an extensive evasion of customs' dues on merchandise passing through Wales and the Marches. Tenants and others in North and South Wales[58] were frequently summoned to pay their debts by instalments, or otherwise to answer for the amounts due from them.

Further, a number of native chieftains were about the same time outlawed or placed under arrest. The ringleader in Carnarvonshire was Evan ap Robin;[59] in the valley of the Dee, Sir Griffith Vaughan;[60] in Carmarthenshire, Owen, the son of Griffith ap Nicholas. The Privy Council ordered Owen to be placed under arrest; Griffith himself and the Abbot of Whitland were summoned to appear before the Privy Council; while some militant monk who had been traversing North and South Wales holding riotous assemblies called *cymmorthau*, narrating Welsh chronicles and traditions, and stirring up the people to rebellion, was immediately 'to be found out and taken'.[61] That this agitator was one of the bardic fraternity may be presumed with a fair degree of certainty. He may, indeed, have been Lewis Glyn Cothi, the most fervid nationalist of his time, whose spirit chafed beneath the miseries and humiliations of political and social servitude. For he himself admits that he was at one time hunted down by the officers of justice, and that he was then sheltered by Owen ap Griffith ap Nicholas.[62] As we have just remarked, Owen was also under the ban of the law at this time; and as Glyn Cothi was his neighbour, both may have been acting together.

This defiance of law and order continued with varying success until the Tudors finally smothered it through the instrumentality of the Court of the President and Council of Wales and the Marches. Meanwhile, the administration of justice rested with the sheriffs of the counties and the lords of the Marches. They failed notoriously, either from self-interest, or gross absenteeism, or ineptitude. Consequently the Privy Council was constrained to interfere.

Court of the Exchequer at Westminster, from a law treatise of Henry VI's reign. The court is presided over by the Lord High Treasurer, probably John Tiptopt, earl of Worcester, and four other judges. Around the table are clerks and officers of the court, and in the foreground two prisoners in a shuttered cage (Society of Antiquaries).

Although empty proclamations rather than energetic action generally characterized its proceedings, the Privy Council was obviously apprehensive about Wales. One of the royal castles might at any time fall into the hands of the lawless element; and a reduction of castles held by Welsh rebels had been a costly business during Glyndwr's wars.[63] The efficiency of the castle garrisons in North Wales, therefore, had been a matter of concern to Henry V. He stipulated that no burgess should be received into the king's wages at the castle, and any who had been so received were to be discharged and replaced by others. The burgess was not as efficient as the professional soldier; and as the burgesses constituted themselves into an armed force at need, the employment of a burgess as a castle soldier implied a weakening of the combined force of town and castle. Another difficulty which Henry V had tried to grapple with was the absenteeism of sheriffs, for it was enacted that none were to be appointed to that office who would not perform their duties in person.[64]

On the death of Henry V, the minority of his son and the continuance of the French war multiplied the difficulties of the Privy Council. Sometimes, as in 1422, commissions would be appointed to try to secure peace. But, with grim irony, the chief members were themselves the advocates and propellors of incendiarism, such as the Talbots.[65] On one occasion it was proposed to place the administration of private lands, namely those of the Skydmores of Herefordshire, in the power of the council itself, 'lest riots and other inconveniences should arise'.[66] But there were too many cross-currents of interest, and privilege was too well fortified, for the extension of such a project. Another time an attempt was made to check absenteeism: all the constables of castles in Wales were directed to return to their posts, and the lords-marcher to hold their courts on one day, and to see that the law was duly obeyed within their own jurisdictions.[67]

In 1437 a more comprehensive scheme was lodged. It was proposed to ascertain who the lords-marcher were, and to appoint a special committee to deal solely with the affairs of the Principality and the Marches.[68] In pursuance of this plan, the lords were summoned to the Privy Council in the following year to assist in the formation of the proposed committee.[69] But, probably on account of the lethargy and the selfishness of those concerned, nothing was done. Nevertheless, the proposal is of constitutional interest as being apparently the first suggestion that the affairs of Wales and the Marches should be administered by a distinct council, the plan which subsequently materialized in the shape of the Council of Wales and the Marches. Five years later, in 1442, when the political temperature of the Marches was inordinately high, the laws of Edward I with regard to the administration of justice in Wales were examined, and the lords of the Marches were ordered to confer and take instant action, a task in which the duke of York promised actively to assist. In case they refused, the government threatened to find some drastic remedy. This was no empty boast. For on 12 August 1443, a conference actually took place at Harlech between Henry Norris, the deputy-chamberlain of Carnarvon, and the gentry of Merionethshire, to try to still the tempest of feud and riot. In October they came before the council.[70]

It may be remarked that other provincial assemblies are recorded in the reign of

Edward IV. But they were summoned to vote money rather than to restore order. In 1466 the freeholders and townspeople of Anglesey agreed upon a subsidy of 400 marks to be paid within six years; while in 1473 Cardiganshire and Carmarthenshire voted a tollage to the Prince of Wales in honour of his first visit to the country.[71]

One result of the prevailing anarchy was a periodical tightening of the penal fetters. The statutes against the Welsh were confirmed in 1431, and again two years later;[72] though it was not until 1447 that the most elaborate and ponderous engine of oppression which the bigoted tyranny of officials could conceive was brought to bear upon the native element. This was at the parliament of Bury, which was assembled at the time of the death of Humphrey, duke of Gloucester; and we shall be able to understand the circumstances more clearly if we consider the relations between Wales and the duke.

Humphrey had acquired a personal interest in Wales as far back as 1414, when he was created earl of Pembroke. He was lord of Tenby and Cilgerran; and his possessions included the castle of Llanstephan, near Carmarthen, which he had obtained as a reward for his services at Agincourt. The place had been forfeited to the Crown by the treason of its possessor, Henry Gwyn, who had fought for the French in that battle.[73] In 1427 Gloucester was made justice of North Wales. He came to Chester in that year, presumably in his capacity as chief justice,[74] while in the following year we find him holding an inquisition at Bala.[75] In 1433 he held a court at Pembroke, and investigated a case of disputed inheritance. In 1437 he was appointed a justice in Anglesey.[76]

In 1440 the office of chief justice of South Wales was conferred upon him, and in August of the following year he held sessions at Carmarthen and Cardigan 'to settle the disturbances and quarrels which existed between the inhabitants of those parts', a task which involved him in 'great costs and labour'.[77]

As we have seen, the years 1441 to 1443 were a period of unusual unrest and insecurity. Gloucester hoped to turn it to some advantage and to release his wife, Eleanor Cobham, who had been removed from Kent to Chester in 1442. At least, the wording of a pardon which was granted to Thomas Herbert, one of Gloucester's retinue, after the duke's death, states as much; and it is significant that Eleanor was removed from Chester to Kenilworth next year, although she again returned to Wales (probably Flint Castle) in 1447, the year in which Humphrey died.[78] It is unnecessary to enter fully into the bitter court factions which culminated in the death of the duke of Gloucester. He condemned the cession of Maine, and led the opposition to Queen Margaret and Suffolk, who were determined to silence him. His impeachment was prepared. Parliament was summoned to meet at Bury St Edmunds in February 1447. Gloucester came to Bury with a bodyguard of eighty horsemen.[79] One authority states that he came up directly from Wales, a statement to which the large number of Welshmen in his retinue lends support.[80] On his way he passed through Greenwich.[81]

On their arrival at Bury on 18 February, Gloucester and some of his most prominent attendants were arrested. Among these were Sir Henry Wogan, the duke's steward in the earldom of Pembroke,[82] Thomas Herbert, the elder brother

Effigies in Slebech Church of Sir Henry Wogan of Wiston and his wife Margaret, daughter of Sir William ap Thomas of Raglan.

of William Herbert (afterwards earl of Pembroke), John Wogan and Howel ap David ap Thomas.[83] Three days later, which was Shrove Tuesday, twenty-eight more of his retainers were sent to various places of confinement. Gloucester died on 23 February and was buried at St Albans, being accompanied thither by about twenty of his own entourage.[84]

One of the charges levelled by his accusers against Humphrey was that he had endeavoured to raise a rebellion in Wales. They 'enformed falsli the king, and sayde that he wolde raise the Welshmenne for to distresse him (Suffolk) and destroie him'.[85] There is no reliable evidence of the existence of such a plot; his servants certainly did not suspect that anything untoward was maturing until they had been placed under arrest.[86] On the other hand it is easy to realize how plausible such a charge would appear when once put forward. Wales had acquired unenviable notoriety as the nursery of treasonable enterprises. Dark suspicion attached to the very name. Throughout the reign she had been the cause of much anxiety to the central government. At this very moment the Marches were a welter of implacable feuds and national acerbities. A few years before one of Gloucester's retinue, Griffith ap Nicholas, had been summoned before the council, and the family implicated in riots.

Moreover, Humphrey's enthusiastic and liberal patronage of learning appealed with special force to the Welsh poets, and he found favour among them. Lewis Glyn Cothi, in an ode to Roger Kynaston, alludes to him in terms of admiration.[87] One of these bards had been traversing the country preaching insurrection, and that about the time when Eleanor Cobham was removed from Chester to Kenilworth. The duke of Gloucester was chief justice of South Wales, and, as we have seen, paid several visits to the country. Such a combination of circumstances made admirable soil in which to sow the seed of a charge of conspiracy.

Of the prisoners, Sir Henry Wogan and Thomas Herbert were sent to London, Owen Dwnn to Wallingford, and Griffith ap Nicholas and David ap Thomas to the King's Bench.[88] David ap Thomas had been a prisoner in the Fleet in 1443. He may have been involved in the disturbance in Wales at that period. He was removed to Carmarthen Castle where he was detained until Sir William ap Thomas found the necessary security of a thousand marks.[89] In the following July, five members of Gloucester's retinue, including Richard Middleton and Thomas Herbert, were tried for treason at Deptford, a special commission that was presided over by Suffolk having been appointed for the purpose. They were sentenced to death, and were already strung up at Tyburn when Suffolk arrived with a pardon from the king. Accordingly they were released and for the most part restored to their possessions. Suffolk succeeded Humphrey in the earldom of Pembroke,[90] although he had been made earl in reversion as far back as 1443.

It is an instructive commentary upon the nervous apprehension of parliament with regard to Wales that it now confirmed all the statutes against Welshmen, ordaining that 'all grants of franchises, markets, fairs and other freedoms to buy or sell, or bake or brew to sell in the towns of North Wales, made to any Welshmen before this time, be void and of no value; and that all bondmen of the king be compelled to such services and labours as they were accustomed to; and that the officers have power to compel them to do such labours and services'.[91] Moreover, in March a special edict was issued by the Privy Council enjoining the constables of castles in Wales to see to the safety of their charge.[92]

These drastic measures were in all probability due directly to the number of Welsh squires in the duke of Gloucester's retinue, and indirectly to the state of anarchy in Wales during the four or five years which immediately preceded his arrest. There is not sufficient evidence to prove that Humphrey schemed to turn this anarchy to Suffolk's disadvantage. That seems to have been a mischievous fabrication emanating from the cunning brain of Suffolk. Its only support comes from the statements in Herbert's pardon that Gloucester had endeavoured to release Eleanor Cobham, and the allegation of Suffolk himself at Bury. At the same time, it must be admitted that the circumstances were such as to make the allegation plausible enough.

The state of Wales did not improve afterwards.

Misgoverned persons take divers persons and cattle under colour of distress where they have no manner, fee, or cause to make such distress, but feign actions and quarrels. And many times for taking of such distresses and in such resistance of them, great assemblies of people, riots, maims and murders be made, and if it be not hastily remedied other inconveniences be like to follow, of which takings, bringings, and carryings in this behalf no due punishment is, whereof the people of the said parts daily abound and increase in evil governance.[93]

In 1449, therefore, the duke of Buckingham, who wielded a wide territorial influence in Mid-Wales, was sent to deal with the matter, while the king traversed the Marches to lend support if necessary. But the Wars of the Roses were already at hand to make confusion more confused.[94]

CHAPTER THREE

Wales and the French Wars – Mathew Gough

The part played by Wales in the fifteenth-century wars between England and France has not hitherto received even a cursory examination. During the prolonged duel which followed the battle of Agincourt thousands of Welshmen crossed the sea, the nation's activity expending itself freely in the game of war. Archers and men-at-arms were greatly in request. The archer's pay was twice that of a labourer. Service abroad was a relief from disabilities and bondage at home. The lust for booty added zest to a life not otherwise unattractive. Such were the causes which allured Welshmen to France; and their deeds of valour contributed materially to amplify the little glory which relieves the monotonous dreariness of those arid years.

Although a detailed examination of the Agincourt campaign as it affected Wales is beyond the pale of the present work, it may be of interest to mention the most prominent Welshmen who shared in that triumph.

Sir John Devereux is stated to have brought a force of 250 men-at-arms and a similar number of foot-archers;[1] Sir John Skydmore of Herefordshire had with him four men-at-arms and twelve foot-archers;[2] John ap Henry[3] and Thomas ap Henry two men-at-arms and six foot-archers each; David Gam, esquire, three foot-archers. The greatest number of Welsh levies, however, was drawn from Cardiganshire, Carmarthenshire and Brecknock, and served under John Merbury who was Chamberlain of South Wales at the time.[4] He is credited with having had beneath his standard over five hundred Welshmen.[5] Thomas Carew also had with him a large body of Welshmen.[6]

Edward Stradling[7] of Glamorgan, John Perot[8] of Pembrokeshire, and William Wogan were with the duke of Gloucester; Henry Wogan[9] with the duke of York; John Griffith and John ap Thomas with Sir William Bourchier; John Glyn and Nicholas Griffith with Lord Talbot; John Edward[10] with Michael de la Pole, son of the earl of Suffolk; Rees ap Rhydderch with Sir Rowland Lenthal of Herefordshire; John Lloyd[11] and John ap Rhys[12] of Carmarthen were with the king. Sir Rowland Lenthal subsequently became lord of Haverfordwest.

Of these warriors none perhaps is so well known as David Gam, the ancestor of William Herbert, earl of Pembroke. He was one of the few men of note who were slain at Agincourt.[13] There is extant a tradition that he was knighted as he lay expiring on the field of battle. There is no conclusive evidence that the story is true. But the anonymous priest who accompanied the expedition, and afterwards gave an account of it, makes a vague statement that two newly made knights were included among the slain.[14] The only knight mentioned by him is Sir Richard Kighley, and it may be presumed that he had been knighted before. Now, if two of the three of inferior rank who were slain were knighted on the battlefield, we may reasonably suppose that David Gam was one, for he is given pride of place by every writer of the period. Our inference is strengthened by the fact that his son-in-law, Sir William ap Thomas, was soon afterwards a favourite at court, and was knighted at the same time as Henry VI.

The belief is fondly cherished that a number of other Welshmen were honoured with a knighthood on this historic field, notably Roger Vaughan of Bredwardine, Watkin Vaughan of Brecknock, and Watkin Lloyd of the same county. But we cannot escape a strong suspicion that these knighthoods have been fathered upon history by family pride. There certainly exists no reliable evidence. Indeed, Watkin Lloyd, alone of the trio, figures in the list of warriors[15] which has survived.

On the death of Henry V the control of English affairs in France fell to the lot of the duke of Bedford who, during the first few years of the reign, wrested from the French practically all districts north of the Loire. Meanwhile, a large number of Welshmen had joined the standards and a few were already holding responsible positions as captains and commanders.

One of these was Sir David Howel whom we have already had occasion to mention in connection with the conspiracy of the earl of Cambridge. He was a native of Pembrokeshire. He went abroad on the king's service in June 1416, fought at Verneuil, and was a captain under the duke of Bedford in 1435.[16] Sometime afterwards we find him in the retinue of the duke of York, designated as a knight. The records do not reveal the time or the occasion of his knighthood. In the following year, 1438, he was associated with Sir William Pyrton.[17]

Another who wrote his name in the annals of the time and in the literature of the land of his birth was Sir Richard Gethin. He was a son of Rhys Gethin, a native of Builth, although one authority describes him as of North Wales.[18] He fought at Crevant (1423) and at Verneuil (1424).[19] After Verneuil he was made captain of St Cales, one of the towns captured by the earl of Salisbury.[20] He was also captain of Hièmes in 1424. In 1428 he played a distinguished part at the siege of Orleans with the earl of Salisbury, and four years later was raised to the command of the important fortress of Mantes,[21] where, in 1433–4, he had under his command 21 mounted lances, 12 foot-lances, and 145 archers. Guto'r Glyn commemorates in song his elevation to this post, and elsewhere mentions a rumour that he had been taken prisoner in Normandy.[22] The fact affords additional evidence of the frequent and reliable communications between the Welsh bards and their heroes abroad.

Of the rest[23] a few played a prominent part in the later events of the period, notably Sir John Skydmore, and the Wogans of West Wales. Sir John Skydmore received protection to cross over to France with his son John, in the king's retinue, on 8 April 1422. He was retained, as we have seen, with ten lances and thirty archers for service at Harfleur.[24] Later (May 1435–6) he was in the retinue of the duke of York.[25] Sir John Wogan was in the service of the duke of Clarence in 1418.[26] He held a commission to array the duke's troops in 1419 (9 August).[27] In 1420 he appears in the king's retinue.[28] Owen Tudor was in the retinue of Sir Walter Hungerford.

None of his compatriots, however, and few of his contemporaries, achieved the fame of Mathew Gough. The lustrous splendour of his deeds shone in almost solitary brilliance in those sunless days. The prominence given to him by the chroniclers of the Tudor period, from whom Shakespeare drew the material for his historical plays, is such that Gough may well have inspired the dramatist in the creation of Fluellen. A native of Maelor, in the lower valley of the Dee, he crossed to France in the enthusiasm of youth. His father was Owen Gough, bailiff of the manor of Hanmer, near Whitchurch, in North

Drawing of Thomas Montacute, earl of Salisbury, from John Lydgate's poem, 'The Pilgrim' (British Library).

Wales. His mother was a daughter of David Hanmer, the nurse of John, Lord Talbot, afterwards earl of Shrewsbury. It is not unlikely, therefore, that Gough from the first came into close touch with that gallant soldier.

His name first appears in the list of the principal personages who fought at Crevant and at Verneuil, where fell two of his countrymen, Richard ap Madoc and David Lloyd.[29] He may have joined the English forces in France with the levies of the Earl Marshal which were mustered by Sir John Skydmore in May 1423.[30] This was the army which, reinforced by some Burgundians, gave battle to the French at Crevant and routed them.[31] Gough distinguished himself in the pursuit and capture of the Bastard de la Baume, a brave Savoyard ally of the French. For this exploit the earl of Salisbury gave him 'a goodly courser'.[32] After Verneuil we find him captain of some of the fortresses which had been taken by the earl of Salisbury. He then played a prominent part in the military operations which culminated in the reduction of Maine and Anjou.[33]

In 1428 he was put in command of the important fortress of Laval, on the border between those two provinces, which had been captured by Talbot in March of that year. At this period the most trivial incidents in his life are not allowed to pass unnoticed, an infallible symptom of growing popularity or

Posthumous portrait of John Talbot, earl of Shrewsbury (d. 1453) (Compton Wynyates).

accomplished fame. During the military operations in Maine in that year, he was sent out by Talbot to reconnoitre the enemy's position on the borders of Brittany. He set off in the dead of night, achieved his object by consummate tactics, and returned with complete information, having in the meantime 'eaten only a little bread and drunk a little wine to comfort his stomach'.[34]

In the same year he and his countryman, Richard Gethin, accompanied the earl of Salisbury in his advance on the Loire. On 25 September Salisbury captured the castle of Beaugency, and pursued his advantage by laying siege to Orleans. The relief of that fortress by Joan of Arc is one of the romantic chapters in French history. Beaugency had been placed in the keeping of Gough as Talbot's lieutenant, but the relief of Orleans seriously imperilled its safety. In June 1429 it was completely surrounded by the triumphant Joan of Arc. Gough's position became precarious, and Talbot sent him an assurance that he would immediately be reinforced.

Sir John Fastolf, realizing the hopelessness of holding the place against such odds, although it was defended by 'men of good stuff', advised the garrison to surrender.[35] The impetuous Talbot, however, resolved to challenge the supremacy of the French with a relieving force. But his army was soon in retreat, and Gough had no alternative but to sign articles of surrender. The French took possession on 18 June, the garrison being allowed to carry out all their belongings. On hearing of this disaster, Talbot and the whole army retreated towards Patay where he was himself defeated and taken prisoner.[36] Gough then tried to stem the French advance at Senlis; and while he was there engaged, Laval was betrayed to the enemy by a neighbouring miller.

The swelling tide of French advance rolled onward with resistless force towards the Norman frontier. The war no longer provided material for heroism. It had become a dreary succession of sieges and the raising of sieges. After the loss of Laval, Gough endeavoured to raise a bulwark of defence in Maine. For six weeks in the summer of 1432 he and Lord Willoughby pounded fruitlessly at the citadel of St Céneri. At the end of that period, a French relieving force which offered battle near Vivain on the Sarthe, opposite Beaumont, was repulsed with considerable loss. On returning with their spoils and a number of prisoners Gough and Willoughby were unexpectedly attacked by another division of the French army under Ambrose Delore. Gough was taken prisoner, and the siege was abandoned in consequence.[37]

Great was the distress in Wales when news of his captivity reached the circle of bards. Their solicitude found expression in a chorus of grief, panegyric and appeal. Ieuan Deulwyn soars to lofty heights of eulogy. Lewis Glyn Cothi sets him up as a standard of valour. Guto'r Glyn appeals for funds to ransom him. Gough was not long in captivity. He was redeemed, and it is not impossible that he may have found financial assistance in his native land.[38]

During the next few years the records are all but silent with regard to his movements. When he does appear, he is in the vortex of the storm on the borders of Normandy and Maine; now with Thomas Kyriel as captain of St Denis, a place which was yielded to the French in June 1435; at another time as joint lieutenant of the important fortress of Le Mans, under Sir John Fastolf, governor of Anjou and Maine.[39] An official attestation of two indentures relative to the custody of this stronghold enumerates his personal bodyguard: 60 mounted lances, 14 foot-lances, and 222 archers.[40]

Meanwhile, Joan of Arc, after the defeat of Talbot near Patay, had met with a series of glittering successes. But she failed in her assault on Paris and thereby lost prestige. In 1430 she escaped from the French court, was taken prisoner by the Burgundians, and in the following year burnt by the English at Rouen. In 1435, at the Congress of Arras, the English refused conditions of peace, and in consequence lost the alliance of Burgundy. In 1436 they were expelled from Paris. During the next fifteen years the interest of the war was concentrated in Normandy.

In 1440 Gough assisted Somerset and Talbot in the reduction of Harfleur which had been captured by the French in 1435. The French garrison made a gallant defence. A relieving force was despatched to raise the siege under Gaucourt, one of the most distinguished of those who took part in the reduction of Normandy. Gaucourt[41] was lagging behind when he was unexpectedly set upon by a body of Welshmen under Griffith Dwnn, and taken prisoner.[42] The reverse was such a severe blow to the garrison that they were immediately forced to surrender.

In 1442 Gough was at Chartres, and was one of the commanders to whom a large sum was paid by Dunois touching the demolition of the two fortresses of Gallardon and Tourville, the surrender of which had become the military necessity of a languishing cause.[43]

English dominion in France now gasped fitfully to its close. The need for reinforcements and a directing genius had become an imperative necessity. Thus it was that in June 1441 the duke of York, having been appointed Lieutenant and Governor-General of Normandy, sailed from Portsmouth. He landed at Harfleur, and marched through Rouen to take part with Sir John Talbot around Pontoise. Among those who constituted his retinue were Sir Walter Devereux and Sir John Skydmore, while Sir William ap Thomas of Raglan was a member of his military council.[44] Sir William ap Thomas was the father of William Herbert, afterwards earl of Pembroke. He was a courtier and councillor rather than a warrior. We have no record of his having achieved military fame. The prowess of Mathew Gough was popularized in the odes of an enthusiastic bardic circle. A curious tale of a later day immortalized David ap Einon, the hero of Harlech. Sir William ap Thomas can claim neither the real glory of the one, nor the legendary renown of the other.

Early in the century his family had cast their lot with the English opposition to the rising of Owen Glyndwr. David Gam, Sir William's father-in-law, had carried his enmity to such lengths that he made an ignoble and malicious attempt to assassinate the Welsh leader, a dark project which almost succeeded. The renewal of the French war by Henry V opened out for him a more honourable field of enterprise which he and his immediate descendants turned to considerable advantage. In the course of years, the family regained their esteem in the public opinion of Wales. Sir William ap Thomas was familiarly known as the 'Blue Knight of Gwent', while his wife Gwladys was hailed as the lodestar of a new nationalism.[45]

Authentic details of his career are few and unimportant. He served on a number of commissions in South Wales, which throw a lurid light on the flagitious piracy that infested the estuary of the Severn. In 1426 he was enrolled among the thirty-six young gentlemen who were knighted in honour of Henry VI's knighthood.[46] The prevailing opinion that he was knighted by Henry V for his valour in the wars of France is therefore erroneous.[47] It is conceivable that his path to honour was largely paved by the prowess of David Gam. We see no reason to refuse to identify him with the person of the same name and title who was sheriff of Glamorgan in 1440, a position which was held by his more distinguished son, William Herbert, some years later.[48] In 1450 he was joint ward of the lands of the countess of Warwick. This is apparently the last recorded notice of him in published records.

To return to the war and Mathew Gough. In 1444 a truce was agreed upon at Tours between England and France to celebrate the betrothal of Henry VI and Margaret of Anjou. One of the conditions of this marriage alliance was the cession to the French of Anjou and Maine. The duke of York endeavoured to reap personal advantage from the alliance by a projected betrothal of his own son to a French princess;[49] and to enhance his prospects in that object he sent Gough to assist the dauphin in an expedition against the Swiss in Alsace.[50]

The negotiations for the cession of Maine did not find Gough in any humour of acquiescence. His conduct on this occasion exhibited a tenacity as inflexible as his patriotism was fervid. It was a galling experience to so valiant a captain to be summoned meekly to transfer to his enemy a district through the conquest of which he had won for himself undying renown; and it did not fail to reveal in him a resourcefulness worthy of a better cause.[51] He doubted the expediency of such a surrender. The glory of British arms had not shone brightly since Crevant and Verneuil, and he dreaded the pernicious effects of a diplomatic check. Even Margaret, herself not devoid of combativeness, was captivated by his vigour and zeal.[52]

The fateful promise to concede Maine was extorted from Somerset in 1444. It had not been fulfilled a year later, and the French began to press their demand. In December 1445 Henry signed an undertaking to surrender Le Mans and his possessions in Maine by the following April. Meanwhile a truce was agreed upon. Gough was now captain of Bayeux.[53]

In July 1446 it appears that he was in England,[54] perhaps in connection with the surrender. In the following year the question had already assumed an exacting predominance. On 28 July 1447 he and Fulk Eyton were commissioned to receive Le Mans from the hands of the earl of Dorset (afterwards earl of Somerset) and deliver it to the representatives of Charles VII of France.[55] They were to use force if necessary. Gough adopted dilatory tactics and, far from appealing to the sword, did not even present his demand till 23 September.[56] When this was formally done, Osbern Mundeford, Dorset's lieutenant in Le Mans, refused to surrender on the technical ground that no letters of discharge were enclosed for him.

On 23 October Henry VI wrote to Gough and Eyton: 'We have been informed of the diligence which by our command you have done to have and recover unto our hands the town and castle of Le Mans.'[57] But if Henry and his advisers thus put a specious interpretation upon their conduct, the king of France was nettled by their arbitrary and fearless evasiveness.

On 1 November a conference was held at Le Mans between the French and

William Ayscough, bishop of Salisbury, marries Henry VI to Margaret of Anjou in Titchfield Abbey.

English representatives to discuss the question of compensation. Gough and Eyton, who were to have made the formal surrender, conveniently absented themselves, and the cession was again postponed. French authorities interpreted their conduct as deliberate shuffling. Charles wrote to Henry complaining of their delay and studied disobedience: 'And seeing the subterfuges, pretences, and dissimulations to which they resorted, we sent our accredited messengers to your great Council at Rouen;

and, in consequence of the wrong, we have been moved to proceed against them.'[58]

On 30 December the count of Dunois extracted from Gough a promise that he would surrender the town on 15 January 1448. Gough again prevaricated. Consequently Charles obtained from the English Council at Rouen an undertaking that if the province was not delivered into his hands by 10 February, Gough would be held guilty of treason. The French were now prepared to enforce their demands at the point of the sword. On 13 February an army under the count of Dunois appeared before Le Mans. Gough was still stubborn, alleging that he awaited further orders from Adam Moleyns. On 16 March, however, he yielded. He was allowed to march out with bag and baggage and substantial compensation. On the previous day he issued a protest in the king's name that the cession was only made in consideration of a secure peace, and that Henry did not resign the sovereignty of Maine.[59] Such a protest did not weigh a feather with the aggressive captains of France, but it revealed the bitter distress with which a born soldier accepted a rebuff of the making of others. It was sorry consolation to him that the Council issued a proclamation that he had done his duty as to the delivery of this rich province.[60]

The disbanded garrison of Le Mans endeavoured to counterbalance this loss by establishing a new fortress at St James de Beuvron, in Brittany. Charles protested, and lengthy discussions followed. The question was still in the crucible of debate when the English sacked Fougères. In the meantime Gough had tried to rescue Giles of Brittany, a loyal ally of England, who had been cast into prison when the duke of Brittany threw his influence on the side of the French.[61] Charles of France, resolved on the complete expulsion of the English from Normandy, suddenly put an end to this travesty of a peace, and in July active war once more began.

St James de Beuvron had been recaptured a few weeks previously, the garrison being allowed to leave with all their goods.[62] On the resumption of hostilities the English strongholds submitted in rapid succession, among them La Roche Guyon, an almost impregnable fortress in central Normandy, situated on the Seine. Its captain was the Welshman, John Edward, who had so far advanced his personal fortunes that he had married a French woman of considerable property, and a relative of the powerful French count, Denis de Chailly. Perceiving that English dominion in France was nearing its close, and being anxious not to jeopardize his wife's property, Edward, with tender discretion, became a vassal of the French king, and surrendered the fortress, 'at the advice, prayer and entreaty of his wife, on condition that he should enjoy his wife's lands, and become a subject of king Charles'.[63] We may assume that he was the same person who fought at Agincourt in the retinue of the earl of Suffolk's son. There were doubtless many other Welshmen who now transferred their allegiance to the French king.[64]

St Lo surrendered on 15 September. Gough, who was at the time captain of Bayeux, was so incensed at the conduct of the burgesses in admitting the French that he threatened to put their town and its suburbs to the flames.[65] Carentan submitted to the duke of Brittany on 30 September. Gough shared the command of this fortress with his countryman, William Herbert. This, apparently, is the first, and one of the very few authentic notices we have of the latter in connection with French affairs.[66]

Meanwhile, the duke of Alençon surrounded Bellême, of which, too, Gough was

Adam Moleyns, bishop of Chichester. From a series of painted wooden panel portraits by Lambert Barnard, 1519, in Chichester Cathedral.

captain and bailly, The garrison, numbering about two hundred,[67] seeing that resistance was futile unless reinforcements arrived, of which they had no hope, surrendered the town by composition. They were allowed to leave with their goods and chattels. This was 20 November. Before the close of 1449, Renneville, the captain of which was 'Griffith ap Meredith, Welshman', surrendered by composition.[68]

Gough was now approaching the zenith of his splendid military career. His heroism flowed like an electric current through those who served beneath him. To have passed unsinged through a furnace of hostile French criticism could not have been expected of a far less vigorous protagonist. Blondel, a contemporary writer, was especially inflamed against Gough. With him Gough's rigour spelt savagery, though he could not deny the stout hardihood with which he inspired his men. Wavrin makes the interesting admission that for years afterwards the name 'Matago', a French contraction of 'Mathew Gough', was fondly cherished by the inhabitants of Bellême in memory of their erstwhile captain.[69]

On 15 March 1450 Sir Thomas Kyriel landed at Cherbourg with reinforcements, and proceeded to lay siege to Valognes.[70] The duke of Somerset immediately sent him assistance under Sir Robert Vere, while Gough had to proceed from Bayeux, in command of about 800 men. Their combined efforts compelled the garrison to submit, on 10 April 1450.[71] The English forces then set out in the direction of Bayeux. Along their line of march they had to ford the quicksands between the sea and Carentan, leaving this town on the right. The inhabitants of that place made a strenuous effort to cut off their rear, but Gough's irresistible dash swept them aside. 'We have crossed in spite of the dogs,' he exclaimed on reaching safety, and thereupon kissed the ground he had won.[72]

They reached Formigny without further mishap, though the rapid concentration of French forces prevented any further general advance. Gough's contingent proceeded on its way to Bayeux, but were immediately recalled when it was seen that an engagement was imminent at Formigny. Here, on 15 April 1450, English domination in Normandy closed for ever. The French historian makes Gough address his troops on the eve of battle as follows:

> Your valour, my brave men, has been steeled in many fires. Show how unconquerable it is in this day's conflict. Vengeance, rather than courage, inspires your foes. Let strength of limb and intrepidity of heart win for you a glorious victory. If you play the lamb they will savagely cut your throats with blood-stained knives. Remember that your fathers, greatly outnumbered, vanquished countless hosts of Frenchmen. Your ranks are firm, and if you have the same indomitable spirit as they, you will scatter in headlong flight yonder disorderly and unbridled host. Flight on your part can only mean captivity or death. Seize the spoils of the Frenchmen! See how they glitter effulgent in silver and gold ! Enrich yourselves abundantly, or embrace death.[73]

Thus does the French writer of those days conceive Gough to have been swayed by alternating moods of fear, doubt, hope, cupidity, and the memory of past glory. That the speech was put in the mouth of Gough rather than of Kyriel, the nominal leader, shows how the former had captured the imagination of his enemies.

The day served to give additional proof of his courage. When the last gleam of hope of victory had disappeared, he cut his way through the French lines at the head of the left wing, which consisted of about 1,500 men, and reached Bayeux in safety. The bulk of the forces under Kyriel were either slaughtered in position or taken prisoner.[74] William Herbert and Kyriel were among the captured.[75] Gough himself all but fell into the hands of his enemy. He was rescued in a moment of extreme peril by his comrade and countryman, Gwilym Gwent, who was perhaps William Herbert ap Norman, a half-brother of William Herbert, afterwards earl of Pembroke.[76]

The remaining English strongholds fell in rapid succession. On 16 May Gough surrendered Bayeux to the count of Dunois, 'after severe assaults and skirmishes, the walls being pierced by great cannon'.[77] The pitiful sufferings of the garrison on their march to Cherbourg form one of the saddest episodes in this tale of disasters.[78] They were eight or nine hundred in number,[79] including the best and bravest of the English soldiers in Normandy. They were allowed a white staff for their weary way. There were about three hundred women besides children. Some of the latter were carried in little cradles on their mothers' heads; others clung around their mothers' necks. Some were led by the hand; many had to shift as best they could. Moved by their wretched plight, compassionate Frenchmen came to their assistance, some with horses, others with conveyances; for many of the women were French born, and were now abandoning their country for a foreign land.[80]

'What great booty dost thou, O Mathew Gough, thus ignominiously expelled from France, now carry to England? Bereft of thy plunder, thou, a weary wayfarer, seekest thy home, wielding a slender staff, not a quivering lance. Thy miserable end is an example to tyrants, who always die in the midst of calamities.'[81] Such were the biting comments of the French contemporary historian.

The remnants of the English forces gathered around Somerset at Caen after the defeat at Formigny. On 24 June that city capitulated,[82] and Somerset retired for a while to Calais. On 12 August Cherbourg, the last English foothold in Normandy, submitted to Charles of France. Sir John Gough refused to surrender without adequate compensation.

To bring Gough's career to a close. After the fall of Bayeux he crossed immediately to England from Cherbourg. He was then placed in command of the Tower of London with Lord Scales. Early in July he was called upon to defend the city against the insurgent Kentishmen under Jack Cade, 'because he was of manhood and experience greatly renowned and noised'.[83]

Cade's rebels entered the city on 2 July. Three days later Gough issued forth by night at the head of a body of troops, dispersed the rioters, and attacked London Bridge, which was in the hands of Cade's men. The battle raged fiercely through the night,[84] and many were hurled into the Thames to receive a watery grave in their heavy armour. Meanwhile, in the darkness lit up only by the blaze of burning houses, Mathew Gough was slain, fighting desperately to hold the bridge which he had succeeded in wresting from the men of Kent. He was honourably buried in the choir of St Mary's, of the Carmelite Friars. William of Worcester gave expression to the grief in Wales on the death of the hero in a curious Latin couplet:

On the death of Mathew Goch
Wales, in deepest gloom, cried, Och![85]

'He was a man of great wit and much experience in feats of chivalry, the which in continual wars had valiantly served the king and his father beyond the seas.'[86] Contemporary chroniclers unite in a chorus of praise and admiration. A native of a land of mountains and castles, he possessed in an eminent degree those qualities which make for success in a system of guerrilla warfare, in which the assault and defence of castles were the outstanding features. He warred in France for more than a quarter of a century; and he was one of the very few who emerged from that cauldron of blundering, incapacity, waste and havoc, with a name resplendent with brilliant achievements.[87]

Contemporary poetical allusions to him are numerous in the vernacular, and afford ample proof of his popularity in Wales, though, as far as we know, he never revisited the land of his birth. Ieuan Deulwyn, Guto'r Glyn, and Lewis Glyn Cothi are unanimous in appraising him as the most daring and successful soldier of his day.

A number of Welshmen sought means at the conclusion of the war to defray their ransom. Edward Stradling and his family were given licence to ship wool to Brittany for this purpose; Robert Dwnn traded with Normandy to defray Lord Falconberg's ransom. His vessel, the *James* of Tenby, while coming to England laden with wines from Bordeaux, was captured by the French near Winchelsea, which involved him in another journey to France. John Derell exported wool to ransom his son who was a hostage in France. Lewis Howel traded with Normandy through certain merchants.[88]

APPENDIX I

For a list of those who received protection see Calendar French Rolls in *Record Reports* 1885, 545–637, and Calendar Norman Rolls, *Record Reports* 1880, 1881. The following is a list of the Welshmen; the dates given in brackets are those on which they received protection: Thomas ap Prene of Aberystwyth (23 March 1418); David ap Rhys of Pencoed, Herefordshire, who was on a commission to redress infractions of the truce with Burgundy, 2 June 1418. He was in the retinue of Thomas Barre (21 February 1419) and with John, Lord Furnivale (2 June 1421); John Hall of Wales, in Gloucester's retinue (15 May 1421); John Henbury of Denbigh in Lord Scales's retinue (14 May 1431); David Gronow of Tenby in Sir John Kyderowe's (28 May 1421); Owen ap Thomas in the earl of Worcester's (8 June 1421); various Welshmen (unnamed) in the king's and Lord Audley's retinues (6 July 1417 and 16 February 1419); William Porter of Cardigan in John Popham's (23 February 1416); John Aylward of Kidwely in Henry Gwyn's (4 August 1419); William ap Griffith of Iscennin, Carmarthenshire, in Sir John Steward's; Meredith ap William ap Patrick of Carnwallon, Carmarthenshire, in Thomas Rempston's, who was captain of Meulan, 22 November 1419; Henry ap Walter of Llanelly (16 August 1419); Henry ap Ieuan Gwynne in the king's (18 October); Thomas ap David ap William of Wales, yeoman in Sir John Steward's retinue in Normandy (26 June), who was then captain of Nully-L'evêque. In 1418 Thomas Carew had a band of Welshmen in his retinue. Rymer IX. 596. During 1420–1 several commissions were issued to array Welsh archers. Sir Edward Stradling of Glamorgan received letters of attorney (24 May 1426–7); Roger Cause of Tenby in Sir John Kighley's retinue (8 December); Thomas Llywelyn in the earl of Ormond's (13 March 1429–30); Ithel Llywelyn of Flintshire and Hugh Penllyn in Lord Fitzwalter's (February 1430–1); Lewis ap Rhys Gethin of South Wales in Walter Cressener's (January 1437–8); Edward ap Howel, assessor of taxes in Normandy (1430); Stephenson II. 130, also 299, 437; Thomas Griffith, in Bedford's retinue (1435); John Vaughan, in Bedford's retinue (May 1422–3); David, son of John Parker of Chirk, in John de Burgh's, captain of Vernon on the Seine (7 May 1424–5); Thomas Toker of Tenby, merchant, in William FitzHenry's, captain of Honfleur (12 December 1422–4); William Wolf of Wales, knight, in Bedford's (1435), Stephenson II. 433; Geoffrey Dwnn and William Vaughan of Cheshire (13 May 1421, and May 1435–6); Gregory ap Heulyn of Denbigh, and Owen Dwnn in Lord Talbot's (8 February 1434–5); Ednyfed Vaughan of Anglesey (January 1435–6) in the earl of Mortain's retinue; Thomas Gamage of Caldecot and Cardiff in the earl of Suffolk's (May 1435–6); Geoffrey ap Rhys accompanied the bishop of St David's to the Congress of Arras in 1435. Robert Lewis of Cardiff, alias Vaughan of London, in Somerset's retinue (May–June 1442–3); Henry Michael of Cardiff in the retinue of William Pyrton, lieutenant of Guisnes (1 February 1443–4); Stephenson II 331–2. Lewis ap Meredith was Marshal of Mantes in 1444, ibid. I. 461; and in the special service of the queen.

Letters of Margaret of Anjou, 116.

APPENDIX II

Virtus enim vestra, fortissimi viri, hodierno conflictu quanta sit in hostium pugnam variis periculis retro probata ostendet. Si virili animo et corpore robusto adversus istos plus vindictae calore quam virtute concitos dimicet, ab hostibus praeclaram victoriam reportabit. Si ignave, veluti pecorum hostes inhumani versa guttura cruentis mucronibus abscindent. Estote memores ut vestri partes cum paucis innumeram Gallorum multitudinem vicerunt et nunc multo plures si animi vigor insit istam effraenatam turbam sine ordine in vos ruentem maximam in fugam disperget, a qua fugax nullus strictam captionem aut subitam mortem evadere poterit. Nam vada jam mari cumulata Carentonium fugientibus viam praecludent. Fusis enim Gallis omnis vobis et posteritati vestrae comparata animi praestantia perpetua nobilitatis insignia consequemini. Ditia Gallorum spolia, quae argento auroque praefulgere conspicitis, non mediocri sorte vestras fortunas augebunt, quae vos non ambigo consecuturos si animi praestantia in conflictu, veluti fortes proavi, in adversos pedem teneat fixum.

Blondel, 171–2.

APPENDIX III

O Matthaeum Goth! Spoliis agrorum et urbium raptu et tortura exactis tuas fortunas fecisti locupletissimas; an ista afflicti populi oppressione cumulatas armis conservare potes? Quid de tanta praeda nunc de Francia foede expulsus in Angliam defers? Fractis enim corporis robore et animi virtute, armaturam, equos et quaecumque castrensia patriae direptione extorta victori Karolo, ut vitam a stricto gladio redimas compulsus cessisti; et raptis omnibus exutus, non eques vibratam lanceam manu, sed tenuem stepitem ad tuos penates pedester portas. Pro sorte gloriae regni tui extollenda vincula, carceres, vulnera, et gravissimas labores, noctu diuque tolerasti. Pro tantis rebus angore gestis, tametsi exteriora fortunae caduca amisisti, saltem summum virtute praemium honorem consecutus es, et labore tot periculis repetito tui principis gratiam et populi Anglici favorem habes, ut beneficiis pro remuneratione elargitis tuae calamitati condoleant. Tua enim foeda a bello Forminiaco fuga sempiterna ignominiae sorde tuam famam, tui nominis aestimationem deturpavit. Et quia fugiens proeliorum ordines dis solvisse accusaris (cujus occasione aiunt conflictum exitu sibi adversum et Gallis prosperum fuisse) et ob hoc tuo principi invisus et a populo implacabili furore concito reversus caede ferocissima necaris. In armis igitur perniciosus tibi, Mathaee, labor fuit, qui egestatem non divitias, qui dedecus non laudem, qui tandem crudele exitum non vitae securitatem attulit. Exitus vitae tuae miserrimus tyrannum semper emori calamitose ostendit.

Blondel, 211–12.

CHAPTER FOUR

Herbert and Tudor

Of the luminaries who appeared in the political firmament during these stormy days of faction and war, none shone with a steadier light than Jasper Tudor. He was the son of Owen Tudor, an Anglesey gentleman who traced his descent from the old Welsh king, Cadwaladr. Owen was tall, handsome, and endowed with extraordinary charm of manner. He was also imbued with a lofty chivalry that continued to ennoble his life in spite of many hazardous vicissitudes during a period of fierce political convulsions, when chivalry degenerated into brutality and selfish lust of power.

It has been supposed that he was one of the band of hardy Welsh warriors who did service at Agincourt.[1] Reliable records, however, do not carry us back further than his appearance in the retinue of Hungerford late in the reign of Henry V.[2] He must soon have abandoned the fields of war for the alluring avenues of court life; for during the infancy of the king he was at Windsor, in close attendance upon Queen Catherine and her child.

It appears that Catherine might have married Edmund Beaufort, earl of Mortain (afterwards duke of Somerset), but for the opposition of Humphrey, duke of Gloucester, who saw in the proposal the dangerous ascendancy of the family of his rival, Cardinal Beaufort. Accordingly it was decreed by act of parliament, apparently about the year 1427–8 that a marriage with a queen dowager without a special permission should be illegal. But it could not have been many years after the death of Henry V before Catherine bestowed her affections upon Owen Tudor in bold defiance of parliamentary decrees and courtly traditions. They were married secretly. We need not suspect the validity of the marriage,[3] though we cannot trace any legal ceremony. During the proceedings instituted by the Privy Council against Owen there was no suggestion of illicit relations between him and the queen dowager. Nor was there any question raised as to the legitimacy of the children. In fact the legality of the marriage is tacitly admitted. However, when the relations between rival parties became more strained, Edmund and Jasper Tudor, who had then been raised to the earldoms of Richmond and Pembroke respectively, deemed it prudent to obtain a parliamentary ratification of their titles, and a formal declaration that they were the king's half-brothers. A technical illegality may, indeed, have been committed if, as has been generally supposed, the marriage took place about 1430.

Left: Victorian stained glass picture of Jasper Tudor, Cardiff Castle.
Right: Memorial brass of Edmund Tudor, earl of Richmond, father of Henry VII, St David's Cathedral, Dyfed. This replaces the lost original on his tomb brought from Greyfriars, Carmarthen, c. 1538.

Intermarriage with Welshmen was contrary to law, and Owen did not receive denizenship till 1432. The date of this grant, and the unusually stringent conditions attached to it, suggest that the marriage was known to a limited circle of courtiers who were not averse to shielding Owen while Catherine lived.[4] The statement of the London chronicler appears to corroborate this view.[5]

Four children were born to Owen and Catherine, three sons and a daughter, 'unwetyng the common people tyl that she were dead and buried': Edmund of Hadham, who was afterwards created earl of Richmond and married Margaret Beaufort (their son was Henry VII); Jasper Tudor of Hatfield who became earl of Pembroke; Thomas who was a monk at Westminster and 'lived a small time'; and a daughter Margaret, who died young.[6] Hadham and Hatfield were royal residences. Many stories have naturally gathered around the romance of Owen and Catherine. Among the tares of tradition must be assigned the tale that Owen on one occasion introduced to the queen a number of his compatriots whom she playfully described as the 'goodliest dumb creatures she ever knew', on account of their ignorance of any language but Welsh.[7]

Soon after the death of Catherine, in January 1437, Owen Tudor was summoned before the Privy Council to answer for his conduct. He was then at Daventry, and refused to come without an assurance that he would be allowed 'freely to come and freely to go'.[8] Though he received a verbal promise to this effect from the duke of

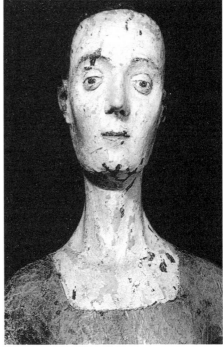

The recently restored head of the wooden figure of Henry V on his tomb in Westminster Abbey contrasts with that of his wife Catherine, from her funeral effigy in the Undercroft Museum.

Gloucester, he justly refused to admit the validity of it unless it were put in writing. Having thus incurred the danger of arrest, he came up to London and took sanctuary in Westminster. He remained there for some days, refusing to abandon his refuge, 'eschewing to leave it although many persons out of friendship and fellowship stirred him to come out thereof and desport himself in a tavern at Westminster gate'.[9] Malicious representations were then circulated accusing him of disloyalty. In his eagerness to belie his traducers he came out of sanctuary and appeared before the Council, where he protested that he had done nothing to give offence to the king, and offered to 'byde the law' with reference to any charge brought against him. He was then permitted to retire to Wales.

He was not allowed his liberty for long. In contravention of the assurance which had been given him he was placed under arrest, taken to London, and consigned to Newgate. The council, recognizing that an unwarranted breach of faith had been committed, drew up a statement, as lame as it is laboured, to prove that the royal assurance had not been violated. The charge preferred against him was that he had married the queen dowager without the king's consent. It was stated that the undertaking given by him to answer any indictment involved the forfeiture of the royal promise of safe-conduct; that at the time the promise was given neither the king nor Gloucester was aware of his hostile designs; and that having already appeared before the council and been allowed to retire to Wales, he had forfeited the benefit of the assurance given.[10] The document is unconvincing. In February of the following year, Owen Tudor and his servant contrived to break out of Newgate 'in the night at searching time through the help of his priest, and went his way, hurting foul his keeper'.[11] Having been recaptured by Lord Beaumont, who was given a special grant of twenty marks for his expenses in the business,[12] he was once more summoned before the Council. The priest was found to have £90 in his possession, which was confiscated to the exchequer.[13] The priest was sent to Newgate, whither Owen Tudor also, after having been placed temporarily under the charge of the duke of Suffolk at Wallingford, was eventually removed. He contrived to elude his keepers once again and escaped to Wales, where, presumably, he remained till the outbreak of civil war.[14] He received a full pardon in November 1439.[15]

The intimate knowledge of Owen's misfortunes possessed by the swarthy bard of remote Anglesey, Robin Ddu, suggests that Owen repaired to his native land on his first release. In an angry lament, which internal evidence proves to have been written during Owen's captivity, the poet mourns his champion's confinement. 'Neither a thief nor a robber, neither debtor nor traitor, he is the victim of unrighteous wrath. His only fault was to have won the affection of a princess of France.' The bard further gives vent to his anxiety for the welfare of Owen's children in lines which show that the soul of chivalry had not departed from the hills, though courtly circles knew it no more. The ode also corroborates the assertion of the annalist Stow, that the attachment between Catherine and Owen began at a dance.[16]

An entirely different, though hardly less romantic, tale of their early relations is given by the Welsh Tudor chronicler:

Now Catherine had been a widow for some years. The council forbade her to marry again, a prohibition which she openly resented. At that time a squire of Gwynedd, who was chief butler at court, conceived an attachment for the queen's maid of honour. One day in summer he and his friends were bathing in the stream which skirts the castle walls. The queen, observing them, saw that Owen – for that was the squire's name – surpassed the others in skill, and was more handsome of figure. Whereupon she turned to her maid and said, 'Yonder then is thy lover?' 'In truth,' replied the maid, 'no sooner am I alone than he plagues me with his attentions.' 'Let me,' replied Catherine, 'take your place in disguise to-night, and he shall harass you no more.'

Now Owen and the maid used to meet on the gallery not far from the queen's chamber. Thither the queen made her way stealthily at nightfall. Owen had already arrived. Only a few words had passed between them when they saw a light approaching as though the queen, as Owen thought, was on her way to her chamber. The maid's demeanour was strange, he thought, and he began to suspect that he was being deceived. He would have kissed her lips; but Catherine, who wished to conceal her face, struggled, and received a slight wound on her cheek. Meanwhile the light was coming nearer, and they parted.

Next day Catherine instructed her chamberlain to command Owen to serve her in person at dinner. Then it was that Owen discovered that the queen herself was the fair intruder, and he bent his head at the thought that he had wounded her. According to some, he would immediately have returned to his native land; according to others, the queen herself detained him at court, and having ascertained his descent from the old British kings, married him secretly.[17]

After the disgrace of Owen, his two sons were placed under the care of the abbess of Barking, Catherine de la Pole, sister of the earl of Suffolk, who occasionally complains of the non-payment of arrears that were due on their account.[18] The boys apparently remained there until 1440.[19] Although Catherine made no direct reference to the Tudors in her will, it is conceivable that her appeal to Henry VI to fulfil 'her intent tenderly and favourably' had a direct bearing upon the lot of the unfortunate boys.[20] It is certain that he afterwards shadowed their education and welfare with a tenderness and solicitude which were perhaps the only gleams that played upon their early life. He placed them under the guardianship of 'discreet persons to be brought up chastely and virtuously'.[21]

Nor did the king, Henry VI, neglect their father, Owen Tudor. He allowed him an annuity of £40, 'which for certain causes him moving he gave out of his privy purse by especial grace'.[22] The generosity of his royal half-brother was not lost upon Jasper, who served the dynasty of the Lancastrians in its hour of need with unflinching loyalty and exemplary devotion. The support which the Lancastrians found in Wales was due primarily to him. When his power waned, public opinion veered largely to William Herbert, who had meanwhile risen to eminence in the councils of Edward IV.

William Herbert was one of the few men who left an abiding impress on the history of his time. Like Jasper Tudor he did not catch the imagination of contemporary writers except during the last few years of his life, for his work was more in secret than in the open. The ponderous tread of armies of retainers afforded a more effective means of publicity; his was the silent voice of the inner council chamber. The eyes of generations of historians have been so dazzled by the glamour of a Warwick that they have failed to see in Herbert the forerunner of the Tudor ministers. It is agreed that the absolutism of the Tudors originated with Edward IV, but the part played by the ministers of that monarch has not been adequately appreciated.

We need not inquire into the ancestry of William Herbert. The task is the province of biography rather than of history. The Welsh gentry of the sixteenth century, anxious that their family trees should appear to have their roots deep in the annals of old Wales or Norman England, forged pedigrees which gave many of them a spurious origin. The existing pedigree of William Herbert, which traces him back to the FitzHerberts of the twelfth century, cannot escape this taint of forgery. It is based on a manuscript which is supposed to have been in the possession of Lord Herbert of Cherbury, who flourished in the seventeenth century.[23]

He was the son of Sir William ap Thomas and Gwladys, the daughter of David Gam;[24] and it is purely a matter of conjecture why the children were given the name of Herbert. It is possible that they wished to avoid the cloud of suspicion which enveloped their countrymen after the cataclysm of Glyndwr's wars. A Welsh name had a foreign sound and was, to many, suggestive of rebellion. The family had been vigorous and aggressive in their hostility to the Welsh leader, and had in consequence been anathematized by their countrymen. It was therefore a stroke of discretion to enter into a wider and more remunerative field of activity than Wales could afford, and to parade an English name.

Sir William ap Thomas must have spent much of his time in London. His eldest son Thomas, who figured prominently among the followers of Humphrey, duke of Gloucester, first appears as 'Thomas Herbert of Greenwich'; while William is introduced on the stage of history as 'William Herbert of London, chapman'. This epithet suggests – and the fact is corroborated by the contemporary Welsh poet Howel Swrdwal – that the Herberts entered into those commercial activities which did much to undermine the ascendancy of the feudal nobility, and to lay the foundations of the new. It was in 1440 that William Herbert received the epithet 'chapman'.[25] The protection which he had received two months before 'as going to Calais, there to abide in the company of Thomas Kyriel, knight, lieutenant of the town, and engage in victualling the same' was revoked, because he tarried in the city of London and its suburbs. This was the time when the duke of York and Sir William ap Thomas went over to Normandy. A few years later we find him engaged in importing Gascon wines into the port of Bristol.[26] Moreover, the Herberts, in 1462, were in command of certain vessels for the defence of Bristol and other ports in the west against the Lancastrians.[27]

We cannot be certain whether William Herbert accompanied York on his expedition in 1440, or whether he joined Kyriel in Calais, and we need not attempt to erect an aerial fabric of assumptions. He is lost to view for some years. When he reappears towards the close of the Hundred Years War, when the French were following hard upon the track of the retreating English, he was under the vigilant eye of his distinguished countryman, Mathew Gough, as joint-captain of Carentan, in 1449.[28]

From this circumstance it may safely be inferred that he had been in Normandy for some time.[29] After the reverse at Carentan he may have served with Gough at Fougères and Bellême. He was taken prisoner at Formigny. For this reason he probably did not return to England until the remnants of the English army crossed the Channel under Somerset in September 1450. Henceforth we must follow his course in the main stream of political life.

On the expiration of the duke of York's term as lieutenant of France in 1445, Dorset, who soon afterwards was raised to the dukedom of Somerset, was appointed to succeed him. York was made lieutenant of Ireland for ten years, a specious form of exile. Certain individuals were appointed to seize and imprison him at Conway on his way to his new post in 1447, Sir John Talbot at Holt Castle, Sir Thomas Stanley in Cheshire, and one Richard 'groom of our chamber' at Beaumaris. Sir Walter Devereux also was to be arrested. Nothing untoward happened.[30] Meanwhile the government of Margaret and Suffolk went from bad to worse. The popular opposition to them culminated in the banishment and death of Suffolk in 1450. Events then rushed onwards with perilous foreboding. Jack Cade raised the Kentishmen with temporary success, and was killed in a scuffle in July. In the confusion the duke of York abandoned his post with the avowed object of reforming the ministry, and landed in Beaumaris in August.[31] The duke of Somerset, who had succeeded Suffolk as leader of the court party, was summoned from Calais to deal with him, and was made constable of England in September.[32] This grant further inflamed public resentment against the queen and her friends.

Instructions had been issued to Henry Norris, deputy to the chamberlain of North Wales (Sir Thomas Stanley), Bartholomew Bold, who had succeeded John Norris as captain of Conway in 1441,[33] William Bulkeley, who was a sergeant-at-arms in Anglesey and may have held some office at Beaumaris,[34] and a few others, to arrest the progress of the duke of York on his return, and prevent his entry into Chester, Shrewsbury and the border towns. But York once again eluded their vigilance, reached his estates in the Marches of Wales, collected a strong body of followers and reached London safely.[35]

However, there was bloodshed. Sir William Tresham, Speaker of the House of Commons in the parliament of Bury, and one of York's most prominent supporters, was hastening to join his leader when he collided with the retainers of Lord Grey of Ruthin near Moulton, in Northamptonshire. Tresham was murdered.[36] In Wales, at least, the name of Grey of Ruthin was already synonymous with perfidy. There is hardly a more revolting figure in the annals of the war.

Parliament met in November, William Oldhall, formerly a colleague of Sir William ap Thomas on the duke of York's council in Normandy, being chosen Speaker. Violent scenes took place between Somerset and York, the latter having the House of Commons on his side, the former relying on his supremacy at court. York subsequently retired to Ludlow.[37] Early in September an attempt was made to arrest Somerset at Blackfriars. It proved futile, and Somerset remained at the wheel during the Christmas adjournment.

This fact is of importance; for it shows that the flash of Athenian acuteness which illumined the recess emanated apparently from the favourite. We refer to the honours conferred during the Christmas festival at Greenwich. The king's half-brothers, Edmund and Jasper Tudor, two sons of the earl of Salisbury, namely Thomas and John Neville, and William Herbert, were knighted.[38] It has hitherto been supposed that Herbert was knighted at Christmas 1449. This is an impossible date; for, apart from the fact that Herbert was then in Normandy, authorities are clear in their assertion that the knighthoods were bestowed after the return of York from Ireland and Somerset from Calais. Except perhaps the Tudors, these were men whose sympathies were presumably with the duke of York. In conferring favours upon them the court party may have hoped to detach the Nevilles and Herbert from their friendship with the duke, and thus to weaken his influence at a most vital point, namely the Marches. The position in south-east Wales was as follows: In 1449 Richard, earl of Warwick, had become possessed of the rich lordship of Glamorgan and Morgannwg.[39] The numerous ramifications of the families of Herbert and Roger Vaughan dominated Raglan and the surrounding district. Monmouth was part of the Lancastrian heritage.[40] Abergavenny was held by a Neville in the person of Edward Neville, son of Ralph, first earl of Westmorland.[41] Humphrey Stafford, duke of Buckingham, was lord of Brecknock and Newport, and an adherent of the House of Lancaster.[42] The Mortimer estates of the duke of York lay to the north, stretching roughly from Builth to Denbigh and including Builth, Clifford, Ewyas Lacy, Maeliennydd, Radnor, and Denbigh, with Ludlow as their centre, and at times Montgomery.[43]

The court party realized that these estates, extending in an almost unbroken phalanx from Cardiff to Chester, would, if united under the duke of York, constitute a very serious danger. For, apart from the personnel of the leaders, these March lordships harboured a restless population whose chief occupation was petty warfare. On the other hand, if Somerset could retain the allegiance of the Nevilles and Herbert, the Marches would be divided almost equally into two opposing camps. This circumstance will serve to explain also the unusual activity of Margaret on the borders of Wales during the next five years.

The duke of York did not remain idle. When the feud between the earl of Devon and Lord Bonville broke out in the west in 1451, he took Herbert with him to settle the dispute,[44] though the importance of this association need not be over-estimated, inasmuch as the duty of suppressing riots in the west would naturally devolve upon the lords of those parts. In the winter of 1451/2 York's designs assumed a more menacing aspect. From Ludlow he issued a manifesto to the burgesses of Shrewsbury denouncing Somerset, and proclaiming his intention of marching on London to destroy him.[45] Having collected an army in the Marches[46] he advanced on the capital. He found less encouragement than he had anticipated from the citizens, and was placed under arrest. Soon he was released and pardoned. His release is said to have been due to the rumour that another force was being mustered in Wales under his son, Edward, earl of March.[47] In the summer of 1452 the court party began their activities in the Marches. In July the king, accompanied by the queen and Somerset, went on a progress through the west, visiting Gloucester, Ross and Monmouth, in order to strengthen the fibres of loyalty and punish the guilty.[48] Walter Devereux of Weobley in Herefordshire, who

Seal of Richard Neville, earl of Warwick, as lord of Glamorgan and Morgannwg. The obverse shows him mounted on a horse bearing the arms of Montacute and Monthermer on the shoulder, with the rear caparison showing Clare, Despenser, Newburgh and Beauchamp. The reverse shows the many quarterings of his arms as borne on the horse's caparison, on a shield supported by his bear badge and surmounted by two helmets with the crests of Beauchamp and Monthermer.

was sheriff of that county in 1447, and some others were indicted for treasonable acts committed in the previous February. Bearing in mind that this was the month in which the duke of York issued his manifesto to the burgesses of Shrewsbury, the charge in all probability referred to the active participation of Devereux with York. Devereux was arraigned before justices Audley and Yelverton, but obtained the benefit of the act of grace pardoning all who had abetted York on that occasion.[49]

In October a general pardon was granted also to 'William Herbert of Ragland, in South Wales, of all offences before August 8 last, and any subsequent outlawries and forfeitures';[50] and shortly before to Owen ap Griffith, the son of Griffith ap Nicholas, and Philip ap Rees, 'for trespasses against the statute of liveries'.[51] These were also the outcome of the king's visit, and may reasonably be regarded as part of a deliberate plan to conciliate the minor gentry and undermine the predominant influence of the duke of York. Whether these had shared in York's immature enterprise the previous winter is a matter of conjecture. There is a strong presumption that William Herbert was implicated. We have seen that he accompanied York to the west in the previous year. He was also on terms of intimacy with Devereux. Moreover, there is extant a proclamation against him in which he is denounced as a notable rebel and forbidding any to give him encouragement or support. The proclamation is undated; but as this appears to have been the only occasion on which he was thus circumstanced, the reference is doubtless to his association with York.[52]

Further to strengthen and consolidate South Wales in the interest of the Crown, the king conferred the earldom of Pembroke upon his half-brother Jasper Tudor,

Edmund at the same time receiving the earldom of Richmond.[53] Their titles and legitimacy were confirmed in the parliament which met at Reading on 6 March 1453.[54] In this declaration the name of their father, Owen Tudor, is significantly omitted, although there is a veiled reference to the fact that some of their ancestors were not English born, and to the disability under which they might have laboured as Welshmen,[55] disabilities which perhaps occasioned this strange declaration. It states that the king confers these grants upon his half-brothers of his own free will, and not at the instance of any other person. They were to take precedence of all other earls.[56]

It is important to observe that the earldom of Pembroke was given to Jasper in spite of Margaret's having hitherto enjoyed the issues thereof.[57] The important castles of Pembroke, Tenby, Cilgerran, and Llanstephan were now therefore in Jasper's hands.[58]

Henceforth he took an active part in the deliberations of the government. In this parliament he introduced a bill into the Lower House asking, among other things, for a grant of the priory of St Nicholas at Pembroke. Intercession was made in favour of the monks of St Albans to whom a previous grant had been made by Humphrey, duke of Gloucester, and a provision was inserted in the bill saving the rights of the monastery.[59] When parliament rose for the Easter recess the Tudors kept in close touch with the king. One of them was at Norwich on 20 April 1453,[60] and in communication with the Pastons.

Meanwhile the government became alive to the need of stringent supervision in Wales. Sir Thomas Stanley, chamberlain of North Wales, was commissioned to compel the payment of arrears of debts and revenues from Merionethshire, Carnarvonshire, and Anglesey,[61] and to make inquisition in those counties touching trespasses, services, and customs concealed from the king, officers negligent of their duties etc.[62] Cymmer Abbey was committed to the charge of the duke of Somerset, and Ellis ap Griffith ap Einon, which abbey 'was endowed to the sum of £60 a year, though now the endowment does not exceed the value of 20 marks a year; and the abbey, through dissensions between certain lords of the marches there, has suffered distraints at the hands of persons on either side and abductions of goods and chattels so that no ministers thereof dare occupy the lands of old collated to the abbey'.[63]

During the year 1453 the court party made renewed efforts to strengthen their hold on Wales. Sir Walter Devereux had risked his life in the cause of York when the latter passed over to Ireland. In spite of this he was now favourably entertained by Margaret and Somerset. In March he was allowed to enter into possession of his wife's lands; in May he was given a moiety of the castle and lordship of Narberth; in December he was commissioned to make inquisition in Herefordshire touching all escapes of prisoners. Jasper Tudor received in addition to numerous grants in Warwickshire, Herefordshire, Lincolnshire, Surrey and elsewhere, the confiscated lands of William Oldhall who was accused of treason, and a fee farm of £113. 6s 8d, paid by the heirs of Roger Mortimer for the castle of Builth, and of £42 of the farm of Hereford, paid by the citizens,[64] as well as the lordship of Magor, in South Wales.[65]

Jasper Tudor had not as yet definitely associated himself with Margaret and Somerset. He was constantly at the king's side, and it is a tribute to the genuineness of the duke of York's protestations of loyalty that Jasper Tudor inclined to his side during this period of uncertainty and suspense. While York had no deeper purpose than the deposition of Somerset, he could, apparently, rely on the half-brothers.

The birth of a prince to Queen Margaret in October 1453 intensified an already strained situation. In November Jasper attended the council for the first time as a privy councillor, York being present, and Somerset absent; and he attended again in December.[66] A more significant proof of the half-brothers' faith in the duke of York occurred a

Edward of Lancaster, prince of Wales, only son of Henry VI and Margaret of Anjou. Victorian engraving, based on his portrait in the 'Beauchamp Pageant' family tree.

few weeks later. For when, in January 1454, the nobles were swept to London by the news of the king's imbecility, both were reported to have come in the company of the duke of York and the earl of Warwick with a large following, and to have been in danger of being arrested.[67] York was expected in London on 25 January.[68] There is no valid reason for doubting this statement as to the friendly relations between the Tudors and York. The grant of the Pembroke estates to Jasper probably gave offence to Margaret. There is no evidence to show that he had the least sympathy with Somerset, whose unpopularity increased with the final loss of France in the previous year; while during York's protectorate, although many Lancastrian lords were placed under guard, Jasper and Edmund were in attendance on the king.[69]

The duke of York became Protector in March 1454. Somerset was put in prison. Jasper Tudor frequently attended the meetings of the Privy Council,[70] and in November signed a series of arrangements for regulating the royal household, although in effect they considerably reduced the retinue of the king.[71]

Henry recovered in December; Somerset was released and acquitted of the charges brought against him.[72] In May 1455 a council was called to meet at

Leicester, nominally 'to provide for the safety of the king's person against his enemies'. The duke of York looked upon it as a declaration of war, marched on London from Wales,[73] and defeated the royal troops at the first battle of St Albans (22 May 1455). Somerset was slain.

The duke of Buckingham, lord of Brecknock, was with the royalists. Jasper possibly accompanied the king to St Albans[74] though he does not appear to have taken any part in the fight. He was among those who took the oath to Henry VI soon afterwards.[75] His brother Edmund's name does not appear; nor did he subscribe to the general oath of allegiance. As we shall see he was busy in West Wales. Jasper meanwhile remained in attendance on his royal master. In June 1456 he was at Sheen with the king, and no other lords were present.[76]

Among the offices assumed by the duke of York after the battle of St Albans were those of constable of Carmarthen Castle, steward of Wydegada and Elvet, and captain and constable of Aberystwyth,[77] with as many soldiers as were wont to stay there. Jasper Tudor did not witness the grant of the protectorate to him.[78]

York summoned parliament, and part of its business was 'to ordain and purvey for the restfull and sadde rule in Wales, and set apart such riots and disobeisances as have been there afore this time'.[79] Lawlessness was everywhere rampant in Wales, and Merionethshire subsisted on cattle stealing, private feuds, burning of houses and murders. Market day at Dolgelly and Conway was a festival of looting and plunder.[80]

APPENDIX

Y modd i doeth kariad hrwng Ywain Tudur ar vrenhines.

Ynn ol proses hrai o lyvre lloygyr ac opiniwn y saesson ni oddevai y kyngor o loegyr ir vrenhines gattrin briodi neb yn lloegyr ac ir ydoedd hi ynni chwnnychu or achos i bu hi yn weddw serttain o amser ynn yr amser ir ydoedd ysgwier o wynedd yn wasnaethwr ac yn sewer i ennaur vrenhines yr hwnn a oedd yn karu un o law vorynion y vrenhines yr hon a ganvu y matter. Ac ar ddiwrnod garllaw llys y vrenhines ynn amser haaf i digwyddodd ir asgwier hwnn vynd i novio i avon a oedd yn llithro gan ysdlys mur y llys y neb a ganvu llaw vorwyn y vrenhines yn vuan yr hon a ddanges y mater ir vrenhines yr hwnn a ddoeth i ffenesdyr i edrych ar y gwyr yn novio ymysg yr hrain i gwelai y vrenhines un or gwyr yn rhagori i gymdeithion o degwch knawd or achos i govynnodd y vrenhines wel dackw wr ysydd yn yckaru chwi yn vawr yn wir heber y verch vonheddig velly i mae ef yn dywedud ac yn wir ni chaaf i fynned i le ynn y byd och golwg chwi ar ni bo ef ynn vyngorllwyn i. Wele hebyr y vrenvines gad imi vynned noswaith yn dy rrith di ynnlle y boch i ynn arver o gyvarvod a myvi a wnaf iddo ef nad amyro ef arnatti o hynny allan ac o vewn ychydig o amser ynnol hyn i gwnaeth y llaw vorwyn oed ar gyvarvod ac ywain mewn galerie gerllaw sdavell y vrenhines Ir hon i dangoses y llaw vorwyn gwbwl or kyvrang a oedd hryngthi hi ac ywain: ar vrenhines a gymerth archennad i llaw vorwyn ac ynny tywyll y hi a aeth ir galerey ynnyman ir ydoedd ywain yn disgwyl i gariad yn lle yr hon i kymerth ef y vrenhines erbynn i mwnnwgyl i ymkannu hroddi kussann yw gennau hi yr hon a droes i grudd att i enau ef ac ynnol uddunt hwy ymddiddan serttain o eiriau bob un ai gilidd y vo a ganvu oleuad yn dyvod megis pedviasiai y vrenhines ynn dyvod yw shiambyr or achos i keishiodd ef roddi kusan yw min hi wrth ymadel yr hon a droes i grudd atto ef ynnyr un modd or achos i tybiodd ef nad y hi aeodd i gariad el or achos y vo a vrathodd i grudd hi ai ddanedd megis ac i gallai ef wybod o gweled yn ynnysbys pwy a oedd ynni watwar ef ynny modd ar yr hyn yr ymadewis ywain ar vrenhines arsswyd y goleuad ynnol yr hyn Ir aeth y vrenhines yw shiambyr ac ywain yw letty. A thrannoeth i gorchmynodd y vrenhines yw shiambyr len orchymyn ywain i vod yn sewer iddi hi ar ginnio y dethwn hwnnw yr hyn gyvlownoedd. Ac ynnol i ywain osod o bwyd ar y bwrdd ynni ordyr megis ac ir ydoedd i swydd ef yw wneuthud y vo a droes i wyneb at y vrenhines yr hon aoedd yn ymolchi i vynned yw chinio yn yr amser ir adrychodd hi'n ffyrnig ar ywain drwy roddi i bys ar i grudd ar yr hwn i gwelai ef blasdyr or achos i gosdyngodd ef i ben drwy aadde ynnigalon mae y vrenhines a vrathassai ef i grudd ynnos ynnyblaen or achos ynnol opiniwn hrau o lyvre ir ymkanodd ef gymerud i varch a marchogaeth yw wlad hrag ovon y vrenhines yr hon ynnol opiniwn hrai eraill or bobyl a ddanvonasai orchymyn ar y porthorion ar gadw ywain o vewn pyrth y llys onnid ni wna mater pa un or ddau vodd i dykpwyd y vo garbron y vrenhines yr hon o vewn ychydig amser ynnol a wnaeth gymaint o honaw ef ac iddi ymkanu i briodi ef or achos ynnol opiniwn y bobyl y hi a ddanvones un oi herawds i Gymru i ymovun pa wr i gennedlaeth oydd ef yr hwn a ddoeth i dy i fam ef ynn ddisymwth ac y hi yn eisde wrth y tan ac yn bwytta i chinio oddiar i gliniau ai harffed ar neb ac ymhlith boneddigion y wlad ir ymovynodd yr herawd am i ach ywain.

(Owen's genealogy follows.)

Ac ni bu haiach o ennyd ynol hyn nes ir vrenhines briodi ywain yn ddirgel. Mostyn MS 158; p. 306.

CHAPTER FIVE

The Campaign of Ludford

It has been customary, in dealing with the disposition of forces in Wales during the Wars of the Roses, to assign the west to the Lancastrians and the east to the Yorkists. Broadly speaking, this invasion represents accurately enough the strength of the rival parties at the commencement of hostilities; for the extensive Mortimer estates gave the duke of York a striking predominance in the Marches; while the Lancastrians could claim supremacy in the Principality (Anglesey, Carnarvonshire and Merionethshire), in the royal counties of South Wales (Cardiganshire and Carmarthenshire), and in the county-palatine of Pembroke under Jasper Tudor. But when we come to details the Marches do not present a uniform political complexion. The wide lordship of Brecknock belonged to the Staffords, at the head of whom was the duke of Buckingham, a prominent and consistent Lancastrian. He was thus wedged in between the earl of Warwick in Glamorgan and the duke of York in Mid-Wales. There were Lancastrian estates, too, at Monmouth and in the lower valley of the Wye. The loyalist Talbot, earl of Shrewsbury, was situated between Shrewsbury and Montgomery, and was supported by the Beauforts and the Mowbrays in the valley of the Dee. Of the lesser gentry in the Marches, the Skydmores of Herefordshire and the Pulestons of Denbighshire gave effective support to the cause of the dynasty. On the other hand, south-west Wales from Gower to Pembroke and northwards to Aberystwyth was more uniformly Lancastrian, the Dwnns of the neighbourhood of Kidwely being the only conspicuous Yorkists.

For a few years after the battle of St Albans the centre of gravity of the war was transferred to Wales and the Marches. York's chief citadels were at Wigmore and Ludlow, which dominated Mid-Wales. Margaret, with a skilful analysis of the military situation, realized that if she would triumph she must challenge him where his resources were greatest. To do this it would be necessary to mobilize her friends there and brush up recruits, a task in which she showed conspicuous ardour and resolution. She could naturally rely upon the Principality; and she became personally responsible for the loyalty of Cheshire and the border counties. In Cheshire and the surrounding districts she was conciliatory; in Mid-Wales, where York was most powerful, she was exacting and defiant. With profound tact and practical sense she sent Edmund Tudor, earl of Richmond, to Wales. Nothing could have been more opportune than the choice of a Tudor for a recruiting mission in these parts.

Edmund's Welsh pedigree was a key which would throw wide open the hearts of men. His father, Owen Tudor, had within recent years come among them as a refugee, a fact which rendered still more charitable the public conscience of the Welsh.

Edmund Tudor came to Pembroke early in 1456. The most representative chieftain in these parts was Griffith ap Nicholas, with whom Richmond would have to reckon sooner or later. It happened sooner. Griffith's unhappy entanglement in the affairs of Humphrey, duke of Gloucester, had revealed to him the treacherous quicksands of politics, though it lifted him to a higher plane of public recognition. In 1449 he came under the vigilant eye of the duke of York, who entrusted him with the important castle of Narberth in Pembrokeshire. In October 1450 he was on a commission 'to array all men-at-arms, hobelers and archers in West Wales, and bring them to the sea-coast to expel the king's enemies, and to set up beacons and survey the muster and keep watches'. Others on the commission were Sir James Audley, Sir Henry Wogan, Sir John Skydmore and Thomas ap Griffith ap Nicholas.[1] Griffith was thus at the zenith of his power when he presided over the famous eisteddfod of Carmarthen, which is said to have been held about 1453, and the proceedings of which constitute an important landmark in the history of Welsh literature. In such circumstances the advent of Edmund Tudor was not altogether free from embarrassments. Heroes of small communities are proverbially intolerant of rivals, and Griffith at first regarded the earl of Richmond as a rival. The latter may have been insidious, and was certainly rash; for within a few months of his arrival there was a fierce clash between him and Griffith, which resounded in the east of England. Although ten years had elapsed since the Gloucester affair, Richmond may have viewed Griffith as a prospective adherent of the duke of York, the political successor of Humphrey. On the other hand, he might have reflected that on the commission of 1450 Griffith was the colleague of such unflinching loyalists as Audley and Skydmore. However, in June 1456 Griffith and the earl of Richmond were 'at war greatly'.[2] Whatever may have been the origin of the feud there were no dregs of bitterness. In October Griffith and his two sons Thomas and Owen received a full pardon, which emanated from the new government of the queen.[3] The Yorkist ministry had been dismissed earlier in the month. Henceforth the family was loyal to the cause of the Tudors. The allegiance of such an enthusiastic and enlightened patriot as Griffith ap Nicholas was a guarantee that the bards whom he liberally patronized would be won over; and they could become a powerful weapon in the hands of a capable leader. They traversed the country frequently, and with great industry and ingenuity preached the fiery doctrine of nationality. In doing so they, for the time being, necessarily cried up the cause of the dynasty as represented by the Tudors. For the first time, though not for the last in the history of Wales, Welsh nationalism was used as a lever in the party politics of England.

Edmund Tudor was not destined long to remain at the head of the Lancastrians of West Wales. Within a month of the peace between him and Griffith he died at Pembroke, in November 1456. At the same place two months later (28 January 1457) his wife, Margaret Beaufort, gave birth to a son, Henry Tudor, afterwards Henry VII. Edmund's place was immediately taken by his brother Jasper, who

Margaret Beaufort, countess of Richmond, in later life (National Portrait Gallery).

continued and amplified the project already begun. Hitherto Jasper had kept in close touch with the king.[4]

Jasper Tudor has not received from historians in general the attention which he deserves. He certainly did not dazzle contemporary chroniclers. With modern writers he cuts a meagre figure, and has been relegated to a series of brackets or a note of interrogation. It is the penalty he has had to pay for having chosen Wales as his sphere of action. None showed more unselfish loyalty to the cause of the Crown, or greater resource in defending it. Sleepless in his devotion to his party for nearly thirty years, he laboured more assiduously than any other to shape its destiny. His achievements in the open field

Henry VII tower, Pembroke Castle. Birthplace of Henry Tudor.

were negligible; the only victory in which he could claim a share was the final triumph of his cause at Bosworth. But, from his entry into political life he displayed extraordinary skill and tenacity in reorganizing his forces after defeat, as well as a keen zest for the shifts of statecraft. His strategy was that of timely retreat when victory had eluded his grasp. He alone of the leaders on either side lived through the struggle and witnessed its close. Sometimes lurking in caverns and woods, sometimes traversing lonely mountain paths, sometimes stranded on a deserted shore, he continued to hold in his hands the thread of Lancastrian hopes. Shrewd, adroit, and persevering, he was undaunted by the caprice of fortune, and successfully braved the perilous vicissitudes incident to his arduous undertaking. And in an age of brutal passion he emerged with his fame untarnished by any deed of cruelty or wrong; while the affectionate care which he bestowed upon his fatherless nephew, Henry Tudor, throws into relief the hideous ferocity that surrounded him.[5]

> Ther is a sayle-yeard fulle good and sure,
> To the shyp a grete tresour,
> For alle stormes it wolle endure,
> It is trusty atte nede.
> Now the sayle-yeard I wolle reherse,
> The Erle of Pembroke, curtys and ferce,
> Across the mast he hycthe travers,
> The good ship for to lede.[6]

His first task was to fortify the allegiance of Griffith ap Nicholas. That he succeeded in this there can be no doubt; for, apart from the evidence of William of Worcester, there is sufficient testimony in contemporary Welsh writings. It will be necessary to substantiate this, because the only existing life of Griffith portrays him as a martyr in the cause of York at Mortimer's Cross.[7]

In an ode written about 1457–8 Lewis Glyn Cothi says: 'That warrior we love who will bring support to the Crown.'[8] Again, 'He [Griffith] is staunch and faithful to the throne.'[9] In another ode written about the same time, the poet refers to Owen, the son of Griffith ap Nicholas, as a captain in the royal army.[10]

Under the influence of the same set of circumstances the poet wrote an ode to Jasper, in which he does something more than eulogize the generosity of his subject after the fashion then in vogue. He gives proof of profound intimacy with the political situation in that year – the hopes centred in the young Prince Edward, the memory of Queen Catherine, the care of Jasper for his young ward Henry of Richmond, the treasonable designs of the Yorkists, the royal blood in Jasper's veins, his Welsh extraction, and above all his efforts to unite Wales for his king.[11] It is characteristic of the poet to appropriate him as a Welshman, and to make him the leader and champion not of a faction, but of the Welsh against the English.[12] Other contemporary Welsh poets also give indirect evidence of Griffith's loyalty to Henry.[13]

The most influential Yorkist in West Wales was John Dwnn, although he does not figure prominently till later in the struggle. However, on 1 March 1459, Jasper Tudor, Owen Tudor, and the two sons of Griffith ap Nicholas, Thomas and Owen, were commissioned to arrest certain individuals, among whom were some of the servants of John Dwnn.[14] We may not be justified in attaching political significance to the affair; but it certainly affords additional evidence of a complete reconciliation between the Tudors and the family of Griffith ap Nicholas; while its chronological proximity to the Ludford campaign gives it additional piquancy. By that time Jasper's sleepless assiduity had achieved the virtual unity of south-west Wales.

It is not always safe to argue from marriage alliances at this period. Still, it is suggestive that Maud, a daughter of Griffith ap Nicholas, was the wife of the consistent Lancastrian, Sir John Skydmore of Herefordshire, who held Pembroke Castle for Jasper Tudor against Herbert a few years later than the time with which we are now dealing. Another daughter married Philip Mansel, also a consistent Lancastrian.

Having secured Griffith, Jasper entered upon another phase of activity, namely, to strengthen his own earldom and take possession of other strongholds in West Wales. His immediate predecessors in the earldom, Humphrey, duke of Gloucester, and the earl of Suffolk, did not appreciate its military value. Humphrey, indeed, had drawn a considerable following from the surrounding districts, but his visits and those of his successor were casual. The Tudors made it their base of operations. It was the expansive genius of Jasper that realized the vast importance of Pembroke and Tenby Castles, and how they might be made a connecting link between England on the one hand, and France, Ireland and Scotland on the other. By means of them he was able, on many occasions, to escape his pursuers and draw support from beyond the sea.

Assigning Pembroke to the countess of Richmond and her son, he apparently made Tenby his own headquarters. His letters that have survived the destructive hand of time are both dated from there. He devoted considerable time and expense to raising and strengthening the walls with a view to establishing the place as an important military and naval post.[15] Moreover, in April of that year he seized personal control over the outlying castles of Carregcennen, Carmarthen, and Aberystwyth, by securing the constableship of each for himself.[16] The duke of York, whom he displaced in these vital fortresses, was reported as having relinquished them at the king's desire, receiving in lieu thereof a grant of forty pounds a year.[17] But it is impossible not to perceive in the transaction a hypocritical and intriguing bargain for the aggrandizement of the Tudors in this part of Wales.

Meanwhile the queen herself was in a state of nervous activity. In March 1456 she took measures to put Flint Castle in a state of defence,[18] while she spent the greater part of the spring in the neighbourhood of Chester. She returned again in the autumn, was at Chester on 24 October, and at Shrewsbury from 31 October to 4 November.[19] The duke of York diagnosed the situation in the Marches with equal skill. On the fall of his protectorate early in October he retired to Wigmore. Each kept a close watch on the other, though, as events proved, Margaret acted with greater resolution and used her time to greater advantage.

The seal of Humphrey Stafford, duke of Buckingham. He was taken prisoner at the battle of St Albans and killed at the battle of Northampton, 1460.

In the spring of the following year Margaret, accompanied by the king, the duke
of Buckingham, and the earl of Shrewsbury, once more traversed the borders. They
were at Hereford during April; from there they had removed to Worcester by 4
May.[20] In these parts Sir William Herbert had begun to display sinister
manifestations of restlessness. For some years after his return from Normandy his
lot was cast in the eddies of local affairs rather than in the main stream of political
controversy and feud.[21] Basing her judgment on the friendly relations which she
knew had subsisted between the duke of York and Herbert's father, Margaret may
have looked upon him as a presumptive opponent.[22] On the other hand there is
reason to suspect an early friendship between the Herberts and the Tudors. In 1454
Edmund Tudor, earl of Richmond, had made William Herbert a grant of ten pounds
a year, to be taken from some of the former's English estates;[23] while in the same year
one of the Herberts secured an interest in the royal lordship of Dynevor.[24]

With a clear prevision of the balance of forces in the Marches, Margaret spared
no effort to attach the Herberts to her chariot, for the many branches of his family
and of that of Roger Vaughan would be a valuable asset on one side or the other.
With the assistance of Jasper in West Wales, of the duke of Buckingham in
Brecknock, and of the Herberts in Gwent, she might reasonably hope to
overwhelm the duke of York. Circumstances favoured her project. The Herberts
and Vaughans became involved in some disturbances on the borders in the early
part of 1457, and Margaret's visit to those parts between April and May was made
ostensibly with the object of suppressing them.[25]

It is true that at the sessions of oyer and terminer held at Hereford in that year
Herbert was adjudged guilty of treason, and seven tuns of Gascon wine belonging
to him, then lying at the port of Bristol, were forfeited.[26] On 22 May this property
was restored to him; and on 7 June, at Coventry, he was admitted to a general
pardon.[27] A number of his relatives and associates in Brecknock, Monmouth and
Herefordshire, notably his brothers Richard Herbert of Abergavenny and Thomas
Herbert, and the sons of Roger Vaughan of Tretower, were among those who were
pardoned at the same time.[28] It must be admitted, however, that the duke of York
did not anticipate any wavering allegiance on the part of Herbert, for he was
steward of York's lordship of Usk as late as 11 December 1458.[29]

The reference by a London correspondent to these disturbances suggests that they
were of more than local significance, and that the allegiance of the Herbert connection
was important; but the chief point to be noted is that Herbert promised fidelity to the
Crown. Of this the correspondent referred to, as well as subsequent events, leaves no
doubt.[30] Herbert, it is stated, would appear at Leicester on condition that his life was
spared and his estates secured to him. The letter is as follows:

> The Queen and the King at Hereford, the lords Buckingham, Shrewsbury and
> others. . . . And now it is stated that Herbert shall come in and appear at
> Leicester before the King and the lords, his life granted and goods, so he make
> amends to them he hath offended. Many be indicted, some causeless which
> maketh Herbert party strong. And the burgess and gentlemen about Hereford
> will go with the King, wife and child, unless a peace be made before the King

depart thence; for else Herbert and his affinity will acquit them, as it is said. . . .
I send a bill of the names indicted to my master and you to see and laugh at
their Welsh names descended of old pedigrees.[31]

Henceforth, till after the panic at Ludford in 1459, he was an associate of
Lancaster rather than of York, a fact which helps partly to explain that calamity.

There is striking evidence of Herbert's loyalty to the throne at this period in
contemporary Welsh literature. In one of his odes Lewis Glyn Cothi refers to Gwilym
Gwent as an ardent partisan of Jasper Tudor. 'If Jasper should strike, Gwilym also
would strike for the Crown, a mighty eagle in the ranks of Jasper of Pembroke.' In
another couplet of the same ode the poet states Gwilym was also one of the party of
Herbert: 'A thousand blessings on William, a party to the earl Herbert.'[32]

The same poet has another ode to one Henry ap Gwilym, probably the same
who became a pledge for the William Herbert who was farmer of the lordship of
Dynevor.[33] In this ode the poet states in effect that the lord of Gwent, William,
entered the service of Prince Edward.[34] When we come to deal with the disposal
of the lands and offices of the Yorkists after the panic of Ludford there will be
forthcoming still more definite proof of Herbert's attitude during these few years.

The situation in south-east Wales was very complicated, and it was evident that
Herbert would have to steer his craft very warily for some time. He was
surrounded by formidable partisans. The earl of Warwick, York's most powerful
ally, held the rich and compact lordship of Glamorgan, with its strong piles at
Cardiff, Caerphilly, Neath, and Llantrissant. The constable of Cardiff at this time
was William's brother, Thomas Herbert.[35] On the north stretched the lordship of
Brecknock, the patrimony of the duke of Buckingham, who was a conspicuous
Lancastrian. In Herefordshire, Sir Walter Devereux had already ranged himself
on the side of York, and Sir John Skydmore on the side of the queen. Being thus
enveloped Sir William Herbert might easily have become a victim to the
Lancastrian Scylla or the Yorkist Charybdis, for his resources were as yet very
limited. Devereux lost his estates after the Ludford campaign in 1459, and
Skydmore suffered confiscation after Mortimer's Cross. Herbert trimmed his
sails so dexterously that he profited from both storms. He was able to convince
Margaret of his loyalty without forfeiting the friendship of York and Warwick.

Meanwhile, the range of Jasper Tudor's influence grew apace. In November 1457
he was empowered to cut down for sale two hundred acres of wood in Sherwood
Forest, Nottinghamshire.[36] In the following January he and John Talbot, earl of
Shrewsbury, were put in possession of the lands of Henry Tudor, earl of Richmond,
during his minority.[37] In April 1459 he has made quit of all fines for charters, letters
patent, and other writs in Chancery. In May he was given 'a tower in the lower end
of the great hall within Westminster Palace, for the communication and easement of
the earl and his council, to hold as the Queen holds the other tower at the end of the
hall at the entry of the Exchequer for her and her council.'[38] These grants were
undoubtedly part of Jasper's equipment for the struggle which was now impending.

In the spring of 1459 the queen turned her attention once more to Cheshire,
where she allied 'to her the knights and squires in these parts, for to have their

The Dunstable swan jewel, gold and enamel livery badge, perhaps connected with the Lancastrian mustering of troops in 1461. The swan was a Lancastrian emblem and badge of Prince Edward (British Museum).

benevolence, and held open household among them, and made her son give a livery blazoned with a swan to all gentlemen of the country, trusting through their strength to make her son king; for she was making privy means to lords of England to stir the king to resign the crown, but she could not bring her purpose about.'[39]

The duke of York was then at Ludlow where 'he gathered to him a strong host of marchmen and other'.[40] The earl of Salisbury, while hastening from Middleham in Yorkshire to join him there, was intercepted at Bloreheath by Margaret's Cheshire levies under Lord Audley (23 September 1459).[41] The Lancastrians, though considerably outnumbering their opponents, were repulsed. The main army of Margaret was close at hand.[42] Salisbury therefore discreetly retired under cover of darkness, 'while an Awstin friar shot off guns all that night in a park at the back of the field, and by this means the earl came to the duke of York. And on the morrow they found neither man nor child in that park save that friar only, and he said it was for fear he abode in that park all that night.'[43]

Sir John Dwnn of Cheshire, who was knighted on that day, was one of the victims on the Lancastrian side. 'In the morning, between the battlefield and Cheshire, his son, who was at home in his father's place, had word that his father was slain. Anon he raised his tenants, and beside a little town named Tarporley took Sir Thomas Neville, Sir John Neville, and Sir Thomas Harrington, and brought them to Chester, and there they abode till the battle of Northampton was fought.'[44] Hall, in commenting on their release, says, 'Such favour had the commons of Wales to the duke of York's band and his affinity that they could suffer no wrong to be done nor evil word to be spoken of him or his friends,' a remark which is not void of truth when applied to Mid-Wales.

Lord Stanley, whose influence in North Wales and Cheshire was considerable, set an example of gross double-dealing during this campaign. He had about two thousand men within six miles of Bloreheath when the fight was in progress. He afterwards excused himself to the queen for his dilatoriness, and at the same time despatched a message to the earl of Salisbury thanking God for his success.[45]

Roger Kynaston of Middle, Salop, constable of Denbigh for the duke of York (1454), and eulogized in contemporary Welsh poetry as a scion of the house of Powys, is said to have added lustre to the name under Salisbury's flag on that day; and it is asserted that in honour of his deeds the Audley arms were inscribed on the Kynaston shield.[46] He was afterwards, at any rate, a steady Yorkist, and may well have helped Salisbury in the fight. On the other hand, the queen had not at first distrusted him. For in July 1453, when she was battling vigorously with the flames of disorder, he was associated with the stout Lancastrian John Hanmer on a commission 'to bring certain people before the king's Council to answer certain charges'.

The earl of Salisbury reached Ludlow in safety after Bloreheath. A few days later he was joined by his son, the earl of Warwick, who, at the head of a well-disciplined body of veterans from the Calais garrison, had traversed the breadth of England unmolested. Edward, earl of March, eldest son of the duke of York, was also at Ludlow. So also were Lord Grey of Ruthin, Richard Grey (Lord Powys)[47] and Sir Walter Devereux. In fact the duke of York had summoned hither the stoutest of his supporters, 'that their coming together might make a mightier array'.[48] It appears from what immediately followed, however, that the response to his appeal was very disappointing.

The Lancastrians, having concentrated at Worcester, marched on Ludlow with a numerous army, 'for every town hath waged and sent forth, and are ready to send forth, as many as they did when the King sent for them before the field of Ludlow'.[49] The duke of York took up an entrenched position at Ludford Bridge, in front of Ludlow, digging a deep ditch and fortifying it with guns and stakes.[50] On 9 October the king was at Leominster. Next day the duke of York issued a manifesto protesting his loyalty to the king's person. He was already aware of his weakness. On previous occasions, notably in 1452 and 1455, he had raised in the Marches a force sufficiently strong to overawe the government; yet now, in his own stronghold, reinforced by Salisbury's victorious contingent and Warwick's veterans, he could muster only 'such as he had blinded and assembled by wages, promises, and other exquisite means'. His 'party was over-weak,' says Gregory. He was so despondent that on the near approach of the enemy he 'brought in certain persons before the people to swear that the king was deceased, doing mass to be said, and offering all, to make the people the less to dread to take the field'.[51] Henry offered a pardon to all who would join his standard within six days. On 12 October the two armies were posted one on each side of the Teme, and at dusk a few shots were exchanged. During the night the Yorkist force dissolved. Taking advantage of the royal pardon many deserted to the king, among them some of the troops brought by Warwick from Calais. Others fled under cover of darkness, including the Yorkist leaders. The duchess of York and her two youngest sons, George and Richard, became prisoners and were placed under the care of Anne, duchess of Buckingham, the duke of York's sister. 'There was not so much a battle as a semblance of a battle.'[52]

The duke, with his second son Edmund, earl of Rutland, 'fled from place to place in Wales, and broke down the bridges so that the king's men should not come after them', and having 'bought a ship for much money, passed over to Ireland'.[53] When parliament met at Coventry on 20 November, it was as yet uncertain whether he had succeeded in escaping the clutches of the pursuing Lancastrians. Salisbury, Warwick, and the duke of York's eldest son Edward, earl of March, fled to Calais.

When the Lancastrians reached Ludlow 'they drank enough of wine that was in taverns and other places, and full ungodly smote out the heads of the hogsheads of wine, that men went wet-shod in wine, and then they robbed the town and bare away bedding and other stuff'.[54] The morning after the calamity, Lord Grey of Ruthin submitted to the king; also Walter Devereux, 'and with him many knights and squires in their shirts and halters in their hands, falling before the king, and all had grace and mercy both of life and limb'.[55]

The traditional view ascribes the rout of the Yorkists at Ludford to the sudden defection of the professional troops which, under the command of Andrew Trollope, had been brought over from Calais by Warwick. 'That made the Duke full sore afraid when he wyste that sum olde soudyers went from him unto the kynge.'[56] The moral effect of the discipline of a few professional soldiers upon amateur retainers would be considerable. Wavering or defection on their part would have enormous influence, and might easily have provoked a rout. It is likely, too, that his father's contingent of Yorkshiremen would be particularly sensitive to the conduct of Warwick's veterans. So much must at once be admitted.

But why should this abrupt and damaging treachery have occurred at this particular juncture? The Croyland Continuator attributes it to the fact that Trollope had been deceived by Warwick into believing that they had been brought over to fight for the king. 'For finding that contrary to their expectations they had really been brought to act against the king they left the duke.'[57] This explanation cannot be entertained with confidence; for Trollope must have been well enough acquainted with the trend of party feud, and the unequivocal position of Warwick as a partisan of York, not to be deluded so easily. Two important contemporary writers pass by the defection in silence;[58] most of them emphasize the weakness of the duke of York's own following. We shall probably not diverge far from the truth, therefore, if we ascribe both the defection and the rout to this primary cause – the weakness of York.

The abject expedients to which the duke resorted on the near approach of the royalists suggest very forcibly that the desertion was part of the general demoralization which had been apparent for some time. Hitherto he had always found in the Marches an enthusiastic response to his appeals, and had relied upon them with complete assurance and security. Devereux and Lord Powys had, indeed, shown a tardy adherence, but the aloofness of Sir William Herbert was probably typical of the attitude of many others. This freezing apathy, where he had been wont to find such warm sympathy, was due to the foresight and assiduity of Margaret and Jasper during the three preceding years. The completeness of their triumph now was the measure of the success of their preliminary efforts there.

The queen, during her frequent visits to the borders, had temporarily undermined the Mortimer influence in the Marches. Nor should we underrate the invaluable contribution of Jasper Tudor. His diligence in West Wales not only secured those parts for the Lancastrians, but also provided a force which threatened the Yorkists in the rear. His movements are no doubt obscure. There is no record of him till his arrival at the Coventry parliament on 6 December, a few weeks after

Ludford. But he could hardly have been inactive while such great events were on the anvil. His force must have been advancing upon Ludlow from Pembroke while the king and queen attacked in front; and we may reasonably argue that his was the army that went in pursuit of the duke.[59] If this was so, it accounts for two significant facts in the situation which have hitherto been neglected, namely, that Jasper did not appear in the parliament at Coventry till a fortnight after the opening of the session, and that he came there with a large following.[60] It is conceivable, and not at all improbable, that the Yorkists had become aware of his approach, and that this inspired them with additional fear, and increased their panic.

Immediately after their triumph the king and queen had summoned a parliament at Coventry. Here the Yorkist leaders were attainted. Lord Powys and Sir Walter Devereux were spared their lives though their estates were confiscated; Richard Croft of Herefordshire and Roger Kynaston[61] were pardoned. Among

Tomb and effigies of Sir Richard and Lady Eleanor Croft in Croft Castle, Herefordshire. The tomb must have been made before the church was enlarged in 1515. The accession of Edward IV after the battle of Mortimer's Cross brought the Crofts to high office at the court in Ludlow.

The painted effigy of Sir John Fortescue, Lancastrian chief justice and tutor to Edward of Lancaster, in Ebrington church, Gloucestershire. He was one of the Lancastrians pardoned by Edward IV after the battle of Tewkesbury.

those attainted was Sir Thomas Vaughan.[62] Sir Walter Devereux had apparently been active gathering men for the duke of York; for on 8 November 1459 certain persons were indicted before Sir John Fortescue for having each received at Weobley,[63] Herefordshire, 'a gown of Walter Devereux contrary to the statute of liveries'. He was bound to the king in 500 marks for his rebellion, which sum was paid to Humphrey, duke of Buckingham, 'for his costs in attendance on the king in Kent and against other rebels'.[64]

A glance at the grants bestowed by the Crown in the flush of victory will help us to understand who were its friends at this period. Of these the most prominent in Wales was unquestionably Sir William Herbert. And if we had no further proof of his Lancastrian proclivities, the favours showered upon him on this occasion should be sufficient. His reward was a grant for life of the offices of sheriff of the county of Glamorgan and Morgannwg, steward of the lordship and its members,[65] steward of the lordships of Abergavenny, Elvel, Ewyas Lacy, Dinas, Usk, and Caerleon, and constable of Usk, 'in the king's hands by the forfeiture of Richard, duke of York, and Richard, earl of Warwick'. The grant was amplified in the following March, when he received power to appoint to all offices in these lordships.[66]

Owen Tudor received an annuity of one hundred pounds from certain manors in Kent and Surrey.[67] A little later he was given the custody of Moelwick and other parks in the lordship of Denbigh.[68] While the court was still at Coventry (12

December 1459) Sir Henry Wogan esquire, and William ap Owen of Pembrokeshire, were commissioned to investigate the treasonable proceedings of certain individuals in the lordship of Haverfordwest.[69] Therefore, the Wogans who later became enthusiastic Yorkists were so far supporters of Jasper and the king. John Owen was made steward and constable of Narberth, forfeited by the duke of York.[70] John Milewater was made receiver of the duke's lands in the Marches and Herefordshire, and of Warwick's lordship of Glamorgan.[71] John Middleton, 'king's yeoman harbinger', became keeper of Cleobury Park, Salop, York's confiscated property.[72] Henry ap Griffith, who was among the Welsh squires pardoned by the queen in 1457, at the same time as Herbert, and who, like him, was on the Yorkist side at Mortimer's Cross, was given the stewardship of Ewyas Lacy.[73] Builth was reserved for the Prince of Wales, as well as Montgomery, Ceri, and Cedewain; and he was also given 500 marks yearly out of the issues of Usk, Caerleon, Glamorgan, and Abergavenny, 'to the intent that knights and squires may be retained with the king and prince, that the said lordships may be brought back the more speedily to the king's obedience'.[74] Lastly, Nicholas ap Rees, 'for his good service in the repression of the rebellion', was granted the office of rhaglaw of the lordship of Denbigh.[75]

The arduous task of reducing the Marches to subjection had yet to be accomplished. Bands of rebels wandered through Wales inciting the people to rebellion, while the castle garrisons on York's estates refused to surrender. Consequently, frequent commissions were issued to bring the recalcitrant lordships to obedience, and to reduce the castles to the king's hands.[76]

Denbigh[77] offered a stubborn resistance to the victorious Lancastrians. Jasper may have begun the siege before leaving Wales for the Coventry parliament. On the rising of parliament, and having signed the oath of allegiance, he immediately repaired to Wales to extinguish this last flame of rebellion. Meanwhile, he had been appointed constable of the castle and steward of the lordship.[78] At the end of seven weeks the garrison was still defiant. On 22 February Jasper was given a special commission with extensive powers to bring about its speedy reduction. When this had been done he was to hold the town 'as of our gift', to take all the movable goods belonging to the garrison, and to distribute them according to his own discretion among the soldiers. Meanwhile he was assigned a force of men-at-arms and archers,[79] with full power to raise more troops in Wales, and to pardon or execute the rebels, 'and on the first approach of our first-born Prince Edward in Wales, to receive into our favour any rebels of the castle of Denbigh or outside, except certain English and Irish holding and defending the same castle against us; except also certain Welshmen outlawed and attainted'. These measures proved effective. The castle submitted before 13 March.[80] On that day a special grant of £1,000 was made on account of the expenses incurred in reducing the town and other places in Wales, the sum to be raised from the Welsh estates of the duke of York and the earl of Warwick. In April Jasper was made a knight of the Garter in recognition of his splendid services.

The Coventry parliament had to consider a novel petition from Wales.[81] It stated that in Chester, Flint, and other counties in Wales 'great extortions and misprisions' were continually being done by the sheriffs and other royal officers 'which have estate term of life in the said offices, and that the king's subjects dare not sue nor complain upon the said misdoers for the defaults as long as those men are in office'. The petition was received sympathetically. Former petitions from Wales, almost without exception, were directed against Welshmen, and proceeded from the official element in town and shire. This petition, on the contrary, made direct reference to the 'unjust exactions and cruelties of English officials in Wales'. The voice of Wales was beginning to be heard, and it may not improbably have been due to the influence of Jasper Tudor, and to the assistance he had already received in Wales.

It is instructive to compare with this petition a 'precipe' of Richard, earl of Warwick, to his sheriff and officers in Glamorgan, saying that he had received complaints of official oppression of the abbots of Margam Abbey by 'certain of our bailiffs and ministers with a great multitude of men and horses'.[82]

APPENDIX

THE VAUGHANS OF BREDWARDINE

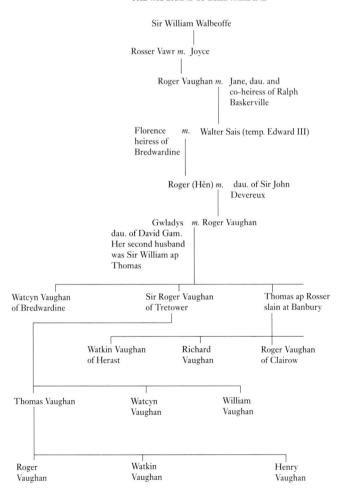

CHAPTER SIX

Mortimer's Cross

At Ludford Bridge the Yorkists received a short but rude shock. Nearly a year elapsed before their complete recovery. Meanwhile vague rumours were on the wing that a mysterious conference had taken place at Dublin, the vast import of which was not revealed till Warwick, Salisbury, and the earl of March landed at Sandwich towards the end of June 1460, and thence marched to London, which they reached on 2 July. Warwick had risked a perilous voyage from Calais to the Irish capital to contrive this new scheme with the duke of York.

Leaving his father, the earl of Salisbury, to blockade the Tower, Warwick advanced swiftly on Northampton, then the Lancastrian headquarters. Margaret was taken completely unawares and fled to Wales, trusting to the Lancastrian lords to do battle for the dynasty. On 10 July 1460 the battle of Northampton was fought. The air was thick and dark with treason; for hardly had the fight begun when Lord Grey of Ruthin[1] admitted the earl of March and the Yorkist vanguard into the royalist entrenchments. In the sordid annals of even these sterile wars there is no deed of shame so foul. The Lancastrians were overwhelmed. The duke of Buckingham, lord of Brecon, was among the slain. King Henry, a pitiable wreck, had to accompany Warwick to London.

Queen Margaret, who had moved to Eccleshall, reached Cheshire in safety. Beside the castle of Malpas a servant of her own,[2] that she had made both yeoman and gentleman, and afterwards appointed to be in office with her son, the prince, spoiled her and robbed her and put her so in doubt of her life and her son's life also. And then she came to the castle of Harlech[3] in Wales, and she had many great gifts and was greatly comforted; for she had need thereof, for she had a full easy many about her, the number of four persons.[4] And most commonly she rode behind a young poor gentleman of fourteen years of age. And there hence she removed full privily unto the Lord Jasper, lord and earl of Pembroke, for she durst not abide in no place that was open, but in private.

The cause was that counterfeit tokens were sent unto her as though they had come from her most dread lord the king, Henry VI; but it was not of his sending, neither of his doing, but forged things; for they that brought the tokens were of the king's house, and some of the prince's house, and some of her own house, and

Harlech Castle, drawn by Sir Richard Colt Hoare in the early nineteenth century.

bade her beware of the tokens, that she gave no credence thereto. For at the king's departing from Coventry toward the field of Northampton he kissed her and blessed the prince, and commanded her that she should not come unto him till that he sent a special token unto her that no man knew but the king and she.[5]

With the assurance of one who had rendered his cause unquestionable service, Warwick seized the government and immediately gave his attention to Wales and the Marches, the vital importance of which had been forced upon him in the campaign of the preceding autumn. In July commissions were issued to Walter Devereux, Henry Griffith, and Richard Croft in Herefordshire, and to Roger Kynaston, Corbet, and others in Shropshire.[6] A fortnight afterwards Devereux was commanded to seize Thomas Fitzharry.[7] Acting through the Privy Council, the earl of Warwick called upon Jasper Tudor, earl of Pembroke, and Roger Puleston, his deputy at Denbigh, to surrender that fortress to the duke of York's nominee, at the same time assuring them of his belief in the loyal intentions of the duke.[8] The constables of Beaumaris, Conway, Flint, Hawarden, Holt, and Ruthin, were directed to provide for the safety of those places. This precaution may have been considered especially important in view of the fact that the duke of York would soon be returning from Ireland. Also Richard Grey, Lord Powys, who had submitted to Henry VI after Ludford, was enjoined to surrender Montgomery Castle to Warwick's nominee, Edward Bourchier.[9] Policy dictated that such wavering allegiance as that of Lord Powys should not be sheltered in so impregnable and advantageous a fort.

Sir Walter Devereux was similarly circumstanced.[10] He had acted with the Yorkists in the recent campaign and had been attainted at Coventry. Both had escaped the full penalties of treason. Yet on the return of the Yorkists to power

Devereux was admitted to their confidence, while Lord Powys was visited with disfavour. It is conceivable that the indulgence shown to Walter Devereux was in some measure due to Herbert. For, in the course of the year 1459–60, Herbert had married Anne Devereux, sister of Walter.[11] This was a stroke of address in that the Yorkists may have regarded it as the first link which bound the fortunes of Herbert afresh to those of the duke of York, while Margaret may easily have interpreted it as a step towards the complete reconciliation of Devereux with the Lancastrians. As late as June 1460, William Herbert was a reputed Lancastrian; for, while the king was at Coventry, almost on the eve of the battle of Northampton, a further bond of union was effected between Herbert and the court party.[12] Unlike Sir Walter Devereux, he had veiled his own political intentions in such mysterious secrecy that he was able to shield his brother-in-law from the consequences of his apostasy as well with the Yorkists as with the Lancastrians.

Yet, when the moment for an irretrievable decision came, Sir William Herbert struck boldly. Family associations, fear, ambition, stratagem, the slender thread upon which hung the royalist hopes, everything conspired to urge him to throw aside his Lancastrian weeds. His transitory association with that party had been elusive, though sufficient to humour Margaret without alienating York. He had steered his craft skilfully between the rival sirens of faction. The new situation which was created by the overwhelming victory of the Yorkists at Northampton offered him boundless scope, and a rare opportunity which he seized with promptitude, and pursued with an intrepidity all his own.

Two circumstances now favoured his rise to eminence. The death of the duke of Buckingham at Northampton left the lordship of Brecon in the hands of a minor, Henry Stafford, whose father Humphrey, the duke's son and heir, had been slain at St Albans in 1455; this removed from Herbert's neighbourhood the most considerable Lancastrian in the Marches. If the duke had lived, Herbert would have found himself between the hammer and the anvil – Buckingham at Brecon, and Warwick at Cardiff. The removal of the one and the favour of the other enabled him to extend his influence in south-east Wales just as the attainder of Jasper, at a later period, brought him to Pembroke. The other circumstance was the proximity of Herbert's patrimony to Warwick's lordship of Glamorgan. It enhanced his value to the earl as an ally.

Warwick was the first to appreciate his supple genius as a most formidable asset in Wales. Whether aware or not of his Lancastrian leanings during the Ludford campaign, he now gave him his unqualified confidence. He gave him priority even over Sir Walter Devereux. He threw upon him, primarily, the responsibility for the loyalty of South Wales, a task in which his Welsh birth gave him an advantage over Devereux. On 17 August Warwick, through the Privy Council, gave William Herbert, Walter Devereux, and Roger Vaughan authority to prevent all unlawful assemblies, arrest all such persons as should, in defiance of the king's commands, attempt to victual or fortify castles, towns, or strongholds in Wales, and adopt adequate measures for the safe custody of those castles, until they received further instructions. The trend of the letter leaves no doubt that Herbert and his associates were vested with absolute and practically unlimited powers of raising troops and extinguishing the embers of rebellion in South Wales. It is a curious document when we bear in mind that Herbert at that moment held as a gift from Margaret certain offices in Warwick's Welsh dominions:[13]

> To Sir William Herbert, Walter Devereux and Roger Vaughan. We have understande by audible reporte made unto us nowe late how that divers persons without our will or commandement and expressly contrary to our laws and place usurp and take upon them to victual and fortify divers castles, places, and strengths in our country of Wales and over make great assemblies, routes and gaderyng of people in riotious wise whereby, unless than it were soon purveyed for the ceasing thereof great hurt and inconvenience is like to ensue both to our said countrie of Wales, and to all this our land. Wherefore we straightly charge you and each of you and give you full authority and power that in all possible haste after the sight hereof ye putte you in effectual devoir and diligence by all ways and means possible to you to repress and subdue all those persons – not only letting them of their purpose in that behalf, but also putting such as are the leaders, principal doers, and stirrers of them in sure hold and keeping, so to remain and dwell till further knowledge from us – unless ye can without danger or peril bring or send them to us – the which if ye may we will ye do so – and ye take all manner such castles unto our hands and surely keep them to our use till we have ordained otherwise. Besides we command all sheriffs, mayors, bailiffs, constables, etc. – to assist you, and that ye and they and none of you fail herein as our perfect trust is in you and as ye desire to be recommended of good and diligent obeissance and to stand in our especial favour and have singular thanks of us.

In the beginning of September the duke of York landed at Redcliffe in Lancashire.[14] On previous journeys his route had been through North Wales. The change was a reflex of his bitter experiences during the previous autumn. Wales was still more insecure now, for Denbigh was in the hands of Jasper Tudor's lieutenant, Roger Puleston, and probably harboured some Lancastrian refugees. Realizing the insecurity of his hold on the affections of the Marches the duke of York traversed the borders leisurely and cautiously, holding sessions at Shrewsbury, Ludlow, and Hereford, where he was to be joined by the duchess. Having confirmed the loyalty of these parts he marched on London, and reached the city on 9 October, accompanied by a strong bodyguard of Welshmen from his estates in the Marches.[15]

Parliament had already assembled, Sir William Herbert being member for Hereford.[16] To the amazement of the lords the duke of York laid claim to the throne. Friendly representations, in which the earl of Warwick played a prominent part, convinced him of the unpopularity and unwisdom of the step. He therefore agreed that Henry should be king during his lifetime, and that he should succeed him. York therefore became Protector. The Principality of Wales was assigned to him. When parliament was dissolved he left London for his Yorkshire estates, on 9 December. Warwick remained in London. York's eldest son, the earl of March, came to the Marches of Wales to raise forces.

On 12 October Queen Margaret and her son were still in Wales. The duke of

Duke of York's monument, Sandal Magna, marks the spot where he is said to have fallen during the battle of Wakefield, 1460.

St George's Chapel. Garter stall-plate of Richard Neville, earl of Salisbury, c. 1436–60.

Exeter was with her with a good following.[17] Her headquarters were probably Pembroke, whence she sailed to Scotland.[18]

The most explicit statement as to her movements in Wales comes from Gregory, who says that she moved to Jasper, lord of Pembroke. Denbigh had been reduced by the Lancastrians since March 1459, but Jasper Tudor made Tenby and Pembroke his headquarters. From Pembroke Margaret could sail to Scotland more conveniently than if she had been at Denbigh. Before sailing she had sent urgent messages to Somerset and Devon to join her as speedily as possible 'with their tenants as strong in their harness as men of war'.[19] It was reported that the great muster was to be in Wales,[20] but the activity of the queen's friends in the north of England drew the duke of Somerset and the earl of Devon thither. They passed through Bath, Cirencester, Evesham, and Coventry on their journey northwards, but did not touch the Welsh border.[21] Apparently Margaret intended Yorkshire to be the venue of the next campaign, for she hoped to bring reinforcements from Scotland.[22] Jasper Tudor was to remain in Wales.

While Margaret was recuperating in Scotland the duke of York was attacked by her northern supporters with disastrous promptitude at Wakefield. There, on 30 December, his army was annihilated, and he himself put to death. Next morning the earl of Salisbury was beheaded. Seven weeks later, on 17 February, Margaret with an army of 'Scots, Welsh, and Northmen'[23] defeated

Warwick at St Albans and put him to flight with a remnant of his host.

Such in brief are two of the acts of this drama of feud, which were enacted in the winter 1460/1. The third, and the most decisive, took place on the borders of Wales, at Mortimer's Cross. Let us consider it.

News of his father's death at Wakefield reached young Edward, earl of March, at Gloucester.[24] He thereupon set about gathering an army in the Marches and the border counties, and was soon at the head of a numerous host. He had been well acquainted with the borders from his boyhood, having been under the tutelage of Richard Croft of Herefordshire. He was a lusty youth of nineteen, but he had not yet organized a campaign in person, although he had taken a prominent part at Northampton. He was now the chief of the Yorkist faction, and under his standard Wales wrote herself in capital letters.

Of Edward's lieutenants and advisers the most conspicuous were Sir William Herbert, Sir Walter Devereux (Lord Ferrers of Chartley) and Sir Roger Vaughan,[25] the three who had been collectively commissioned to look after Yorkist interests in Wales in the previous August; and of these the recognized chief was Herbert. To him, who had an end in view and an eye to means, the fact that Edward was heir to the title and pretensions of Richard, duke of York, appealed with tremendous force. To be associated with his prospective sovereign in his first campaign, and to turn that campaign into a triumph, was an alluring prospect for future eminence. He therefore threw himself with inflexible resolution into the task. He and Walter Devereux were men of experience. Both had served in the French wars, Herbert under the most daring and consistently successful captain of his day in France, Mathew Gough. What was more important for the enterprise then being forged, both were familiar with the turbid politics of the Marches. Moreover, Herbert and Roger Vaughan especially could appeal with effect to Welsh sentiment, which was never more intense or more general than in the second half of the fifteenth century. With them were William Herbert's brother Richard, Henry ap Griffith, Philip Vaughan captain of Hay, William Thomas, John Dwnn, and three knights from Herefordshire, namely, Sir Richard Croft, Sir John Lynell and Sir William Knylle.[26] In a letter written a few weeks after the engagement Jasper Tudor attributes his reverse to 'March, Herbert, and the Dwnns'.[27]

It will thus be seen that the forces of Edward, earl of March, in this campaign were drawn mainly from what are now the shires of Glamorgan, Brecknock, Monmouth, Radnor, and Montgomery, and the border county of Hereford. Lord Audley, the son of him who was slain on the Lancastrian side at Bloreheath, is also mentioned as having been with Edward. He had estates in Cemmaes, Pembrokeshire; but as Jasper, earl of Pembroke, was gathering fuel for war in these parts, it is hardly possible that Audley could have sought material there. He had been taken prisoner by the earl of Warwick in Calais after the panic of Ludford, had crossed the Channel with him in June 1460, and was with the Yorkists at Northampton. He may therefore have accompanied the earl of March to the borders of Wales at Christmas.

Against this compact, homogeneous force, the Lancastrians brought a motley body of Welsh, Irish, French and Bretons, under the leadership of Jasper, earl of Pembroke, and the earl of Wiltshire and Ormond (James Butler).[28] With them were Jasper's father, old Owen Tudor,[29] Sir John Skydmore, who had a personal bodyguard of thirty men;[30] Sir Thomas Perot of Haverfordwest; two of the sons of Griffith ap Nicholas, Owen and Thomas; Lewis ap Rhys of Carmarthen; Philip Mansel and Hopkin ap Rhys of Gower; Rheinallt Gwynedd of Harlech; Lewis Powys of Powysland; Hopkin Davy of Carmarthen; Thomas Fitzharry; James Skydmore and Sir Harry Skydmore, sons of Sir John Skydmore; Sir William Skydmore, his brother.[31]

If we except the Hereford contingent these men were drawn mainly from Pembrokeshire and Carmarthenshire. There was also a large body of foreigners who came by sea, and who formed the bulk of the Lancastrian army. At least they were so numerous that one contemporary chronicler makes no mention whatever of the Welsh contingent.[32] These Irish, French, and Bretons were probably the reinforcements brought by the earl of Wiltshire, unless we may suppose, what is quite feasible, and actually suggested by Lewis Glyn Cothi, that Jasper himself had left for Ireland and perhaps for France, when Margaret sailed for Scotland.[33]

Moreover, it is suggested by Lewis Glyn Cothi that Jasper landed at Milford Haven about 27 December. If so, there arises a strong presumption that his attack from Wales and that of his allies from the north were timed to take place simultaneously; for the battle of Wakefield was fought on 30 December.

The most probable conclusion from the few fragments of records that are

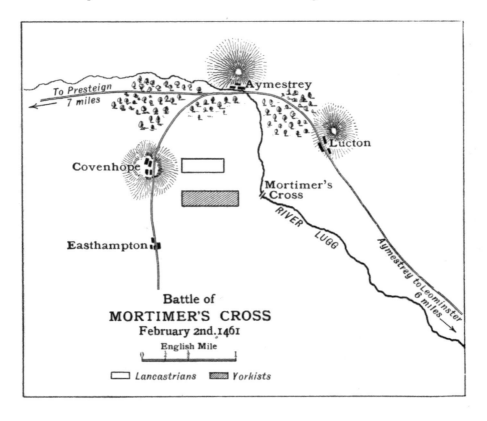

Battle of
MORTIMER'S CROSS
February 2nd, 1461

available seems to be that, while Jasper mustered his supporters in Wales, the earl of Wiltshire, having enlisted troops on his Irish estates and abroad, landed in Wales, probably at Milford Haven;[34] that the combined force, moving up the valley of the Towy, passed through Radnorshire, and, having reached Presteign, which is about seven miles from Aymestrey, followed the valley of the Lugg in the direction of Leominster. But they found their further progress barred by the Yorkists at Mortimer's Cross. This route would serve to explain the predominance of the levies of Carmarthenshire and Pembrokeshire. The earl of Wiltshire was sheriff of the former county as well as of Cardiganshire.[35] It should be remembered, moreover, that some time previously he had fitted out a fleet of five ships at Genoa, with which to act against the Yorkists; and, having been appointed captain to guard the sea in April 1454, he was presumably in command of a fleet.[36] In short, the Lancastrian plan of campaign was a repetition of what we conceive to have been their strategy during the manoeuvres which culminated at Ludford.

Edward, earl of March, was advancing eastwards when he heard of the Lancastrian advance in his rear. He turned to meet them, advancing probably from Hereford and Leominster towards Presteign.[37] The two armies came face to face at Mortimer's Cross on the Lugg, about six miles north-west of Leominster, on 2 February 1461.[38] About ten o'clock on the morning of the day of battle a strange portent was seen in the heavens; for 'there were seen three suns in the firmament shining full clear, whereof the people had great marvel, and thereof were aghast. The noble earl Edward them comforted and said, – "Be of good cheer and dread not; this is a good sign."'[39] Another reports 'a shower of rain of the colour of blood', as well as a three-fold sun.[40]

The Yorkists, who considerably outnumbered their opponents,[41] obtained the victory, and a large number of the Lancastrians were slain. Jasper Tudor and the earl of Wiltshire stole away in disguise; and Sir John Perot also made good his escape.[42]

Owen Tudor was among the prisoners who were taken to Hereford and there put to death. It is said that he was brought to the place of execution by his countryman Sir Roger Vaughan.[43]

> And he was beheaded in the market-place, and his head set upon the highest grise of the market cross; and a mad woman combed his hair and washed away the blood of his face. And she got candles and set about him burning, more than a hundred. This Owen Tudor was the father unto the earl of Pembroke and had wedded Queen Catherine, King Henry VI's mother, weening and trusting all the time that he should not be beheaded, till he saw the axe and the block; and when that he was in his doublet he trusted on pardon and grace till the collar of his red velvet doublet was ripped off. Then he said – That head shall lie on the stock that was wont to lie on Queen Catherine's lap; and put his heart and mind wholly unto God, and full meekly took his death.

He was buried in the chapel of the Grey Friars in Hereford.[44]

Owen Tudor typifies that spirit of adventure and chivalry which in the fifteenth century sent Welshmen abroad to win fame on the battlefields of Europe or in the courts of princes. He carried to the grave that intrepidity and dignified bearing which had characterized him in life. But he mistook the age, not indeed in which he had lived, but in which he was to die. The age of chivalry was passing by and giving way to the ungovernable passions and truculent savagery of meaner days. Owen Tudor bridges the two; he lived in the one, and died in the other.

It has been supposed that eight other captains were put to death at Hereford with Owen Tudor.[45] It can be shown, however, that the lists of the chroniclers are inaccurate in many respects. It is certain that there escaped several of those whose names are given as having been either beheaded or captured. For instance, Phillip Mansel, Hopkyn ap Rhys of Gower, and Lewis ap Rhys of Strata Florida were in the field again a few years after these events; Sir John Skydmore subsequently held Pembroke Castle against Sir William Herbert, and must have made good his escape; the two sons of Griffith ap Nicholas also found safety in flight.[46]

The battle aroused even less interest in Wales than in England. There are but few references to it in the poets. In one of his odes Howel Swrdwal alludes to an important fight in Herefordshire, in which Watcyn Vaughan of Bredwardine was slain. He may have Mortimer's Cross in mind, but there is nothing to prove it.[47] But the very paucity of allusions to the fight shows how little the country generally was moved so far by the quarrel between the factions.

A spurious tale gained currency in later years with regard to Griffith ap Nicholas and his son Owen, which it would be absurd to notice but that responsible writers have given credence to it. It has been stated that Griffith brought to Mortimer's Cross a force of seven or eight hundred followers to assist the Yorkists, men 'well-armed, goodly of stature, and hearts answerable thereto'. When he received a mortal wound, his second son Owen stood at the head of his troops and pursued Jasper. When he returned to acquaint his father of the victory the latter exclaimed: 'Welcome death, since honour and victory make for us.'[48] As has already been said a vein of unreality runs through the whole biography; and its details cannot stand the limelight of historical criticism.[49] Griffith is not mentioned by any contemporary chronicler, though many Welshmen of far less distinction are named. His sons are recorded, but on the Lancastrian side. If the family had accomplished the deeds attributed to them they would probably have found their reward on the accession of Edward IV, as did, for instance, their neighbours, the Dwnns of Carmarthenshire.[50] As a matter of fact Griffith had probably been dead a couple of years. There is no mention of him in authentic records, local or general, after 1456. Moreover, though his two sons, Owen and Thomas, were mentioned in 1459 as assisting the Tudors against the Dwnns, Griffith himself is not mentioned.[51]

Soon after his victory Edward was given a commission by the Privy Council to raise fresh levies in Bristol and the border counties,[52] he having in the meantime moved on to Gloucester.[53] It was on the day on which Edward received his commission that Warwick moved from London to St Albans, accompanied by the king, to meet the hosts of Margaret which were then advancing on the city. As already stated, the earl was defeated by the Lancastrians on 17 February, and, having escaped westwards with the remnants of his army, met Edward five days later at Chipping Norton,[54] or at Burford,[55] in Oxfordshire. Edward was now accompanied by William Hastings and John Wenlok, who must have joined him after the battle at Mortimer's Cross; for they are not reported to have been present at that action.

Heraldic achievement of Sir John Wenlok depicted in stained glass at Ockwells Manor, Berks.

Mortimer's Cross monument, Kingland, Herefordshire, erected in 1799.

Margaret apparently had begun her southward march before news of Jasper's defeat had reached her. Warwick may have received information of her approach on 28 January, the day on which commissions were issued in the king's name to noblemen and sheriffs to raise troops.[56] She was at St Albans before Edward had left the Marches. Edward, who was at the head of a more amenable following than the queen's intoxicated host, must have surmised that the Lancastrians, in the flush of their brilliant triumph at Wakefield, would advance on the capital. And he was not a man who lacked courage in a crisis. Why then did he not strike directly for the seat of government which was still in the hands of his friends, and where his party was strong, so as to endeavour to be in time to assist Warwick? Instead of doing so he tarried on the borders of Wales. From Hereford he moved to Gloucester, where he was on 12 February. These ten days (2–12 February) would have enabled him to cover the distance between Gloucester and London with comparative ease. Yet he delayed another week, received intimation of Warwick's defeat around 19 February, and three days later had only reached the confines of Oxfordshire, meeting Warwick on 22 February.

His movements leave an uncanny suspicion that he was anxious neither to assist

Engraving of Baynard's Castle, the Thames-side residence of the House of York in the fifteenth century.

nor even to meet Warwick. Warwick's voice had been raised with success against the usurpation of the throne by Richard, duke of York; Edward had no reason to hope that he would adopt a different attitude towards himself. The only circumstance that would render Warwick less dictatorial would be a defeat, and Edward astutely let him run the risk. If Warwick were victorious, Edward too had a victory in hand – a valuable asset when he claimed the throne. Fortune, by giving victory to Edward and withholding it from Warwick, made Edward doubly independent.[57]

Mortimer's Cross was sufficient to retrieve the double disaster at Wakefield and St Albans, and Edward did not fail to appreciate it at its true value. It is significant of the importance which he attached to it that he afterwards assumed as his peculiar war-badge 'the rising sun', in allusion to the portent on the day of battle.[58] The measure of its importance was nothing less than the accession of Edward. He could not fail to compare his own success with the failure of Warwick; and it is certain that he afterwards commented upon the earl's want of resource at St Albans. From that moment Warwick ceased to conjure up terrors for either Edward or his associates from the Marches.

On 26 February the combined armies reached London. Margaret had already gone north. On 1 March the citizens joined Edward's Welsh army in St John's Fields, Clerkenwell, and, under the guidance of the chancellor, George Neville, proclaimed Edward king. Two days later the Yorkist leaders met at Baynard's Castle and formally offered Edward the crown.[59] There were present the chancellor, Archbishop Bourchier, the bishop of Salisbury, the duke of Norfolk, the earl of Warwick, Lord Fitz-Walter (Sir John Ratcliffe), Lord Ferrers of Chartley (Walter Devereux), and Sir William Herbert. It is noticeable that special reference is made to Herbert as one of the 'chosen and faithful' of Edward.[60] The political and military storms of the winter had swept him to the highest council in the realm. Edward had already hinted broadly at his appreciation of the services of his friends from the Marches; for on meeting with Warwick in Oxfordshire he had referred to them as men who had come at their own cost.[61]

Warwick raised no objection to Edward's accession. Edward's father owed much to Warwick; Edward himself little, at any rate before his accession. The earl presumed upon his victory at Northampton to resist Richard, duke of York, when he claimed the throne. His defeat at St Albans gave him no alternative but to concede to the son the acquiescence which he had withheld from the father.

Edward was now king. As such he hurried northwards after Margaret. Victorious at a skirmish near Ferrybridge, he completely overwhelmed the Lancastrians at Towton (29 March 1461). Edward had won a throne at Mortimer's Cross; Towton made his throne secure.

CHAPTER SEVEN

The War in Wales

It is unnecessary to enter into a minute description of Edward's campaign in the north of England. He was accompanied by Sir William Herbert; and the Welsh foot-soldiers, the force that had triumphed at Mortimer's Cross, reinforced by the levies of Kent, constituted the nucleus of the army which completed the annihilation of the Lancastrians at Towton.[1] It has been freely assumed, presumably on the authority of Wavrin, not a very faithful chronicler of English affairs, that the Lancastrian army comprised a large body of Welshmen who, led by Andrew Trollope, displayed magnificent dash in the teeth of a blinding snowstorm. Flattering though it be to national pride, it lacks corroboration. Indeed, there could have been but few Welshmen under the banner of Lancaster at that battle. Only a few weeks had passed since Jasper had brought the flower of Lancastrian Wales to Mortimer's Cross; and in spite of his steadfast and insistent zeal he could not possibly have recovered in so short a space. Even now, when the clash of battle resounded in the north, he was quietly engaged in the task of reorganizing and encouraging his adherents in Wales. If any Welshmen were arrayed against Edward at Towton, it seems that they must have been raised either by Margaret when she sought refuge in Wales after Northampton, or by Exeter and others as they passed along the borders of Wales towards Wakefield. But there is no peg on which such an assumption can hang.

After his victory at Towton Edward, leaving to the earl of Warwick the task of reducing the Lancastrian strongholds of the north, returned to the Welsh border, and threw upon Sir William Herbert the responsibility of bringing Wales to obedience. With this object in view he began to invest him and his brothers with considerable power. When at York, on his way to the south, he made William Herbert chief justice and chamberlain of South Wales, and steward and chief forester of Carmarthenshire and Cardiganshire.[2] On the following day (9 May) a commission was given to him and his two brothers Thomas Herbert[3] and John Herbert,[4] and Hugh Huntley,

> to take into the king's hands the county and lordship of Pembroke, with all members in England and Wales and the Marches of Wales, late of Jasper, earl of Pembroke; the castle of Dunster, county Somerset, and other possessions late of

James Luttrell, knight; and the castles and lordships of Gooderich and Archenfield in the county of Hereford and the Marches of Wales adjacent to the county of Gloucester, and all advowsons late of John, earl of Shrewsbury, rebels, with power to appoint stewards and all other officers.

Herbert was also to take possession of the lands of Sir William Mulle; and two days later, 11 May, authority was given to him and Thomas Herbert and John Dwnn 'to take into the king's hands and demise at farm the castles and lordships of Laugharne and Walwyn's Castle, late of James, earl of Wiltshire, in South Wales.'[5] Moreover, Thomas Herbert became constable of Gloucester, while a half-brother William Herbert was made constable of Cardigan.

These offices and honours were conferred on Sir William Herbert while the king was at York. Shortly afterwards both returned to London, passing through Chester on 28 May, and making a circuit of the Welsh border. A month later Edward was crowned with more than usual pomp and splendour. In honour of the occasion the most prominent of his friends from the Marches were raised to the peerage. Sir William Herbert became Lord Herbert of Raglan, Chepstow, and Gower; Sir Walter Devereux was formally recognized as Lord Ferrers of Chartley;[6] Sir William Hastings and Sir John Wenlok became Lord Hastings and Lord Wenlok respectively. Richard, earl of Warwick, was not made a duke as had been confidently anticipated in some quarters. This disappointment was

Seal of William Herbert, earl of Huntingdon, 1479.

the first drop of the torrent which engulfed the Nevilles.

Immediately after the coronation a considerable redistribution of power took place in Wales. Lord Hastings was made chamberlain of North Wales;[7] Richard Grey, Lord Powys, became steward of Ceri, Cedewain, and Montgomery;[8] John, earl of Worcester, became justice of North Wales;[9] John Dwnn was made constable of Aberystwyth and Carmarthen, and sheriff of Carmarthenshire and Cardiganshire, 'with all profits of pasture of Aberystwyth', and the custom called 'prysemayse'.[10]

Preparations now sped onwards for the immediate invasion of Wales. On 8 July Lords Herbert and Ferrers were empowered to array all able-bodied men in the counties of Hereford, Gloucester, and Salop.[11] Early in August they were appointed to inquire into all treasons, insurrections, and rebellions in South Wales, and to pardon all who submitted, except Jasper Tudor, John Skydmore, Thomas Cornwall, and Thomas Fitzhenry.[12] On 12 August Roger Kynaston and a number of others were commissioned to urge the king's subjects of Shropshire to array a force at their own expense for the defence of the county and the adjoining parts of Wales. On that day, also, separate commissions were issued to Thomas, John, and Richard Herbert, to act against Jasper Tudor. The general muster was to be at Hereford.[13]

Parliament was not to meet till November, and Edward decided to spend a considerable portion of the interval in the Marches so as to keep in close touch with the progress of events in Wales; and his movements appear to have attracted considerable attention.[14] He had reached the borders before the end of August. On 4 September he was at Bristol, where he was 'most royally received'. Four days later he left for Gloucester, whence he moved to Ross, Hereford, and Ludlow. He remained at Ludlow for nearly a week, till 26 September.[15] Meanwhile Herbert and Ferrers

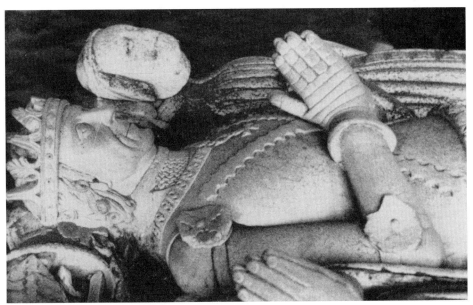

Effigy of John Tiptoft, earl of Worcester, Ely Cathedral, Cambs.

had gone into Wales to extinguish the few flickering Lancastrian lights, with every prospect of success. 'As for any grete doing in Wales I trust God we shal not doubte. The Lord Herbert and the Lord Ferrers of Chartley with divers many other gentilmen ben gone afore to clense the countreye afore us.'[16]

After the reverse at Mortimer's Cross, Jasper Tudor had retired to his estates in Pembrokeshire. On 25 February, three weeks after that battle, he wrote to his stewards at Denbigh, Roger Puleston[17] and John Eyton, exhorting them to be faithful. The letter was written from Tenby; and it shows, what we have already pointed out, that the Herberts and their connections were regarded as the chief engineers of that campaign on the Yorkist side.

> To the right trusty and well-beloved Roger à Puleston and to John Eyton, and to either of them. We suppose that ye have well in remembrance the great dishonour and rebuke that we and ye now late have by traitors March, Herbert, and Dwnns with their affinities, as well in letting us of our journey to the kinge, as in putting my father your kinsman to the death, and their trayterously demeaning we purpose with the might of our Lord and assistance of you and other our kinsmen and friends within short time to avenge. Trusting verily that you will be well willed and put your hands into the same, and of your disposiçon, and with your good advice therein we pray you to ascertayne us in all hast possible as our especiall trust is in you. Written at our town of Tenby the xxv February.[18]

On a previous occasion the Yorkists had held Denbigh with grim tenacity against Jasper. It was now as stubborn on his behalf. The castle was still holding out in July as appears from the letter which follows.

> To Roger Puleston, Keeper of the castle of Denbigh. We have received your letters by Hugh and understand the matter comprised therein; and as touching the keeping of the castle of Denbigh we pray you that you will do your faithful diligence for the safeguard of it, taking the revenue of the lordship there for the vittaling of the same, by the hands of Griffith Vaughan, receyvour there, – we have written unto him that he should make p'veyance therefore; and that ye will understand the goodwill and dispossiçon of the people and that country towards my Lorde Prince, and to send us word as soone as you may. Written at my town of Tenbye, the xxiii July.[19]

Edward, with commendable clemency, had already made overtures of peace to the Pulestons and Griffith Vaughan; for early in July he had enrolled them on a commission in Chirkland with a number of other staunch royalists of North Wales. But his conciliatory efforts were for the present unavailing.[20]

Lords Herbert and Ferrers had already entered upon their task of reducing Wales on 9 September 1461. They had two important strongholds to deal with besides Denbigh; for Harlech was held by David ap Eynon and some English Lancastrian refugees, notably Tunstall, while Pembroke Castle was held for Jasper by Sir John Skydmore.

Herbert attacked Pembroke first. It was the most formidable, and consequently the greatest prize. The fleet was sent to cooperate so that no assistance might reach the castle from beyond the sea.[21] Philip Castle of Pembroke and Thomas Mansel were empowered to man some ships for the purpose. The Yorkist leaders would find no opposition on their march westwards; Oystermouth Castle, near Swansea, one of the gates of Gower, had been placed in the hands of a local Yorkist, Sir Hugh ap John.[22] Like so many others of the Welshmen engaged in these wars he had fought in France, and had been one of the council of Robert Norreys. He was now constable of the castle, and reeve of the lordship of Gower. It was on behalf of Sir Hugh ap John that the earl of Warwick used his influence with Elizabeth Woodville, afterwards the queen of Edward IV, to get her to accept him in marriage.[23]

Tenby apparently offered no resistance, although much care had been bestowed upon its fortifications by Jasper. Pembroke, too, was 'victualled, manned, and apparelled for a long time after'.[24] These preparations notwithstanding, Skydmore, when summoned by Herbert to surrender the castle into his hands, obsequiously delivered it 'without any war or resistance'.[25] This took place on 30 September. Skydmore's conduct was in complete harmony with the general practice during the wars. Impregnable as were many of the castles of England at this period, their history is an uninspiring recital of slavish deference to the will of the conqueror of the moment.

The betrayal was inspired by a natural desire for personal safety and the security of his estates, though it availed him nothing for the moment. He received a written pledge from Herbert and Ferrers that his life would be spared and that his lands would not be confiscated. Both promised to intercede with the king on his behalf. But in spite of this guarantee, when parliament met, a bill of attainder was brought against him. It failed to pass. Nevertheless, at the latter end of the parliament, his estates were forfeited by royal ordinance.[26]

The lords promised that 'he should have better than his livelihood, and he was

Pembroke Castle.

then admitted unto the kyngs good grace as he hath redy to showe in writyng under the seale of the said Lord Herbert'. Herbert was present in the parliament in which the attainder was moved and rejected. But 'after many lords and knights had departed, by mervelous pryvat labour', a bill signed by the king was brought to the Commons containing an ordinance that Sir John Skydmore should forfeit his livelihood saving his life and goods. At the time he was at home in the country 'trusting to the promise of Lords Herbert and Ferrers'.

Jasper probably superintended the affairs of his party in North Wales in person. He was assisted by the duke of Exeter,[27] and Thomas Fitzhenry of Hereford, who had fought with the Lancastrians at Mortimer's Cross. On 4 October it was reported that all resistance was at an end, and that Jasper had taken refuge in the mountains of Snowdon, the last stronghold of so many lost causes, and the nursery of as many new enterprises. 'And all the castles and holds in South Wales and in North Wales are given and yielded up to the king. And the duke of Exeter and the earl of Pembroke [Jasper] are floon and taken the mounteyns and divers lords with great puissance are after them; and the most part of gentlemen and men of worship are comen to the king and have grace, of all Wales.'[28]

The writer was premature. Denbigh seems to have yielded without further pressure. It must have suffered considerable damage during these years. As we have seen, in the previous year a substantial grant was made to repair the disastrous effects of the Lancastrian siege. Early in 1462 Edward IV advanced a sum to enable the burgesses to rebuild their houses 'brent by certain rebells and traytors'.[29]

But Harlech had not yet submitted, and was to remain inexorable for seven years more. Jasper Tudor and the North Wales Lancastrians were brought to bay near Carnarvon. They made a last stand at Tuthill, just outside the walls of that town, on 16 October 1461.[30] As the duke of Exeter had fought at Towton it is probable that he had brought reinforcements to Jasper by sea. The Yorkists once more triumphed, though Jasper again displayed his wonted subtle resourcefulness in eluding pursuit. He escaped to Ireland, where he stirred up strife during the winter.[31] It is curious that the engagement at Tuthill has escaped the notice of every historian of the Wars of the Roses.

The Yorkists did not pursue their advantage by compelling Harlech, the only remaining Lancastrian stronghold in Wales, to surrender.[32] It may be that, the day for the opening of parliament having been fixed for 4 November, they were more desirous to appear there than to traverse the bleak and pathless regions of Snowdonia on the approach of winter. Edward's supine indifference to the existence of this remote garrison kept North Wales in a state of war for several years after the rest of the country had been brought into subjection. An echo of the prevailing anarchy was heard in his first parliament in the form of a petition from the 'Tenants and Commons of North Wales', as follows:

Where many and divers of them been daily taken prisoners and put to fine and ransom as it were in land of war; and many and divers of them daily robbed and spoiled of their goods and cattle contrary to the law by David ap Ieuan ap Eynon, Griffith Vaughan ap Griffith ap Eynon, Jenkyn ap Iorwerth ap Eynon,

Thomas ap Ieuan ap Eynon, Griffith ap Ieuan ap Eynon, John ap Ieuan ap Eynon, John Hanmer, Morys ap David ap Griffith, David ap Ieuan ap Owen, David ap Einon ap Ieuan, Grommys ap Ieuan ap Eynon ap Ieuan, Grommys ap Howel ap Morgan, Edward ap Morgan, John Tother, clerk, Griffith ap Ieuan ap Iorwerth, and Rheinallt ap Griffith ap Bleddyn, and Morys Robert; and over more the said David ap Eynon calleth himself by the name of Constable of Harlech, and that kepeth to the use and behove of him that he calleth his sovereign lord King Henry VI, saying as well by his mouth as by his writing that the said castle was committed to him by his sovereign lord aforesaid and by his sovereign lady Queen Margaret and his right and gracious lord Prince Edward, and sworn to keep it to their use and will not deliver it to no other person saving to such as one of them will assign, notwithstanding the King's commandment is the contrary. And daily the said David and all the aforesaid other misdoers take and repute in all their demeanour the said late king for their sovereign lord and not the king our sovereign lord that now is as their duty is. And moreover all the said misdoers taketh oxen, sheep, wheat, and victuals of the said poor tenants for stuff of the said castle with strong hand and will not deliver it to no such person as the late King hath deputed to be his constable there.

Then follows a specious proclamation that David must surrender the castle before the Feast of Purification; and that if he came to Carnarvon in peaceable wise, and there before the king's justice or chamberlain found sufficient security for his future good conduct, he would be pardoned; otherwise he would be attainted of treason and his lands and title forfeited. This proclamation was to be made in the counties of Carnarvon and Merioneth.[33]

The garrison defied the proclamation, and during the next few years Harlech remained a safe refuge for the Lancastrians, and a convenient link with Ireland and Scotland. Contemporary Welsh poets are unanimous as to the assistance rendered by it to the cause. That it inspired the Lancastrians to renewed efforts became evident very soon. For a new scheme issued from their busy forge, according to which Jasper and the duke of Exeter were to land at Beaumaris, 'by the appointment of Robert Gold, captain of the duke of Burgundy';[34] while simultaneous attacks were to be made from the north and the south-east of England. Edward acted with decision. The scheme was destroyed before it matured. In February 1462 the earl of Oxford and a few others were executed as accomplices. On 1 March Lord Herbert and Lord Ferrers were commanded to array all able-bodied men in South Wales and the Marches, the former and his brother Thomas Herbert being also commissioned to equip a fleet from Bristol and neighbouring ports to clear the coast of Wales of Lancastrian ships.[35] It is not certain whether Jasper actually landed in Wales. During the early part of the year, as we have seen, he was in Ireland causing trouble. 'These three weeks came there neither ship nor boat out of Ireland to bring no tidings, and so it seemeth there is much to doo there by the earl of Pembroke.'[36] Leaving him there for the present, we shall consider what rewards were bestowed upon the Yorkists of Wales for their valuable services to Edward.

A wide redistribution of lands, and consequently of political power, now took place in Wales. The lavish profusion with which Edward enriched the Herbert family is a lucid commentary upon the value which he attached to their services. It was also an augury, clear and palpable, of Edward's intention to raise up a new aristocracy whose secret counsels were to aid him to outwit the old.

The lands of Jasper, earl of Pembroke, the earl of Wiltshire, and Sir John Skydmore had already been confiscated. Lord Herbert received those of Jasper and the earl of Wiltshire in South Wales. They included Pembroke, Tenby, Emlyn, Cilgerran, Llanstephan, and Walwyn's Castle.[37] A few days later, on 12 February, he was given the custody and marriage of Jasper's nephew, Henry, earl of Richmond, then a child of four, 'for a thousand pounds in hand paid'. It was Herbert's intention, as we shall see, to marry him to his daughter Maud.

A few days later he received the custody of the lordships of Swansea, Gower, and Kilvey, during the minority of John, son and heir of the duke of Norfolk, rendering the king 200 marks a year; also the town and castle of Haverfordwest for twenty years, rendering the king 100 marks a year.[38] In April he appeared in the House of Lords, and was made a knight of the Garter.

Richard Herbert received the confiscated lands of Jasper's faithful adherent Fitzhenry, as well as those of Sir John Skydmore, in Herefordshire, including the lordship of Moccas.[39]

Roger Vaughan of Tretower, in Brecknock, received extensive lands in Somerset, Devon, and Dorset.[40] His son Thomas ap Roger Vaughan became receiver of the lordships of Brecknock, Hay, and Huntingdon, during the minority of the heir to the dukedom of Buckingham.[41] John Dwnn received Laugharne, the confiscated property of the earl of Wiltshire, as well as some lands in Northamptonshire, 'for good service to Richard, duke of York, and against Henry VI and Jasper'.[42]

The lands of Thomas Cornwall, in Devon, were shared between John ap Jankyn and Trahaiarn ap Ievan ap Meurig,[43] while one David Gough received Stapleton in the Marches.[44] Thomas and Richard Croft received lands in Oxfordshire; John Milewater found his reward in the receivership of confiscated castles in Wales; Lord Ferrers received Richard's Castle in Herefordshire.[45] Among other grants one of the most interesting was that of 'letters of denization as Englishman for the king's servitor David Middleton one of the yeomen of the Crown, born a Welshman', to him and his heirs.[46] The Middletons of Denbighshire wrote their names large in the annals of the seventeenth century as scholars, engineers, and sailors.

Another recipient of grants was Sir Thomas Vaughan who piloted his craft with much skill through many storms. His parentage is uncertain, though it seems to be generally agreed that he was a son of Sir Roger Vaughan. By some means he came under the protection of the duke of Somerset and Adam Moleyns, through whose influence the Privy Council relieved him of his disabilities as a Welshman. In 1450 he was master of ordnance and was commissioned to equip Carisbrook Castle, Isle of Wight, against the attacks of the French. In 1458 we find him as treasurer of the king's household. Like his kinsman William Herbert he was associated with Jasper Tudor for a time; but he soon took the badge of York, and was attainted at the Coventry Parliament. Edward gave him lands in Surrey, and in 1463 he was sent on an embassy to the duke of Burgundy.[47]

To return to the main stream of events. Though Jasper Tudor had been driven out of Wales, Edward continued to keep a strict watch on the borders. On 1 November 1462, John Paston, junior, who was staying at Holt Castle in Denbighshire, wrote to his father saying that the duke of Norfolk was likely to keep his Christmas in Wales, 'for the king hath desired him to do the same'.[48] Soon, however, Edward summoned him to the north where the scattered Lancastrian parties were once more concentrating. The king was at Durham on 11 December. With him were Herbert, Ferrers, and others of the 'Kyngys house'.[49] This description of the two lords is strikingly suggestive of what they had so far achieved, a position pregnant with superlative possibilities.

We left Jasper stirring up strife in Ireland. We next hear of him in Scotland assisting Somerset, at the head of three hundred men, to defend Bamborough Castle, which was being besieged by the earls of Worcester and Arundel.[50] The castle surrendered on Christmas Eve 1462, whereupon Jasper, unable to obtain the clemency proffered to Somerset and others, retired to Scotland under safe conduct, 'unarmed, with white staves in their hands'.[51] Subsequently he assisted in the operations which culminated in the taking of Alnwick in May 1463.

Lord Herbert's exploits in the north are duly recorded by contemporary Welsh poets. Lewis Glyn Cothi nowhere gives a more glowing picture than that in which, with pardonable poetic licence, he describes his hero urging forward his men, 'his frame ablaze on prancing steed, and his eyes glistening like glowing embers'.[52]

In the summer of 1463 Herbert's attention was once more directed to Wales, where the ashes of war were still smouldering. In June he was made constable of Harlech and chamberlain and chief justice of Merionethshire, with all powers pertaining to the office of chief justice of North Wales, so as to be able to deal more effectively with the recalcitrant garrison there.[53] During Herbert's lifetime the country was to be separated from the jurisdiction of the justice of North Wales. Vindictiveness was certainly not a feature of Edward IV's treatment of his Welsh Lancastrian foes. If any of them even now were disposed to give in their allegiance Lord Herbert, Lord Ferrers, Richard Herbert, and Trahaiarn ap Ievan ap Meurig were empowered to grant them a full pardon.[54]

But in spite of Herbert's vigilance and Edward's clemency, Jasper's enthusiasm, his hardihood, and his towering gift of patience, had not yet failed to inspire his followers to indomitable resistance. During the winter of 1463/4 material was laid for another conflagration. The duke of Somerset who, since his pardon by Edward at the end of 1462, had been kept in semi-confinement, became privy to a scheme which involved simultaneous risings in Wales and in the north of England. He was to engineer the rebellion in the northern counties of England; while Roger Puleston and John Hanmer were entrusted with the leadership in North Wales. In South Wales Jasper relied upon Philip Mansel of Gower, Hopkyn ap Rhys of Llangyfelach near Swansea, and Lewis ap Rhydderch ap Rhys of Strata Florida.[55] They were probably assisted by Philip Castle of Pembroke who was attainted soon afterwards 'because, in spite of previous pardons, he assisted Jasper'.[56] It will be recollected that he and Thomas Mansel had been commissioned to equip some ships during the siege and reduction of Pembroke.

The rising in Wales was apparently premature. John Dwnn, who was now sheriff of the two West Wales counties, and captain of Carmarthen and Aberystwyth, with the help of Roger Vaughan, overwhelmed the insurgents at Dryslwyn in the valley of the Towy, between Carmarthen and Llandilo, before they could become dangerous. These Yorkists were subsequently rewarded with the confiscated estates of the luckless Lancastrians.[57]

It was this engagement at Dryslwyn, probably, that brought Edward once more to the borders of Wales. He was at Gloucester on 9 February, and 'punished his rebellious against the law'.[58] Philip Mansel and Hopkyn ap Rhys were attainted and their estates forfeited.[59] Roger Vaughan entered into possession of the former's lands, namely, Oxwich, Scurla Castle, Nicholston, Reynoldston, Manselton, parts of Llanrhidian, and certain rents from Kidwely; and also of Llangyfelach and Kilvey, near Swansea, the property of Hopkyn ap Rhys.[60] John Dwnn received two parcels of the duchy of Lancaster in the lordship of Kidwely. Henry Dwnn received an annuity of £20 from the issues of Kidwely, Carnwallon, Iscennin, which were also parcel of that duchy in West Wales.[61]

We have no details to show how widely the infection of disloyalty spread in North Wales. Even the measures taken to combat it are swathed in a mantle of obscurity. Whatever was done fell to the lot of the duke of Norfolk, as appears from the following letter, which was written on 1 March from the duke's head-quarters at Holt Castle:

> My lord [the duke of Norfolk] hath great labour and cost here in Walys for to take divers gentlemen which were consenting and helping on to the duke of Somerset's going, and they were appealed of other certain points of treason, and this matter. And because the king sent my lord word to keep this country, is the reason why my lord tarryeth here thus long. And now the king hath given power to my lord whether he will do execution on these gentlemen or pardon them, as he pleases, and as far as I can understand yet they shall have grace. And as soon as these men come in my lord proposes to go to London which will be probably in a fortnight. The men's names that be impeached are these – John Hanmer, William his son, Roger Puleston, and Edward ap Madoc. These be men of worship that shall come in.

The writer was John Paston, the younger.[62]

Somerset's hazardous undertaking in the north of England also met with disaster. He had drawn a large contingent from North Wales with the assistance, as we have seen, of those patient and energetic kinsmen of Jasper Tudor, Roger Puleston and John Hanmer. 'He stole out of Wales with a prevy many toward Newcastle.'[63] At Durham he was detected and barely escaped being arrested in bed. 'He escaped away in hys schyrt and barefote, and ii of hys men were take.'[64] He then took a leading part in the campaigns of Hedgeley Moor (April) and Hexham (May). After the latter engagement he was captured by the servants of John Middleton,[65] and executed. The temporalities of the sees of St Asaph and Bangor were forfeited on account of

Sir John Donne of Kidwelly and his wife Elizabeth kneel before the Virgin and Child. From the triptych by Hans Memlinc (National Gallery, London).

the bishops' participation in these Lancastrian movements.[66]

Herbert was once more empowered to pacify the Lancastrians of Wales. In October 1464 he obtained a commission to receive into the king's allegiance all rebels, with few exceptions, within Harlech Castle and Merionethshire.[67]

Jasper as usual kept in the background during these commotions. He was a consummate engineer of rebellion, who considered his own person too valuable an asset to his cause to allow himself to fall into the clutches of his enemy. Fortunately for him he had many friends in the Principality, while Harlech was still a haven of refuge. His comrades, though dwindling in numbers, were sufficiently loyal to ensure his safety. If we are to credit contemporary poetry, his bard Tudur Penllyn, and his intimate friend Griffith Vaughan of Corsygedol, North Wales, could have revealed his places of hiding. They knew where he slept the night before his

St George's Chapel. Garter stall-plate of John Mowbray, duke of Norfolk and earl marshal KG, 1472–6.

departure, and from what spot on Barmouth shore he sailed away to bide his time, and await the morrow of better hope.[68] 'He moved', says Hall, 'from country to country in Wales, not always at his heart's ease, nor in security of life or surety of living. Such an unstable and blind goods is fortune.'[69]

Ellis Griffith, the Welsh Tudor chronicler, gives more specific details, if we can trust them:

In that time [after the pacification of the north] Jasper, according to what I heard from my elders, took the ship which belonged to a gentleman who lived at Mostyn, in the parish of Chwitford in Flintshire, at a place called Pwll Picton. The earl [Jasper] was constrained to carry a load of pease-straw on his back as he went to the ship lest he should be recognised because there were not wanting those who searched for him, and he betook himself to Brittany more by his own naval skill than by the skill of the sailors of Picton.[70]

Lord Herbert was now further enriched with a grant of Crickhowel and Tretower, to be held in chief by the service of one knight's fee; also of the 'honour, castle, manor and borough of Dunster, together with other possessions of Sir James Luttrell, Sir Walter Rodney, and Sir John Seymour, in Somerset and Devon'.[71] The text of the grant is instructive in parts:

Whereas William Herbert holds to himself and his heirs the castles manors and lordships of Crickhowel and Tretower as of the king's castle and lordship of Dinas and Blaenllyfni which are parcels of the earldom of March, the king now releases all claim in the said castles, and grants that he may hold them in chief by the service of one knight's fee. His tenants shall be quit of attendance at courts within the said lordships, and he shall have power of administering justice.

In 1464 parliament again called upon the Harlech garrison to submit. It was now known that John Dowbeggyng and Thomas Daniel, among the most unpopular of Henry VI's ministers, had taken refuge there. The summons stated that David ap Ieuan ap Eynon and Rheinallt ap Griffith ap Bleddyn harboured refugees, that they inspired commotions and gatherings against the king, and that the castle was used as a means of enabling the Lancastrians to enter the kingdom at their ease. Edward also issued a proclamation to the mayor and sheriff of Chester, which was to be read in the city on three consecutive days, threatening the defenders with the penalty of death unless they submitted before 1 January 1465.[72]

During these years the garrisons of the North Wales towns were strengthened on account of the ever-present danger from the Lancastrians, and from Harlech in particular. Thomas Montgomery, constable of Carnarvon, had to keep 24 soldiers there throughout the reign, while from 1455 to 1458 there existed a separate town garrison of 12 under a distinct captain.[73] At times the two garrisons were united. There were similar town and castle garrisons at Beaumaris during these years, numbering 12 and 24 respectively, under the direction of the constable. So also at Conway.

Stained glass figure of Thomas Montgomery (d. 1495), Long Melford Church, Suffolk.

APPENDIX

The following were protected in the Act of Resumption of 1464–5: John Wynne, officer of the household; Walter Mathew, Richard Gwynedd, Howel David, and John Howel, officers of the household; John Goch, yeoman of the larder; Morris Gethin, of the amobrship of the North Wales counties; William Gronow, of an annuity of 6 marks of the toll Presteign; Rees Vaughan, of an annuity of £7 of the toll of Radyr; John Newborough, keeper of the artillery and gunner of the North Wales towns; John and Hugh Lloyd of Denbigh, of an annuity of 5 marks granted by Richard, duke of York, from the lordship of Denbigh; Henry Trahaiarn ap Ievan ap Meurig, John ap Jankyn ap Madoc, William Cemmaes, William ap Howel ap Thomas, John ap Morgan, Jenkyn ap Thomas, John ap Jankyn, Meredith ap Morgan, William ap Morgan ap David Gam, John ap Gwilym, William ap Morgan, William ap Hopkyn, Howel Davy, Jankyn ap Howel ap Ievan, Jankyn ap Ievan ap Llywelyn; William ap Morgan, David ap Gwilym, Thomas Herbert esquire of the body, of 50 marks a year; Sir Thomas Vaughan, of lands in Kent, etc.; Thomas the elder, of the constableship of Gloucester; Thomas the younger, of the bailiwick of Guisnes in Picardy; John Davy, of an annuity of £20 from the town of Montgomery; Morris Arnold, Howel ap Meredith ap Howel, David Vaughan, Howel Swrdwal, Thomas ap Rosser, Thomas ap Madoc, Henry ap Griffith ap (? of) Ewyas, Griffith ap Richard of Builth, of an annuity of 100s.

Of the above, Thomas Herbert, the younger, was probably the son of Lord Herbert's brother; while Howel Swrdwal was the poet of that name.

CHAPTER EIGHT

Warwick and Herbert – Banbury

At the accession of Edward IV 'old maxims of government and policy were tardily expiring, and the forces of a new era were in their season gathering to a head'. The old maxims implied baronial and feudal supremacy, buttressed by serried ranks of retainers; the new era implied the absolutism of the king, guided by the dark and labyrinthine manoeuvres of men of intellect, many of whom were raised from obscurity for the purpose. 'The king', said Warwick, when he could no longer tolerate the arrogance of the new men, 'estranges great lords from his council and takes about him others not of their blood, inclining only to their counsel.' Against the peril of the new monarchy the ponderous energy of the old aristocracy revived and struggled with desperate resourcefulness and heroism under the leadership of that feudal Goliath, the great earl of Warwick, until, after a last fleeting success at Banbury, it reached its dramatic close at Barnet.

The most aggressive exponent of Edward IV's new principle of absolute rule was William Herbert, his confidential friend and adviser. Others were raised to eminence as a counterpoise to the prodigious might of Warwick, but none from such meagre beginnings as Herbert. Of him it must be said that he owed his advance less to lineage than to sheer ability and proficiency in the tortuous paths of intrigue. He suited the temper of the times. We must regard him as the forerunner of Wolsey and Thomas Cromwell. The victory at Mortimer's Cross, opportunely followed by the accession of the Yorkists, opened before him a startling vista. A man of his silent assiduity and serpentine methods was not slow to grasp opportunities thrown in his way. Herbert and Warwick, then, dominated the crisis which was already looming large in the political firmament, and by a strange irony both protagonists perished in the strife, though it was the cause of Herbert that triumphed.

In some measure Herbert owed his rise to Warwick. After his triumph at the battle of Northampton the latter was supreme in England. His glory had then reached its midday splendour. At that very moment Herbert, as we have seen, held in Glamorgan as a gift from the Lancastrians positions which were

Warwick's to bestow. The earl could easily and rightfully have reclaimed them, and given the leadership of South Wales to another. He did not do so. Instead, he commissioned Herbert to arm South Wales against Jasper. The tale of how that commission fructified at Mortimer's Cross has already been unfolded.

From that moment onwards Warwick and Herbert took divergent ways. Warwick fought the king's battles and largely managed his diplomatic affairs. He therefore cut an imposing figure in the public eye. Herbert, on the contrary, was the courtier. He had the ear of his king. We get a glimpse of his power in the inner circle of court life in 1463. This record narrates how Lord Clynton, in advancing his claim to the patronage of the Benedictine priory of Folkestone, threatens the town with reprisals, and clinches his threat by saying that he had the support of 'Lord Herbert and others of the king's council'.[1] It is a brief though illuminating illustration of the part Herbert was already playing.

We suspect too that the commercial legislation of this year found in Herbert a strong advocate if, indeed, it was not actually inspired by him. It must certainly have been due to the initiative of men who, like himself, were interested in commerce. Parliament enacted, for instance, that trade with foreign countries should not be carried on in foreign bottoms if native ships were available; and Herbert owned a number of merchant ships which traded with Ireland and foreign parts. In this connection we may note a curious piece of information contained in a grant to Lord Herbert 'of all gear, fittings, wines etc. on a great ship called the *Gabriell* which he had sent at great expense to foreign parts and which on its return from thence to England laden with divers wines and merchandise was wrecked on the coast of Ireland'.[2] The king, too, alive to the interest of commerce, did not disdain to take part in trade and to compete with other merchants. The traders were rapidly rising in influence and wealth, and they found in Edward and his confidential adviser not only active supporters, but also at times dangerous competitors. This common interest, while it bound the king and Herbert, was directly antagonistic to the interests and traditions of Warwick and the old aristocracy.

It served Herbert's purpose that the king cherished with enduring loyalty those whom he chose to honour with his friendship. Thus, when the estrangement between Edward and Warwick began to swell to a flood of enmity on the secret marriage with Elizabeth Woodville in May 1464, Herbert's position was strengthened in proportion as that of the earl was weakened. To celebrate the king's marriage, wealth and honours were showered upon the queen's relatives. One was married to the young duke of Buckingham; another to a Bourchier, the son of the earl of Essex; a third to a Grey of Ruthin, the son of the earl of Kent.[3]

Such alliances were a severe strain upon the loyalty of the mightiest baron in England. But whatever Warwick's mortification on their account, it was deeply embittered by the favour shown to Herbert; for Herbert had none of the halo of ancestry which encircled a Stafford or a Bourchier. At Windsor in September 1466 Herbert's son and heir, William, was married to the queen's sister, Mary Woodville, amid profuse magnificence. He was also given the title of Lord Dunster. At the same time Herbert's daughter was given in marriage to the young Lord Lisle. These arrangements, we are told, gave secret displeasure to Warwick.[4]

ELIZABETH VXOR
EDWARDVS IIII

Queen Elizabeth Woodville. Portrait as foundress of Queen's College, Cambridge.

Now Warwick, as heir to the earldom of Salisbury, could have preferred a claim of his own to the title of Lord Mohun of Dunster; and, as already stated, the Dunster estates in Somerset, Dorset, and Devon had already been bestowed upon Lord Herbert in June 1463. Every favour given to Herbert seemed, with peculiar insolence, to detract from the prestige of Warwick. There can be no doubt that the former was now to a large extent wielding the destinies of the House of York. Others might wear the trappings of office, but Herbert was the man at the wheel. He was, as William of Worcester describes him at this period, the king's most trusted adviser; not a plaything like a Gaveston or a Despenser, but a silent, calculating, resolute agent in the hands of Edward to extricate the Crown from the meshes of feudalism. His was the task of fashioning a new monarchy and not of rejuvenating the old.

In 1467 events developed with alarming rapidity. Early in the summer of that year gorgeous jousts were held at Smithfield to grace the visit of the Bastard of Burgundy with whom Edward was negotiating an alliance. The Nevilles stood severely aloof, while Herbert figured prominently among the king's inner circle of friends. Of more sinister significance was the removal of Warwick's brother George, archbishop of York, from the chancellorship. On 8 June Edward, accompanied by Herbert and a few others, went in person to the archbishop's inn at Charing Cross to demand from him the Great Seal.[5] The archbishop was impeached, and some time later Sir Thomas Vaughan and Sir William Parr were sent by the king to take possession of his manor of Moore.[6]

Edward's resolve, on commercial if on no other grounds, to stand for friendship with Burgundy rather than with France, widened the breach between Warwick and Herbert; while the blunt diplomatic proceedings which produced it gave unnecessary ruggedness to the severance. For Warwick, who had been in France negotiating with Louis XI, and incidentally intriguing with him, had been kept in ignorance of the Burgundian embassy to England. When he returned with the

Great seal of Edward IV.

French ambassadors Edward treated them with gross incivility. They had brought with them presents of gold and jewellery; Edward sent them back with presents of hunting-horns and leather bottles.

As they rowed home in their barge the Frenchmen had many discourses with each other. But Warwick was so wrath that he could not contain himself; and he said to the admiral of France, 'Have you not seen what traitors are about the king's person?' But the admiral answered, 'My lord, I pray you, wax not hot; for some day you shall be well avenged.' But the earl said, 'Know that those very traitors were the men who have had my brother displaced from the office of chancellor, and made the king take the seal from him.'[7]

These events, doubtless, convinced Warwick that he must eventually appeal to the arbitrament of the sword. Then an unusual circumstance occurred which made the antagonism between him and Herbert at once more personal and more envenomed. A certain person was captured in Wales carrying letters from Queen Margaret to Harlech. Lord Herbert, whose unsleeping vigilance was equalled only by his unscrupulous daring, had him sent up to London to be examined. In consequence of his depositions Warwick was accused of treachery, and of being in secret communication with the Lancastrians, accusations which the earl indignantly repelled. The prisoner was sent to Middleham to be interrogated by the earl, and the accusations were dismissed as frivolous.[8]

The incident served to sharpen the blade of Warwick's anger against the courtier through whose instrumentality the charge had arisen. The charge raised in his breast a tempest of warring emotions that carried him in poignant rage away from court to his seat at Middleham. For some time he refused to return even under safe conduct. Perhaps this was Herbert's stroke of retaliation; for Warwick, it seems, had been the main obstacle in preventing him receiving the wardship of Lord Bonville's daughter and heiress for his eldest son.[9] Not long afterwards (January 1468) a reconciliation was effected between Warwick, Herbert, and others at Coventry. The reconciliation was short-lived. The situation was now becoming critical. Herbert had been assiduously endeavouring to raise the temperature that his projects might prosper; but the fuel which the spy had added to the flame was such as consumed Herbert himself.

If Herbert was gifted with the more subtle intellect, Warwick was better harnessed for war. The king, no doubt, realized this, and set himself to remedy it as far as possible by lavishing grants upon his favourite. In 1465 Herbert received part of the royal lordship of Usk, 'with certain villeins, bondmen, and bondwomen of the king with their issues';[10] and also part of the royal lordship of Monmouth. These, being added to the Raglan estate, considerably enlarged that patrimony: 'They shall form one united royal lordship called the lordship of Raglan held in chief by the service of one knight's fee, and the said William and his heirs shall have within the said limits all royal rights.' On 26 September 1466 he was given other lands in South Wales, as well as the reversion of the estates of his half-brother William Herbert if he should die without heirs.[11]

On 28 August 1467 he became constable of Denbigh, and steward of Denbigh, Montgomery, Ceri and Cedewain, and chief justice of North Wales.[12] The chief justiceship of North Wales had previously (1461) been given to John, earl of Worcester, who now in compensation received a grant of £200 from the issues of South Wales. About the same time Herbert received the wardship of the lands of Richard Grey, Lord Powys, and of the lands of Sir Thomas Talbot.[13] Further illustration of how the Herberts dominated Wales may be found in the names of the commissioners for North and South Wales touching clippings and falsifications of money. These were Lord Herbert, Devereux, Sir Richard Herbert, Sir Roger Vaughan, Thomas Herbert, John Herbert, Thomas Morgan, John Milewater, Thomas ap Rosser, Henry Griffith, and Morgan ap Jankyn ap Philip.[14]

In North Wales the chief men upon whom Edward could rely were David Mathew, William Griffith, William Bulkeley, and John ap Meredith. In 1466 the three last mentioned, together with Griffith ap Robin, were ordered to inquire into the report that the greater part of the revenues and rents of Carnarvonshire and Merionethshire, and the fines of the great towns in North Wales had not been paid during the reign and that the tenants refused to pay their rents.[15] Harlech largely accounted for this defiance of authority.

The reconciliation between Warwick and the court party was not only short-lived but superficial. The hostility to the Woodvilles was deepening. Edward's alliance with Burgundy, and especially the marriage of his sister Margaret to Duke Charles the Bold, brought Edward to the verge of war with France, whose wily sovereign once more stirred up the dynastic strife in England. There was an active correspondence carried on between the Lancastrian exiles and their friends at home. Several arrests were made in the early summer of 1468.

On this flood-tide of disatisfaction, intrigue, and revolt, Jasper Tudor, about the end of June, landed near Harlech, probably at Barmouth where he had a steady adherent in Griffith Vaughan. Jasper had with him 'fifty persons and a few pence'.[16] The little force had been conveyed in three ships, one of which, on its return to Normandy, was captured by a skilful manoeuvre on the part of Lord Herbert.[17] Jasper probably proceeded to Harlech for reinforcements, for the garrison there was still unsubdued.[18]

We fail to see any authority for Ramsay's statement that Jasper 'was unable to make his way to Harlech because the fortress was beleaguered by Lord Herbert'. As a matter of fact Herbert's force did not arrive in North Wales till later. If Herbert had been there at the time of Jasper's arrival he ought surely to have been able to prevent the landing of such an insignificant party. Tudur Penllyn states that Griffith Vaughan was Jasper's chief agent in North Wales – and he certainly was one of the defenders of Harlech – and that he had a fortified homestead near Barmouth, a convenient landing-place a few miles south of Harlech. It is most likely, therefore, that Jasper landed at Barmouth. Nor was his progress stayed; for he traversed North Wales as far as Denbigh.

The people flocked to his standard, and he was soon at the head of a considerable force,[19] with which he attacked that town. Denbigh was once again plundered and set on fire. The castle, of which Lord Herbert was now captain, apparently did not surrender to the Lancastrians, though Jasper was so far successful that he was able to hold sessions in the name of Henry VI.[20]

It would be fastidious altogether to discard the evidence of contemporary Welsh poets on these events, some of whom give ample evidence of a close familiarity not only with the projects of Jasper himself, but also with the movements, prospective and otherwise, of the Lancastrians in England. Thus, Dafydd Llwyd, who was a man of estate as well as a poet, was obviously aware of Jasper's projected invasion. 'The brave, long-haired invader will come with a fleet, and will hover around the North Wales coast after the Feast. Meanwhile, there will be disturbances in Kent before harvest-time, and the world will be in a turmoil. David ap Eynon [the ode is addressed to him] will keep Harlech true to Jasper and defy Edward.'[21] This statement is substantially verified by William of Worcester who gives the date of Jasper's landing as 'immediately after the Feast of Saint John the Baptist'[22] (24 June). Moreover, there actually were disturbances in the south-east of England, as a result of which the earl of Oxford was sent to the Tower, and a few were put to death.

Edward now realized the supreme importance of reducing Harlech. On 3 July 1468, he commissioned Herbert to array the border counties of Gloucester, Hereford, and Salop, as well as the Marches, against Jasper.[23] There appears to be no record that any previous organized attempt had been made by Edward to subdue Harlech. A number of proclamations had been issued calling upon the garrison to surrender, but nothing further had been done; and every overture had been met by an unequivocal refusal. The captain of the castle, *de facto*, was David ap Eynon, about whom there is no lack of fitting panegyrics in contemporary Welsh literature,[24] as well as in the prose writers of a later day. The latter especially can be consulted with amusement by those who are interested in the picturesque fables which gathered around his name a century or so later. He is supposed to have held castles in France until all the old women of Wales spoke of it.[25] Strangely enough, among the glistening array of Welsh captains who distinguished themselves at one time or another in the French wars, the name of this hero is found wanting. Historically his fame must rest upon his unrivalled loyalty to the cause of Lancaster when every fortress in the kingdom had long since thrown in its lot with the fortunes of the House of York.[26]

Jasper Tudor was still at large in North Wales when he was attacked by the Herberts with a considerable force variously estimated at between seven and ten thousand.[27] There is no great disparity between the estimates of the poets and the chroniclers. The army was divided into two, possibly three, invading forces. One, under Richard Herbert, approached Harlech along the North Wales coast. Having reached Denbigh this force appears to have collided with Jasper's somewhere between that town and the Conway valley. A number of prisoners were taken and twenty of them put to death. There is significant allusion to the executions in the tales of a later day. One story narrates how seven brothers were executed in Anglesey in spite of the prayers and earnest entreaties of the mother that at least one should be spared. Thereupon, with a pair of woollen beads on her arms, she fell on her knees and cursed the earl (Herbert); 'which curse fell upon him at Banbury'.[28]

The army pursued its course up the Conway valley, ravaging it with fire and sword. The entire Snowdon district experienced such unparalleled desolation that it had barely recovered more than a century later. Echoes of the slaughter still survive in song and story. Wynne, writing nearly a century and a half after the events, says 'the print is yet extant, the very stones of manie habitations in and along my demaynes carrying yet the colour of the fire'. The whole borough of Llanrwst in the Conway valley was consumed, and the devastation was followed by a plague.[29]

While Richard Herbert had been dealing with Jasper, Lord Herbert himself had advanced northwards from Pembroke, taking the old Roman road, Sarn Helen. There was very little resistance, though one experienced warrior in Herbert's army, Philip Vaughan of Hay, was killed during the siege.[30] On 14 August the castle surrendered at discretion. 'That castylle ys so stronge that men sayde that hyt was impossybylle unto any man to gete hyt.'[31]

Fifty of the garrison were taken prisoners and conveyed to the Tower of London by Lord Herbert. Among them were three knights, namely, Sir Richard Tunstall, Sir Henry Bellingham, and Sir William Stoke. Two of the prisoners, Troublote and Thomas Elwick, were executed by Rivers who was constable of England.[32] It is noteworthy that the captain David ap Eynon did not suffer the extreme penalty, and tradition ascribes the leniency with which he was treated to the influence of the Herberts. He was received into favour and actually found reward a few years later;[33] as also did the family of Jasper's ardent follower, Griffith Vaughan.[34] Ievan ap Robert ap Meredith of Carnarvonshire was also invited to accept a pardon.[35] He was a sturdy adherent of Jasper, and had wrought considerable mischief to those who had yielded to Edward in North Wales. It is obvious, therefore, that Edward dealt with commendable clemency with this recalcitrant garrison. On 1 December 1468 he issued a general pardon to all.

Herbert found his reward in the earldom of Pembroke, to which he was raised on 8 September 1468.[36] The wily Jasper once more evaded his pursuers. 'The olde Lorde Jasper and sum tyme erle of Pembroke was in Walys. Men wene that he was not oute of Walys whenn that the Lord Herberde come with hys oste; but favyr at sum tyme dothe grete ease, as hit ys prevyd by the hydynge of that lorde sum tyme Erle of Pembroke.'[37] Tradition says that he escaped to Brittany from the house of Griffith Vaughan.

The young earl of Richmond, whom a stroke of luck was soon to make the most important Lancastrian in the realm, came now, if he had not come before, into Herbert's hands. As we have seen, Herbert had already been given the custody of the earl's estates during his minority; but the boy's movements are wrapped in obscurity, and we cannot be certain that Herbert secured his person until after the fall of Harlech. It is interesting to note that Herbert intended to marry him to his daughter Maud; for one of the clauses in his will states: 'I will that Maud my daughter shall be married to the Lord Henry of Richmond.'[38] This project, dictated alike by a natural solicitude for the welfare of his children, and by a clear perception of the possible contingencies of the future, was not too ambitious even for a new man who had married his son to the queen's sister; while it was certainly in harmony with the king's own policy of courting the Lancastrians.

Herbert may have been alive also to the passionate appeal of the leaders of Welsh public opinion that Wales should not be made the cockpit of contending English factions, but should seek to unite in an endeavour to rid the country of the baneful rule of English officials. To the poets there was no dynastic question. Now that Herbert stood in solitary pre-eminence, they appealed to him as fervently as they had appealed to Jasper to achieve unity in Wales. As far as Wales was concerned there could be no happier union than that of the Tudors and the Herberts. In the whole range of fifteenth-century Welsh literature there is no more fervent longing for leadership, unity, and patriotism, than that of Guto'r Glyn in an ode written immediately after the fall of Harlech. 'Tax not Anglesey beyond what it can bear. Let not the Saxon rule in Gwynedd and Flint. Confer no office upon the descendants of Horsa. Appoint as constables of castles throughout Wales men of thine own nation. Make Glamorgan and Gwynedd, from Conway to Neath, a united whole. And should England resent it, Wales will rally to thy side.'[39]

The interests of a large number of Edward's Welsh adherents were safeguarded in the parliament of 1467–8.[40] Many of them received additional grants. In September Lord Herbert acquired Chepstow Castle by a grant from the duke of Norfolk;[41] in October he was given power to make a weir across the Thames from Paternoster Lane to the Surrey side;[42] in November he was made master-forester of Snowdon, and constable of Conway, and captain of the town; in April 1469 he was made chamberlain of North Wales.[43]

Another Welsh Yorkist who remained in favour was Roger Kynaston. He and Roger Eyton, late sheriff of Salop, were given a general pardon in March 1466.[44]

In March of this year Edward pardoned a Pembrokeshire gentleman, Richard Bennet or Hugh of Monkton, who apparently had been Jasper's adherent.[45] His clemency extended even to Roger Puleston,[46] Jasper's old friend, also described as Roger ap John.

The winter of 1468/9 was characterized by disturbances, arrests, and executions, which were due largely to the dark machinations of Warwick. Herbert's supremacy in the councils of the king was now an abiding challenge to aristocatic self-esteem, and Warwick was determined to remove him and his chief associate, Lord Rivers.[47] For their

> mischievous rule, opinion, and assent have caused our sovereign lord and the realm to fall in great poverty, disturbing the ministration of the laws, and only intending to their own promotion and enriching. The said seditious persons have caused our sovereign lord to spend the goods of our holy father, and have advised him to give of his livelihood to them above their degrees. The king estranges great lords from his council and takes about him others not of their blood, inclining only to their counsel.[48]

Although there were other grievances such as the close friendship between Edward and Charles, duke of Burgundy, the kernel of Warwick's complaint was the king's partiality for the new men. 'It is to reasons of this nature that may be attributed the overthrow and slaughter of the Welsh.'[49]

Warwick succeeded in detaching Edward's brother, the duke of Clarence, from the court party, and before committing himself irretrievably he made certain of the allegiance of his royal ally by marrying him to his daughter, Isabella Neville, which was accomplished at Calais on 11 July 1469. On the following day the letter or manifesto already referred to was issued in the names of Clarence and Warwick, allusion being made also to the 'covetous rule and guiding of certain seditious persons'. The two announced their intention of appearing at Canterbury on 16 July, to lay their grievances before the king.

Meanwhile the earl of Warwick had already set his northern friends in motion under the standard of 'Robin of Redesdale'.[50] These marched southwards in strong force. On hearing of their advance Edward summoned Herbert with reinforcements from Wales, whither he had repaired towards the end of October.[51] He himself set out on a progress through the eastern counties, going northwards as far as Stamford and Newark. The attitude of the people becoming increasingly hostile, he returned to Nottingham.[52] There he appears to have stayed for some days after 9 July awaiting reinforcements. Humphrey Stafford of Southwick, who had recently (May) received the earldom of Devon, was ordered to enrol the levies of Somersetshire and Devonshire.[53] These consisted mainly of archers. It is curious, in view of the prominence of the Welsh archer in the French wars, that there were few, if any, of this arm in Herbert's contingent.[54]

Guto'r Glyn introduces us to a feast held by the Herberts on the eve of their departure. Internal evidence proves that the poem was composed at the time, or shortly afterwards, and certainly before the catastrophe at Edgecote. It is here stated that Herbert, at the head of a strong force, marched to Gloucester; and that his objects were the suppression of a rising of the common people, and to defend the king against the earl of Warwick. The poet, moreover, is sincere and candid in his admission that Herbert was the object of intense hatred in England. And there can be no reasonable doubt that Guto'r Glyn derived his information from the Herberts themselves.[55]

From Gloucester the earl of Pembroke (Herbert) advanced to a place called Cottishold.[56] Perhaps the chronicler refers vaguely to the Cotswold Hills. Very possibly the allusion may be to the spot where Cotswold House now stands, five miles from Cirencester, on the line of the Roman road (Ermin Street) from Gloucester, which joins the Fosseway at Cirencester. Curiously enough, there is a lane called the 'Welsh Way' joining the two roads a little above Cirencester. At Cottishold Pembroke was joined by the earl of Devon. The combined armies thereupon continued their march towards Northampton. It seems impossible to give an exact estimate of the numbers of the troops employed; chroniclers' figures are always suspicious, and there appears to be no means of checking them. The estimates of Herbert's contingent vary from 6,000 (Hall) to 13,000 (Warkworth). Meanwhile, the northerners were said to be making for the same point as the royalists – Northampton.

The Welsh contingent were said to be 'the best in Wales'. They were drawn mainly from Gwent (Monmouthshire), Brecknock, Gower, Pembrokeshire, and the neighbourhood of Kidwely. There were no men of note from the royal counties of Carmarthen and Pembroke; while Glamorgan, which belonged to the earl of Warwick, could not be expected to provide fighting material to do battle against its lord. Pembroke county, of course, was represented by its earl, Lord Herbert. With him were John Wogan, son and heir of Sir Henry Wogan,[57] and John Eynon, a warrior who had had experience in France under the duke of York. Kidwely sent another old French warrior in the person of Henry Dwnn, son of Owen Dwnn; also Henry Dwnn of Picton, Meredith ap Gwilym, and Hoskyn Hervey, a companion in arms with Griffith Dwnn in France.[58]

Brecknock was represented by the Havards – William, Lewis, and Thomas; by the Morgans – William, Walter, Walter (another), and Henry; Gwent by Thomas Huntley, another of York's retinue in France; Thomas ap Harry, one of Lord Herbert's retinue; and Thomas Lewis of Chepstow. The Herberts and the Vaughans, whose many ramifications had now spread throughout South Wales, were represented by Sir Richard Herbert; another Richard Herbert, probably of Ewyas, the ancestor of the second line of Herberts, a natural son of Lord Herbert; another William Herbert,[59] a half-brother of Lord Herbert; John ap William, by whom is meant presumably Lord Herbert's brother John; Thomas ap Roger Vaughan, the son of Herbert's mother Gwladys by her first husband Roger Vaughan; and William ap Norman, another of the earl's relatives. The last three are said to have fought in the French wars.[60]

Hall, the chronicler, therefore, was not far from the literal truth when he stated that Herbert came 'with the extremity of all his power'. He adds that the earl 'was not a little joyous of the king's summons, partly to deserve the king's liberality which of a mean gentleman had promoted him to the estate of an earl'.[61]

The earls of Pembroke and Devon came into touch with their enemy somewhere in the neighbourhood of Northampton. On Monday 23 July the earl of Pembroke's brother, Richard Herbert, and the earl of Devon, with a strong force of cavalry, went on in advance to reconnoitre. They unexpectedly collided with the northerners, and a sharp fight ensued in which a number of Welsh gentlemen were slain, notably Thomas ap Roger, son of Roger Vaughan of Bredwardine, Herefordshire. In consequence of this shock the whole force was compelled to retire,[62] and fell back upon the main body, which had taken up its quarters at Banbury.[63]

Meanwhile the northerners must have come into touch with the citizens of Northampton, and perhaps even with the earl of Warwick, who could not have been far distant. The earl, as we have seen, had announced his intention of being at Canterbury on 16 July, his daughter having been married to Clarence five days before at Calais; and he was certainly on the scene the day after the battle. It was probably the assurance that they would receive reinforcements from Northampton that emboldened the northerners to pursue the royalists, a task which they had refrained from attempting after the first day's engagement. It is possible, too, that having ascertained Edward's whereabouts, they hoped to prevent a junction between him and his friends by an immediate attack. At any rate, they moved towards Banbury, and took up a strong position on the hills around Edgecote Lodge, about five miles from that town.

If the earl of Pembroke expected support from Edward he was soon to be disillusioned. Most of the courtiers had fled. Lord Rivers, whose influence in that neighbourhood should have been sufficient to call forth a strong force, had gone to Chepstow; others had found refuge in Norfolk, 'with the connivance of the king as it is generally said'.[64] To add to the difficulties of the royalists Pembroke and Devon engaged in an unseemly quarrel about quarters and a comely wench. The earl of Devon, it appears, had found lodgings before Pembroke's arrival; but the latter managed to oust him. According to Hall's version, who alone narrates this incident, Pembroke was the chief offender. A fierce altercation ensued. 'After many words and cracks' the earl of Devon gave rein to his irritation and marched away from the battlefield with all his men for a distance of ten or twelve miles.[65] Whatever may be thought of Pembroke's arrogance and his indecorous gallantries, nothing can justify Devon's conduct in allowing a personal insult to override his loyalty. Less than two months had elapsed since Edward had bestowed an earldom upon this nobleman. This defection inflamed the anger of contemporary writers in Wales more perhaps than the loss of the battle itself; and many are the envenomed allusions to it. The death of the earl of Devon soon afterwards did something to sweeten Guto'r Glyn's cup of bitterness.[66]

This occurred on 25 July, the day before the great battle, according to Hall, although it seems more probable that it took place on the 24th, the day after the first skirmish with the northerners, when the two sections of the royalists had once more joined hands. However, on 25 July (Wednesday) the earl of Pembroke once more offered battle in spite of his ally's treachery. He may have hoped to destroy the northern army before any reinforcements should reach them from Northampton. If he anticipated that they would receive such assistance his surmise proved to be accurate. There may be some force, too, in the statement of the English chronicler that the Welsh, inspired by the prophecies of their poets that they would one day vindicate their rights, were impetuous and eager for battle, confident of the issue 'as their unwise prophesiers promised them before'.

The truth is that in those parts and throughout Wales there is a celebrated and famous prophecy to the effect that, having expelled the English, the remains of the Britons are once more to obtain the sovereignty of England, as being the proper citizens thereof. This prophecy, which is stated in the chronicles of the Britons to have been pronounced by an angel in the time of king Cadwalladr, in their credulity receives from them universal belief. Accordingly, the present opportunity seeming to be propitious, they imagined that now the long-wished-for hour had arrived, and used every possible exertion to promote its fulfilment. However, by the providence of God, it turned out otherwise, and they remain for the present disappointed of the fulfilment of their desire.[67]

Pembroke had no other alternative than to fight. Like a true soldier he did not think the battle lost until it had been fought. Devon's force had been withdrawn,

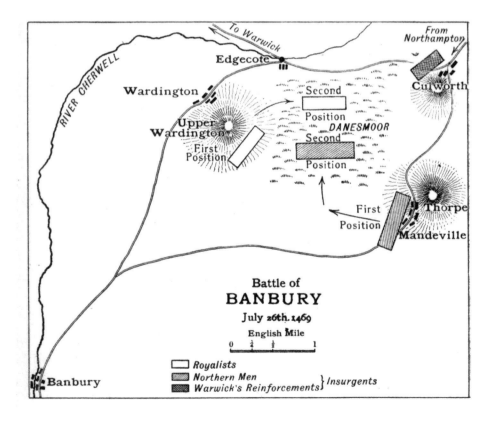

Battle of
BANBURY
July 26th. 1469
English Mile

including the main body of archers. The Welsh were now the only loyal troops in arms. The king was without an effective following and, as events proved, in extreme personal danger from the earl of Warwick and his rebels. An inglorious retreat might have been as disastrous as the battle itself proved to be. In any case, it would justify Edward in impugning the loyalty of one upon whom he had lavished unprecedented wealth and honour. Pembroke was spurred by duty as well as by his innate courage. On 25 July, therefore, he sent forward his vanguard. Some fighting took place. Sir Henry Neville, son of Lord Latimer, was taken prisoner and put to death. The advantage was with the Welshmen, who succeeded in occupying the hill at Upper Wardington before the close of the day.[68]

On the following morning, Thursday 26 July, the two armies were in position to renew hostilities. Hall describes the scene of this day's battle as 'a fair plain near to a town called Hedgecote, three miles from Banbury, wherein there be three hills, not in equal distance, nor yet in equal quantity, but lying in manner although not fully triangle'. Edgecote lies about five miles from Banbury, almost in a direct line between it and Northampton. The three hills referred to are those at Upper Wardington, which we are to understand as the west hill; at Culworth, the east hill; and at Thorpe Mandeville, the south hill. From these hills there extends a gentle slope towards Edgecote and the river Cherwell, a tributary of the Thames. This was the 'fair plain' or moor, called Danesmoor, which also has given its name to the battle. Upper Wardington, on which the Welshmen were encamped on the morning of the battle, is about three miles from Thorpe Mandeville where the northerners had taken up their position, and about a mile from Edgecote. The distance between Thorpe Mandeville and Edgecote across the moor is about two and a half miles, and that between Wardington and Culworth, whence Warwick's auxiliaries advanced, about three.[69]

On the morning of 26 July the northerners opened the attack with a shower of arrows. The Welsh, being deficient in this arm, were compelled to abandon their stronghold and descend to the plain, where a fierce conflict was waged for several hours.

> Pembroke behaved himself like a hardy knight and expert captain; but his brother Sir Richard Herbert so valiantly acquitted himself that with his poleaxe in his hand he twice by fine force passed through the battle of his adversaries and returned without mortal wound. When the Welsh were on the point of victory John Clapham, esquire, servant of the earl of Warwick, mounted the eastern hill with only five hundred men and gathered all the rascal of Northampton and other villages about, bearing before them the standard of the earl of Warwick with the white bear, crying, A Warwick! A Warwick![70]

Some writers have maintained that these reinforcements were royal levies who turned traitors. But, apart altogether from its inherent improbability, the assertion is disproved by Hall, who is substantiated by William of Worcester.[71]

Whatever the strength of these auxiliaries it was sufficient to nullify the splendid valour of the Welshmen, who broke, fled, were pursued, slain, and captured in large numbers. About 168 Welshmen of note are said to have fallen.[72] Pembroke and his brother Richard Herbert were among the prisoners, and were taken to Banbury. The next day, 27 July, the earl made a codicil to his will. On the following day both men were executed at Northampton by the orders of Warwick and Clarence without any opportunity of ransom.[73]

> Entreaty was made for Sir Richard Herbert both for his goodly person which excelled all men there, and also for his chivalry on the field of battle. The earl when he should lay down his head on the block said to John Conyers and Clapham 'Let me die for I am old, but save my brother which is young, lusty, and hardy, mete and apt to serve the greatest prince in christendom.' This battle ever since has been, and yet is continual grudge between the northernmen and the Welsh.[74]

Wavrin's account[75] of the battle appears to agree in the main with that already given. He states that on the evening before the day of battle a preliminary skirmish took place between the combatants along the banks of the river Cherwell.

Two poleaxes dating from the fifteenth century.

This was the fight already alluded to, as a result of which the Welsh occupied the hill at Upper Wardington. They also seized, according to Wavrin, the passage over the river, presumably at Edgecote, and compelled the northerners to retire with great loss. This was on the following morning. In the afternoon, however, the northerners were reinforced to such an extent that the Welsh were considerably outnumbered, and had to retreat with immense loss. Thomas ap Roger was slain, while the two Herberts were taken prisoners.

Guto'r Glyn also gives an interesting account of the battle. Judging from its wealth of detail and its accuracy on points of chronology, it must have been obtained from some of the Welshmen who took part on that fateful day. We have already quoted largely from him in so far as he is corroborated by English authorities. Lewis Glyn Cothi alludes to the Welshmen's onslaught when they cut their way through the enemy's lines, and is confirmed by the graphic account given by Hall. He adds that in the heat of battle 'amidst the clash of lance and shield and the loud clangour of battle, hoarse shouts were heard on every side, some shouting 'Herbert,' others 'Our Edward'; some 'Warwick,' others 'King Harry.' '[76]

Earl Rivers and his son John were captured at Chepstow and, having been brought to Kenilworth, were executed on 12 August. The earl of Devon was also

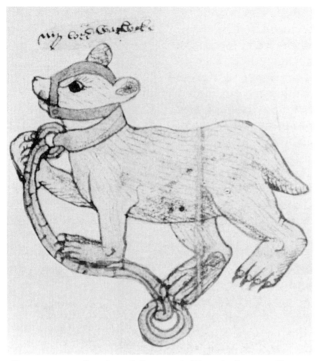

Contemporary drawing of the muzzled bear badge, usually depicted together with a ragged staff, of Richard Neville, earl of Warwick – 'the Kingmaker' (British Library).

taken in Somersetshire and put to death at Kenilworth.   King Edward was seized not far from that town.

Of the Welshmen who were either slain at Banbury or subsequently put to death, the following names are given by both William of Worcester and Warkworth, and they are the only names common to the two lists: Lord Herbert and his brother Sir Richard Herbert, Thomas ap Roger Vaughan,[77] Henry Dwnn of Picton,[78] John Eynon of Pembrokeshire, and William Herbert, half-brother to Lord Herbert.[79] Of the rest, the following are mentioned by William of Worcester: Richard Herbert, bastard; John ap William, a brother of Lord Herbert, who had fought in France;[80] John Wogan, son and heir of Henry Wogan; William Herbert ap Norman; Henry Dwnn of Kidwely; Thomas ap Harry; Thomas Lewis; William, Lewis, and Thomas Havard; William, two Walters, and Henry Morgan; Thomas Glys; Hoskyn Hervey; Meredith ap Gwilym; and Thomas Huntley. Warkworth adds the following: Sir Roger Vaughan; Henry Wogan son and heir;[81] Watkin Thomas, son of Roger Vaughan;[82] Ivan ap John of Merwyke; David ap Jankyn of Lymerwyke; John Dwnn of Kidwely; Rice ap Morgan of Ilston; Jankyn Perrott of Scottesburght; John Contour of Hereford. Of these it is probable that Sir Roger Vaughan did not take part in the battle;[83] he certainly was not slain there, for Lewis Glyn Cothi calls upon him to avenge Banbury, and a few years later he was executed by Jasper at Chepstow. Nor was John Dwnn of Kidwely slain at Banbury, for he, too, played a prominent part later.

When we contemplate this formidable list of dead, comprising the cream of the aristocracy of South Wales, it is easy to understand why the defeat was regarded in Wales as a national calamity. It was not a party reverse. Of this there is no suggestion. 'Let us hasten to the north to avenge our country. My nation is destroyed, now that the earl is slain,' said Guto'r Glyn.[84] 'This greatest of battles was lost by treachery; at Banbury dire vengeance fell upon Wales,' wrote Lewis Glyn Cothi.[85] The defeat convulsed Wales more profoundly than any other battle in which the Welsh had hitherto been engaged, and evoked a universal outburst of fierce, passionate, and tearing rage.

It is not difficult to explain the summary execution of William Herbert by the earl of Warwick. At a critical period in Herbert's career it was Warwick, as we have seen, who supplied the bridge over which he passed to the Yorkist fold; and Herbert had become the chief instrument in driving Warwick himself from that very fold. Edward had chosen to entrust to this meanest born of his courtiers the confidence which the Nevilles regarded as their right by birth, by wealth, and by power. Warwick could not forget the part played by Herbert in displacing his brother from the chancellorship. It was Herbert's informer, too, who had first openly accused Warwick of treachery. It was Herbert who had received the earldom of Pembroke which had long since become the heritage of scions of the royal house. Warwick had crossed the Rubicon with the avowed resolve of destroying him and his associates; and having once launched his craft on a sea of disloyalty, he had no logical alternative but to remove his opponents. We do not thereby justify his rebellion. But if the

Tomb and effigies of Sir Thomas Vaughan of Hergest, killed at the battle of Edgecote, 1469, and his wife Elen, in Kington church, Herefordshire (photograph Benjamin Corbett).

above considerations, and the death of Sir Henry Neville, gave Warwick sufficient cause for putting the earl of Pembroke to death, for the execution of Richard Herbert there was not a shadow of justification. This was the brood of malice.

William Herbert was the ablest of those subtle advisers who stood around the royal person and gave the reign its most distinctive constitutional feature. Warwick, doubtless, with his glittering phalanx of retainers, dazzled his contemporaries; but the statesmanship of the future was to move along the tortuous paths of intrigue, and to depend less on the armoury of feudalism than on the intellectual equipment of royal favourites. The Tudor monarchy had not yet come, but Edward IV and Herbert were its harbingers. Herbert had many of the characteristics of Tudor ministers, not the least of which were his unpopularity and his devotion to the king's service. He justified the confidence reposed in him even on military grounds; for at the moment of greatest peril to the Yorkist dynasty he risked all while Hastings stood aloof and Lord Rivers took ignominious flight. His unpopularity was that of the parvenu who rises to eminence. The eminent churchman who said of another distinguished Welshman of the period, Reginald Pecock, that he was instigated by the Devil, said of Herbert that he was a fierce oppressor of churchmen and others for many years.[86] But there appears no evidence to substantiate the allegation. His interest in commerce coincided with that of Edward and may have inspired it. It certainly foreshadowed the basis on which England's greatness was to rest.

It is easy to overestimate racial characteristics in judging character. But there were moments in Herbert's career when the fire and impulsiveness of the Celt dominated his actions. There is hardly a historic parallel to the fateful explosion of passion which took place on the roadside inn on the eve of Banbury, and culminated so tragically on the morrow. On the other hand, the general tenor of his conduct along the perilous and giddy paths by which he ascended to power discloses a cool, calculating circumspection. The spite of fortune brought him into conflict with the most commanding of medieval barons, and few men would have dogged the track of a Warwick with such inflexible resolution. The son of a Welsh knight, he forged a career which made him the first statesman of a new era, and the most redoubtable antagonist of the last and most formidable of the old.

CHAPTER NINE

The Return of Jasper Tudor – the Council of the Prince of Wales

A few days after the defeat of the royalists at Edgecote Edward himself was taken prisoner at Olney, three miles west of Kenilworth, and thence removed successively to Coventry, Warwick, and Middleham. That the king should thus unceremoniously be paraded over his kingdom at the whim of one of his subjects revealed the obliquity of the political situation. Comedy succeeded the tragic excesses of faction in close proximity.

For the moment Warwick wielded official patronage by right of conquest, and the discomfiture of the most favoured among his rivals put virtually within his gift a number of advantageous positions in Wales. Lord Hastings recovered his former office of chamberlain of North Wales. He was made also constable at Beaumaris.[1] Severe as had been the strain upon his loyalty, the earl of Warwick in the moment of triumph displayed no vindictiveness. The events of the last few years, nevertheless, must have taught him that South Wales was a vast field of combustible material which he should have under his personal control, and his interest in the lordship of Glamorgan gave him a plausible excuse for seizing certain offices. He became justiciar and chamberlain of South Wales, constable of Cardigan and Carmarthen, steward of the two counties, and seneschal of Cantref Mawr, the forest of Glyn Cothi, and of the Welsh courts,[2] offices which had been vacated by the death of Lord Herbert.

Edward's incongruous position soon came to an end. He returned to London in October free from the tutelage of his proud subject, and immediately commenced operations with his usual vigour in a crisis. Eighteen months of strange flux and reflux of fortune followed. He sent the following order to Lord Hastings within a few days of his arrival in the capital:

We charge you that ye make proclamations on our behalf in all necessary places in the shires of Anglesey, Carnarvon, and Merioneth, that they obey the laws and pay their duties of the country ther yerely growing as hath been of old time due and accustomed, certifying us the names of those who were disobedient; and inasmuch as we are informed that Sir Henry Bolde, sheriff of Anglesey, payeth not his duties belonging to his office of sheriff we charge you to put another in his place in that office unless he pays, until ye have other commands from us.[3]

On 7 November Edward made his brother Richard chief justice of North Wales.[4] In South Wales he relied largely upon Lord Ferrers of Chartley. This man had not figured conspicuously for some time, having been completely overshadowed by Lord Herbert. But he had served on a number of commissions; in October Edward gave him a commission of array in the border counties, and a few weeks later the constableship and stewardship of Brecknock, Hay, and Huntingdon during the minority of the duke of Buckingham,[5] and power to seize the lands of rebels in the border counties. Lord Herbert's widow, a sister of Lord Ferrers, received the custody of her late husband's lands during her son's minority.[6]

The most consistent Yorkists in West Wales were the Dwnns. In November John Dwnn was appointed constable of Haverfordwest, and steward of Llanstephan and Cilgerran Castles. The Lancastrian malcontents in this remote district chafed at the

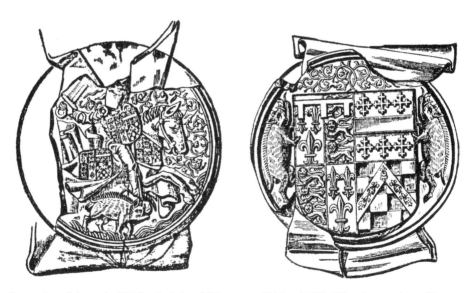

Engraving of the seal of Richard, duke of Gloucester (Richard III). The obverse shows him on horseback with his boar at the foot, and this also occurs as the supporters to the royal shield of arms on the reverse, where his arms as duke of Gloucester are impaled with those of Beauchamp and Newburgh.

ominous rise of the family into favour, and the kindred of Griffith ap Nicholas under the leadership of his two grandsons, Morgan ap Thomas and Henry ap Thomas, seized Carmarthen and Cardigan Castles and held them against royal authority.[7] Richard, duke of Gloucester, was called upon to deal with the danger, and we may presume that his intervention reached its mark. We cannot say whether the outbreak was incited by Warwick and Clarence, but in February the constableship of Cardigan was taken away from Warwick and given to the steady Yorkist Sir Roger Vaughan, while the duke of Gloucester now became chamberlain and steward of Cantref Mawr and the other estates of the duchy of Lancaster in those parts.[8] Further to strengthen his hands in Wales, Edward gave John Dwn, Ferrers, John Herbert, and the young earl of Pembroke power to array men for service, and Robert Griffith similar power in Shropshire. Even Lewis Glyn Cothi urges Sir Roger Vaughan and his son Watkin to stir their kindred on behalf of Edward and to avenge Banbury.[9]

Meanwhile there had become apparent symptoms of impending trouble in various parts of the kingdom. The most serious outbreak took place in Lincolnshire early in March, under the leadership of Sir Robert Welles, one of Warwick's henchmen. The rebels were scattered in an engagement afterwards known as Losecoat Field. Next day (13 March) 'the king, nothing mistrusting the duke [Clarence] and the earl, sent from Stamford toward them John Dwnn, one of the squires of his body, with two letters in his own hand, telling them to come to him and disband their levies. John Dwnn found them at Coventry. The duke and the earl told him that they would come to the king with a thousand or at most fifteen hundred men. Dwnn, noticing that they were not going in the direction of the king, told them of it.'[10] In fact they took the road to Burton to gather troops. Edward thereupon proclaimed them traitors.

They fled to France, where the cynical Louis XI contrived to bring them and Queen Margaret into line. The queen and Jasper met their new allies at Amboise and came to an understanding – a sort of paradox which, though temporarily successful, produced another furious conflagration. The alliance was sealed by the betrothal of Margaret's son to Warwick's daughter, Anne.[11] In due time Jasper and other Lancastrian leaders prepared to launch their craft on an unfathomable sea of uncertainties, piloted by their erstwhile enemy. They landed at Dartmouth on 13 September and proclaimed Henry king. Edward was taken unawares and, being deserted by his northern followers, narrowly escaped capture by crossing the sea. Warwick marched leisurely to London and restored Henry VI. For this reason, and for no other, can the earl of Warwick be called the kingmaker. For, as we have seen, he cannot justly claim to have placed Edward IV on the throne. When Edward was proclaimed king, Warwick was virtually a fugitive seeking shelter beneath his standard. To attribute the victory of Towton to Warwick is to discount unjustifiably the generalship of Edward who was admittedly the better soldier. And with regard to this second enthronement of Henry, it was so fleeting that a title based upon it becomes a grotesque caricature.

The government of the kingdom now devolved upon Warwick and Jasper Tudor. The latter, with discerning promptitude, returned to Wales. We find him at Monmouth on 16 December, writing to his devoted follower, John Puleston, appointing him sheriff of Flint 'for his good services'.[12] On 23 January he was commissioned to array South Wales and the Marches. On 14 February he took the constableship of Gloucester.[13] At Pembroke he found his nephew Henry, earl of Richmond, 'who was kept in manner like a captive but well and honourably educated by Lady Herbert'.[14] The tale runs that he took him to London and presented him to Henry who foretold that he would heal the breach between the factions. This prophecy was, of course, manufactured after the accession of the Tudors.

In March 1471 Edward returned, landing at Ravenspur. With cool audacity he prevailed upon the citizens of York to receive him, not as king, but as a loyal subject of Henry VI. He then passed on by a circuitous route to London, which he reached on 11 April. His backsliding brother Clarence had now come over to his side. Three days later, on Easter Day, Edward and Warwick met at Barnet. After a few hours' fight Edward's strategy prevailed and the earl was slain. That afternoon Edward marched back to London in triumph. He was accompanied by the young earl of Pembroke.[15] The victory kindled a bright flame of enthusiasm in Wales; for Guto'r Glyn, one of the most representative writers of the period, regarded it as an occasion for national rejoicing and the death of Warwick as just retribution for the death of Herbert.[16]

Margaret landed at Weymouth on the day of Barnet. Her chances of success, now very remote, depended largely on her being able to unite her forces with those of Jasper Tudor in Wales. The latter had raised Herefordshire and had seized the castles of Richard Grey, Lord Powys. Edward relied upon Sir Roger Vaughan assisted by Devereux, Roger Kynaston, and Richard Corbet, to thwart the efforts of Jasper, while he himself, having assembled a great muster at Windsor, advanced by long, rapid strides against Margaret.[17]

News of the crushing blow to her cause at Barnet reached the queen soon after her landing. At Cerne Abbey she took counsel with Somerset and other Lancastrian leaders. It is generally assumed that Jasper came from Wales to take part in the conference. But contemporary writers are silent with regard to any such movement on his part, and such an enterprise was practically impossible in so short a time; for only nineteen days intervened between Margaret's landing and the battle of Tewkesbury, which hardly sufficed for the news to reach Jasper in Wales and for him to travel to the south of England and again return to levy troops.

Having gathered a considerable army in Somerset, Wilts, and Dorset, the Lancastrians marched towards Gloucester, 'trusting to be assisted by Welshmen by means of Jasper Tudor who had been sent to array them'.[18] But Edward came across their path at Tewkesbury, and completely routed them. Margaret was taken; and her son Edward, who seems to have fallen into the hands of Sir Richard Croft, was slain. So also was William Hanmer, probably a member of that devoted North Wales Lancastrian house.[19] But Wales was more conspicuously represented on the side of the victors. John Dwnn and Roger Kynaston were knighted on the field of battle.[20]

The hopes of Lancaster once more found refuge in Wales. In spite of the vicissitudes of a long and bitter experience Jasper's faith in the ultimate success of his cause remained constant and undimmed. It was his lot again to avoid the zone of greatest peril, and with prescient wisdom he rescued his party from a third consecutive calamity. He was at Chepstow on his way to join the queen when he received news of the fight at Tewkesbury. To retrace his steps and spin new webs was therefore the better course. Rumours of risings in other parts of the country prevented Edward advancing to Wales, though spies had kept him well informed about the movements of the Welsh Lancastrians.[21] He commissioned Sir Roger Vaughan, 'a man there both strong of people and of friends to the intent by some guile or engine suddenly to surprise and trap the earl'. But Jasper was sufficiently powerful to overawe South Wales. He seized Roger Vaughan and put him to death at Chepstow. But the bishop of Llandaff, who seems to have assisted Jasper, lost the temporalities of his see, though on the accession of Henry VII Jasper gave ample proofs of reciprocal gratitude in lavish grants to the cathedral, which still cherishes his name.[22]

From Chepstow Jasper retreated to Pembroke. It has been said that he was there besieged 'with ditch and trench' by Morgan ap Thomas, a grandson of Griffith ap Nicholas, and a supposed adherent of the House of York; and that Morgan's brother David, a Lancastrian, contrived to gather a strong force, securing many of his brother's supporters by disseminating a false report that Morgan did not really wish to capture Jasper, but only to make a pretence of investing him; and that thus with the assistance of a rude rabble armed with hooks, prongs, and glaives, he succeeded in rescuing him after a siege of eight days.[23] But it may be well to observe that this family had been consistent supporters of Jasper, and that only in the previous December this Morgan ap Thomas had given conspicuous manifestations of hostility to Edward's government. Moreover, if Jasper could have held his own in east Wales where the Herberts and Vaughans were all-powerful, he was not likely to find much difficulty in the west.

Jasper sailed from Tenby to Brittany, taking with him his nephew, the earl of Richmond. They found refuge with Duke Francis II.[24] The escape of Henry, which proved to be a far more momentous stroke than Jasper could have foreseen, was galling to Edward, who made immediate efforts to get hold of him and his elusive uncle. He sent secret messengers to the duke of Brittany, offering lavish rewards for their apprehension and delivery; to which the duke replied that he could not honourably surrender them, but promised to guard them vigilantly so as to prevent them engaging in any movement hostile to Edward's government. Edward sent again 'promising yearly to reward him with a full hand and a well-stuffed purse'. A rumour took wing that Edward was likely to succeed before the year was out: 'Men say that the king will have delivery of him [Jasper] hastily; and some say that the king of France will see him safe and shall set him at liberty again'.[25]

During the next few years Edward's friends in Wales obtained their rewards.[26] Robert Dwnn was made constable of Cardigan. John, earl of Shrewsbury, became chief justice of North Wales, with power to suppress rebels. the earl of Pembroke entered into most of his father's offices 'without proof of age'.[27] William Vaughan received an annuity from Glasbury and other manors in Brecknock. Others who received favours were: Thomas Vaughan, son and heir of Sir Roger Vaughan; David Middleton; John Howel of Montgomery; William Herbert, son and heir of Sir Richard Herbert;[28] Sir John Dwnn; Hugh Conway; Rice Griffith; Richard ap Rhys; and Lord Ferrers of Chartley. The Stanleys were invested with considerable power in North Wales and Anglesey. On 27 August 1471 Lord Ferrers and the earl of Pembroke were given authority to pardon all rebels except Jasper Tudor, the earl of Exeter, John Owen, Hugh Mulle, and Thomas Fitzharry.[29]

The chief interest of the latter part of the reign of Edward IV in its bearing upon Wales lies in the attempts made to secure a more effective administration of the law. The government of Wales was a thorny question, and Edward was no doubt conscious of the magnitude of the task of initiating reforms. Since the time when Earl Warrenne defied Edward I with a rusty sword no king had seriously contemplated any radical changes in the administration of the Marches. The Privy Council of Henry VI groped along many obscure paths before it hit upon the principle of a separate council, which adumbrated what proved to be the real solution. But though the shaft travelled in the right direction it had not sufficient momentum to reach its aim. Years of almost incessant warfare had now wrought abiding change. Though the traditional privileges of the lord-marcher were not yet effete, and alien officials were as narrow and irascible as ever, the numbers of the former had ominously declined, whereas the opponents of the latter had gathered sufficient confidence to render the irritating anti-Welsh laws an anachronism. Moreover, Wales had almost become one vast lordship-marcher. The broad lands of the duchy of Lancaster had fallen to the Yorkist Edward. The rich lordship of Glamorgan had met a similar fate. So that the king, already lord of the Mortimer estates, stood unassailable even as a lord-marcher, his only imposing rival being the duke of Buckingham.

As the chief seat of the Mortimers was Ludlow, that town became a sort of capital for Wales and the Marches when Edward conceived the happy idea of making it a residence for the Prince of Wales, to whom he gave a separate court. The heir apparent was created Prince of Wales on 26 June 1471. He was then nine years of age. In July[30] he received a formal grant of the Principality of Wales and the counties-palatine of Chester and Flint; and a council was assigned to him for the management of his household and the general control of his education, the chief members of which were the queen, the archbishop of Canterbury, the dukes of Clarence and Gloucester, Earl Rivers, Lord Hastings, and Thomas Vaughan, the prince's chamberlain. Any four of these could form a quorum, and their authority was to continue till the prince was fourteen years of age.[31]

The position of Edward as the most considerable of the lords-marcher would naturally invest the council with authority over the greater part of Wales. And there was plenty of work to do, for the volcanoes of anarchy were active. In July it was reported that 'the Walyshmen be busy; what they meane I can not seye'; while in the following January the king himself intended going to Wales.[32]

Further general instructions were issued to the council in February 1473. In the spring of the same year its activity was directed specifically to the pacification of the Marches. This appears to have been its first organized effort in the suppression of disorder. The circumstances were as follows:

'On account of the robberies and murders especially in the counties of Hereford and Salop as well by men of those shires as by men of the Marches of Wales, for which before there was no penalty or remedy, the king sent his queen and the prince with many lords spiritual and temporal, and judges, as commissioners to inquire and determine these defaults; and furthermore for the reformation of the same within the said shires.' The lords put their commission into execution at

Hereford. Inquiries were made by a grand jury of eighteen knights and squires in one inquest; 'which persons with great difficulty and long tarrying at last appeared before the said commissioners, and before taking oaths said openly in the presence of the commissioners that they dared not tell the truth for dread of murder, and to be mischieved in their own houses, considering the great number of misdoers and the bearers up of the same'. Before presenting they demanded a special pledge 'of the king's good grace and assistance of the lords', and a promise that the persons presented should not be lightly delivered without due examination. Certain individuals were thereupon indicted before William Alyngton, justice of the peace for Hereford, and the records were delivered to the king's bench. In spite of this, at the sessions held at Ross, in Herefordshire, 'on the Thursday before the Feast of All Hallows', 1473, before Thomas Braynton and John Wynne, justices of gaol delivery, a number of miscreants were secretly acquitted.[33]

There is no reason to suppose that the lawlessness here referred to had anything to do with the decrepit cause of Lancaster, or with the machinations of the duke of Clarence who was now restive and quarrelsome.[34] It was probably nothing more than a local riot. Miles ap Harry of Newcourt, the only man of position among the accused, had been an associate of the Herberts in similar trouble in 1457. He received a formal pardon in June 1473. There was also some trouble in West Wales where Rhys ap Thomas, grandson of Griffith ap Nicholas, who afterwards figured prominently in the general history of the times, took the lead. One of the charges against him on this occasion was that he entered into his inheritance without licence.[35] These events, if only of local significance, were not without anxiety to Edward, for in the Easter of this year the prince and his court could not leave Wales.[36]

In the winter there was further disorder in which the Herberts were concerned; and an order was issued to Lord Rivers, Walter Devereux, John Devereux, and Richard Croft to array the county of Hereford to suppress them 'because they did not appear before the king and council when summoned, to answer for divers offences committed by them in Wales and the Marches, but withdrew to Wales and stirred up rebellion'.[37]

In 1475 we have another illuminating document: 'Whereas there have been perpetrated great and heinous complaints of robberies, murders, manslaughters, ravishing of women, burning of houses by the inhabitants of the Marches and now of late by errant thieves and rebellious of Oswestry hundred and Chirksland; for redress of same I am commanded to assemble the people to punish the misdoers, and I entrust Thomas, marquis of Dorset and Richard Grey, knight, to do the same. Therefore all men in your bailiwick between 60 and 16 should array themselves as soon as possible.'[38]

The king summoned the council of the prince to be at Ludlow on 24 March 1476, to discuss with the lords of the Marches, to whom the king had sent separately, the best means of restoring order, intimating that he would be there after Easter.[39] In 1478 he required the earl of Pembroke to exchange that earldom for that of Huntingdon, assigning as his reason that it was 'for the reformation of the wele publique, restfull governance, and ministration of justice in South Wales; and for the satisfaction of grete and notable sommes of money diewe by the said earl of

'The Dictes and Sayinges of the Philosophers'. Anthony Woodville, Earl Rivers, kneels before Edward IV to present him with a copy of the book. Next to the king stands his queen, Elizabeth Woodville, with Prince Edward (later Edward V) in the foreground. The figure in coronet and ermine, centre, is probably Richard, duke of Gloucester (later Richard III) (The Archbishop of Canterbury and the Trustees of Lambeth Palace Library).

Huntingdon' to the king.[40] The earldom of Pembroke was given to the Prince of Wales. With a similar object the king purchased Holt Castle from Lord Abergavenny.

These fragmentary details serve to prove how active were they who would establish the negation of order. They manifest also a sincere desire on the part of Edward to evolve order out of chaos. And there seems no doubt that he was to some extent successful, for we hear very little of riots and disorder during the last few years of his reign.

CHAPTER TEN

Henry, Earl of Richmond and the March to Bosworth

We need not enter into the general history of the reign of Richard III, except in so far as that may be necessary to explain events in Wales. At the time of his father's death Prince Edward was at Ludlow with his uncle Earl Rivers, Sir Thomas Vaughan 'an aged knight',[1] and other members of his council. They left immediately for London. Richard, duke of Gloucester, who was at York, also hurried to the capital. At Northampton he met Henry, duke of Buckingham, 'with whom the duke of Gloucester had long conference, in so muche that as is commonly believed he even then discovered to Henry his intent of usurping the kingdome'.[2] Buckingham had lived in obscurity during Edward IV's reign although he had married the queen's sister, Catherine Woodville.

The prince's party had reached Stony Stratford when Rivers and Vaughan were seized by Gloucester and the council of the prince dismissed. The queen, on being informed of these proceedings, took sanctuary at Westminster. Shortly after reaching London Richard was made Protector. He was assisted in his designs by Lord Stanley, the son of the man who was guilty of double-dealing at Bloreheath. Stanley was justiciar of Chester, and he had married Margaret, the countess of Richmond. He was thus stepfather to Henry Tudor.

But of Richard's accomplices the most favoured was the duke of Buckingham. In his anxiety to carry the duke with him Richard sacrificed the advantages which Edward IV had gained in Wales by concentrating authority in royal hands, for he made Buckingham chief justice and chamberlain of North and South Wales, and constable of all the royal castles in Wales and the border counties – Carmarthen, Pembroke, Cardigan, Aberystwyth, Tenby, Dynevor, Cilgerran, Llanstephan, Walwyn's Castle, Haverfordwest, Narberth, Builth, Monmouth, Usk, Caerleon,

Memorial brass to Sir Thomas Vaughan. At the time of Edward's death he was with Prince Edward at Ludlow, but was intercepted on the journey to London by Gloucester and Buckingham; he was arrested and executed at Pontefract in June 1483. His tomb is in the Chapel of St John the Baptist, Westminster Abbey.

Dinas, Ewyas Lacy, Ludlow, Clifford, Radnor, Montgomery, Wigmore, Carnarvon, Conway, Beaumaris, Harlech, Denbigh, and Holt; he had power to garrison these forts, to appoint sheriffs and other officials; to take the customs at Tenby and Mildford; and to levy troops. He was made steward and seneschal of the vast Mortimer estates and of the lands of the duchy of Lancaster.[3]

Certain precautionary measures were taken to secure the effective transference of this authority. Thus Richard sent the following order to the auditors of Wales: 'We considering that the duc shall sustain great costs in executing his authority have granted that he have and retain in his own hands such money as he shall receive to our use by reason of the said office of chamberlain.' The inhabitants of Gower were charged to vacate all offices in that seigniory, to take the duke of Buckingham as their ruler, and to suffer any whom he would appoint to enter into their tasks 'peasibly without interruption'. Hugh Bulkeley, the deputy-constable of Conway, was not disposed to acquiesce in the new arrangements, and Richard wrote to Hugh's father, William, telling him to see that his son gave up possession of the castle. A mandate was given to the people of Carnarvonshire to assist the duke as their sheriff. Somewhat similar measures were taken in Pembroke and the Forest of Dean.[4]

Meanwhile the revolution which Richard and Buckingham contemplated was rapidly maturing, and the latter summoned troops from Wales. The young king was now removed to the Tower and disappeared. Richard preferred a charge of treason against Lord Hastings and summarily put him to death. John Morton, bishop of Ely, who might have proved an obstacle, was sent to Brecon as a prisoner. A few days later the queen was prevailed upon to give up her second son, the duke of York, who was with her in sanctuary. Buckingham received him in Westminster Hall and handed him over to Richard, by whom he was placed in the Tower to share his brother's fate. Then Shaw preached a notorious sermon in St Paul's advocating the claims of Richard to the throne; after which Buckingham held a meeting of the citizens in the Guildhall where he made an eloquent appeal to the Protector to accept the crown. Richard thereupon became king on 26 June. About the same time Sir Thomas Vaughan was put to death at Pontefract, Lord Rivers having suffered a similar fate.[5]

Buckingham continued to advance in favour. In June he was made great chamberlain, and shone conspicuously at the coronation festivities. It was he who bore the king's train in the procession from the palace to the abbey. In July his powers in Wales were confirmed and he became constable of England. He accompanied the king in his progress westwards immediately after the coronation, but at Gloucester he took leave of Richard and retired to Brecon. His departure was the beginning of Richard's anxieties.[6]

From that moment Henry Tudor, earl of Richmond, becomes the central figure in the opposition to the new king. Buckingham and Morton had not been long together at Brecon before they agreed upon a combined movement to dethrone Richard, place Henry on the throne, and marry him to Elizabeth of York, daughter of Edward IV. The late king, as we have seen, had made repeated attempts to get hold of Henry. In 1476 he had sent Dr Styllington and two others to Brittany 'laden with great substance of gold, and that his demand might seem more honest he commanded them to tell the duke that he desired earl Henry because he might make some match with him in marriage, by affinity, whereof the roots of the adverse faction might be utterly pulled up'. The duke at first refused, but 'at the last, wearied with prayer and vanquished with pride, he delivered the earl to the ambassadors, not supposing that he had committed the sheep to the wolf, but the son to the father, as one who thought that king Edward meant simply to marry with Henry, Elizabeth, his eldest daughter'. Richmond was taken to St Malo whence he was to be shipped to England. But at that place Henry was overtaken by fever 'through agony of mind', which necessitated the postponement of the voyage across the Channel. Meanwhile it was represented to the duke by John Chenlet what was likely to be the fate of Henry if he fell into Edward's hands, for Henry VI had recently been put to death. In consequence of these representations the duke once more yielded and sent Peter Landois 'who, counterfeiting some business, while that by long talk devised of purpose he hindered them of their intended voyage, he caused earl Henry, almost dead, to be brought politicly into a most sure sanctuary within the said town and not long after reduced him again to the duke'.[7]

Henry and his Lancastrian friends were now joined by the Woodvilles whom Richard's tyranny had sent abroad. Soon after his accession, therefore, Richard sent Thomas Hutton to Brittany instructing him to propose a conference on commercial affairs between England and the duchy and 'to understand the mind and disposition of the duke anent Sir Richard Woodville and his retinue, and to enserche and know if there be intended any enterprise out of land upon any part of this realm, certifying with all diligence all the news and disposition there from time to time'.[8]

Some weeks elapsed before the duke replied that the king of France had made him substantial offers for the delivery of Henry and threatening war if he refused; and that alone the duke would not be able to withstand the might of France, but would be compelled to deliver Henry unless Richard sent him 4,000 English archers paid for six months, and if necessary 2,000 or 3,000 more at the duke's expense. If Richard agreed to this he would await the fortunes of war rather than deliver Henry.[9] Whether the duke was sincere in his protestations may be doubted; for he actually authorized his treasurer to lend Henry ten thousand crowns of gold to enable him to join Buckingham's enterprise against Richard.

The causes which led Buckingham to desert Richard are obscure. It has been said that the king had refused him the Lancastrian half of the Bohun estates in the Marches,[10] which had become vested in the Crown, the other half being already held by Buckingham as heir of Eleanor Bohun and Thomas of Woodstock. But Richard had virtually conceded this demand in July. It is probable that, being aware of the murder of the two princes in the Tower, Buckingham joined a widespread conspiracy which had already been set on foot by the Lancastrians and the discontented Woodvilles to place Edward V on the throne; and that plan having fallen through by the death of Edward, he entered into Morton's project at Brecon of placing Henry of Richmond on the throne.

It is certain that while Buckingham and Morton were maturing their plans in Wales, Queen Elizabeth and Henry's mother, Margaret, were plotting in London on the same lines through the medium of a learned Welsh physician named Lewis. When the queen had fully concurred, Margaret summoned her friends, raised money, and appointed her servant Reginald Bray to be her chief agent in the conspiracy. She sent Hugh Conway to Brittany with a large sum of money, telling him to advise Henry 'to arrive in Wales where he should find aid in readiness'. When Richard became aware of the conspiracy Buckingham was summoned to court but excused himself 'alleging infirmity of stomach'.[11] On 15 October Richard issued a proclamation against him.

Three days later there were simultaneous revolts at Exeter, Salisbury, and Brecon. From Brecon the duke

Drawing of the figure of Sir Reginald Bray, as donor, from the east window, Great Malvern Priory, Worcs.

marched towards the Severn with an army of Welshmen 'whom he as a sore and hard-dealing man had brought to the field against their wills and without any lust to fight for him, rather by rigorous commandment than for money'.[12] Buckingham's movements were made known to Richard who contrived that armed men should be set around him. In Wales the king relied upon Thomas, son of Sir Roger Vaughan, and his kinsmen. They were to hang on his rear if he should endeavour to advance from Brecon across the border, while Humphrey Stafford was to watch the passes over the Wye and the Severn. Buckingham managed to reach Weobley, the home of Lord Ferrers,[13] where he had to remain for ten days on account of the floods, which carried away bridges, and otherwise made it impossible for him to cross into England. Gradually this enforced inactivity demoralized his army which, having lingered idly and without money, victuals, or wages, suddenly departed. Morton made good his escape to Brittany. Buckingham fled in disguise to Shrewsbury, and was sheltered for some time by Ralph Bannister. Being discovered, he was brought to Richard at Salisbury by John Mytton, sheriff of Shropshire, and executed in the market-place there.[14]

It appears that Buckingham had shown favour to the Vaughans and might reasonably have counted upon their assistance. But no sooner was he well out of reach than they attacked Brecon and robbed the place.

Before my Lord of Buckingham departed out of Weobley Brecon was robbed, and the young ladies and gentlemen were brought to Sir Thomas Vaughan's place, the traitor who was the captain of the said robbing, with Roger Vaughan of Talgarth his brother, and Watkin Vaughan his brother, and John Vaughan; having been rewarded by my lord every one of them, and the least of them had £10 of fee of my lord with other diverse gentlemen which some been alive and some dead.[15]

The Vaughans then went in pursuit of the duke and Sir William Knyvett, a gentleman whom Richard had made steward of Castle Rising.[16] After the duke had been taken they searched for Lord Stafford and Sir William Knyvett, both of whom were in the keeping of Elizabeth Delabeare and William ap Symon. His friends had shaved Lord Stafford's head, dressed him in a maiden's raiment, and conveyed him to Newchurch. They fetched him and Knyvett again to Kynnardsley and kept them there until David Llwelyn Morgan[17] came and placed Delabeare under arrest. But Elizabeth and William ap Symon stealthily conveyed the fugitives to Adeley where they remained four days. Then there came a great army out of Wales, but eventually Stafford and his companion escaped to Hereford, 'Stafford riding behind William ap Symon aside upon a pillow like a gentlewoman rode in gentlewoman's apparel'.[18]

It is necessary here to remove a slight misapprehension. Sir Roger Vaughan of Tretower, the father of Thomas Vaughan, was slain not, as has been supposed, at Edgecote, but at Chepstow by Jasper Tudor in 1471. The assistance given by this family to Richard is the subject of an ode by Lewis Glyn Cothi, where it is stated that Vaughan, having given valiant support to Edward, would help Richard to keep the Rose.[19] The attitude he took up was not unnatural in view of the circumstances in which he was now placed. The extraordinary authority with which Richard had vested Buckingham in Wales was a serious menace to the smaller gentry, and particularly to the Vaughans, not only in Brecknock but also in Gower, where Thomas Vaughan was lord of Oxwich.[20] Men like William Herbert and Jasper Tudor could appeal to a strong national sentiment; Buckingham had no such qualification. Moreover, throughout the reign of Edward IV the Vaughans and the Herberts had been Yorkist, and to this was attributable the predominance they now enjoyed. Buckingham's sympathies, on the other hand, had been Lancastrian, and his sudden rise could not have been welcome to the earl of Huntingdon (William Herbert). Huntingdon was actually justiciar of South Wales when the position was given to Buckingham. After the latter's death the office was again given to him as well as the stewardship of Usk, Caerleon, Ewyas Lacy, and other Mortimer-Lancastrian estates in south-east Wales.[21]

Thomas Vaughan became steward of Brecknock, while Roger Vaughan received Penkelly in Brecknock and Brynllys in Radnor.[22] In West Wales, Rhys ap Thomas received an annuity of 40 marks, while Richard Williams became constable of Pembroke, Tenby, Cilgerran, Haverfordwest, and Manorbier.

Apart from the above grant, which was not given to him immediately after the rebellion, there is no authority for Gairdner's statement that Rhys ap Thomas gave active assistance to Richard. It is true that the 'Life' of Rhys in the *Cambrian*

Register suggests that he was won over through the medium of the countess of Richmond's physician, Lewis, but there is so much deliberate fabrication in that document that it would be dangerous to place any reliance whatever upon it.[23]

Meanwhile, the earl of Richmond had set sail from Brittany with a fleet of fifteen vessels. For some reason he had been delayed; and when at last he took to sea his ships were scattered by a violent tempest which drove some of them back on the French coast and others on to the coast of Cornwall and Devon. Henry, however, succeeded in coming to anchor off Poole or Plymouth about the time that Richard had reached Exeter (12 November).

> [Henry,] seeing the shore beset with soldiers which King Richard had everywhere disposed, commanded that no man should land before the residue of his ships should come together. While he tarried he sent out a boat to see whether they were his friends who were arrayed on land. They were informed that they were sent from the duke of Buckingham to be ready to accompany Henry safe unto the camp. But Henry, suspecting it to be a trap, as it was indeed, hoisted sail and returned to Normandy. Thence he returned on foot to Brittany, having received permission to pass through Normandy from the king of France, and also money to bear his charges.[24]

When he reached Brittany he received intelligence that the duke of Buckingham had been beheaded, and that a large number of English refugees were at Vannes, in Brittany. At Rennes during the Christmas of 1483 he was joined by his friends, who proclaimed him king, he promising to marry Elizabeth of York. He received further promises of help from the duke of Brittany, and prepared for another invasion.

Parliament met in January 1484. Henry and Jasper were attainted, while Henry's mother, the countess of Richmond, was declared incapable of holding or inheriting any estate or dignity. Her husband, Lord Stanley, had proved loyal to Richard thus far. It was anticipated that another attempt would be made by Henry in March, and the king became increasingly anxious for his expulsion from the confines of Brittany. He offered the duke the revenues of the English estates of Henry and the refugees if he kept them in ward. At last, in June 1484, Peter Landois, on behalf of the duke, negotiated a truce favourable to Richard.[25] But Henry, through the sleepless vigilance of John Morton, became aware of it and decided to cross into France. Jasper and a few friends immediately entered Anjou.

> [Henry,] two days after departing from Vannes, and accompanied by only five servants, feigned to go unto a friend who had a manor not far off, and, because a huge multitude of English people were left in the town, nobody suspected his voyage; but when he had journeyed almost five miles he withdrew hastily out of the highway into the next wood, and putting on a serving-man's apparel, he as a servant followed his own servant (who was his guide in that journey), as though he had been his master and rode on with so great celerity, keeping yet no certain way, that he made no stay anywhere, except it were to bate his horses, before he had gotten himself to his company within the bounds of Anjou.[26]

The company then proceeded to Angers and thence to Paris, passing the winter as the guests of Charles VIII of France.

Richard's anxious suspicions were intensified when Lord Stanley wished to excuse himself from court, a request which Richard granted only on condition that he left his son Lord Strange behind as a hostage.[27] In June 1485 he issued a proclamation against Henry, in which it was stated that Jasper, John earl of Oxford, Sir Edward Woodville, and others had fled from Brittany because the duke would not agree to their plans; that they had taken refuge in France; had chosen as their leader Henry Tudor who, in return for the assistance he was to receive, was prepared to relinquish the claim of the kings of England to the title of king of France. It is to be observed that this proclamation, though it asserts that both Owen Tudor and Henry's mother were of illegitimate descent, does not impute any illegality to the marriage of Owen Tudor and Catherine, the widow of Henry V.[28]

Richard's activity was not confined to proclamations. There seems to have been current a prophecy that Richmond would land at Milford. There is a small village of that name in Hampshire, and Richard may have been deceived into believing that that was the place intended, for Lord Lovel was sent with the fleet to the Solent. More probably the object of this move was to keep an eye on Henry's preparations at the mouth of the Seine on the opposite coast. At any rate, Richard did not lose sight of the magnificent natural harbour of Milford Haven in Pembrokeshire as a possible landing-place. For

> he commanded noblemen and gentlemen dwelling about the seacoast, and chiefly the Welshmen, to keep watch by course after their country's manner, to the intent that his adversaries should not have ready recovery of the shore and come a land; for the inhabitants about the seacoasts place, in the time of war especially, on the hills adjoining, lamps fastened upon frames of timber, and when any great or notable matter happeneth, by reason of the approach of enemies, they suddenly light the lamps, and with shouts through town and field give notice thereof; from thence others afterwards receive and utter unto their neighbours notice after the same sort. Thus is the fame thereof carried speedily to all villages and towns, and both country and town arm themselves against the enemy.[29]

In West Wales Richard took very minute precautions which he might reasonably have expected would have made it invulnerable. In Pembrokeshire he placed his trust in Richard Williams, whom, as we have seen, he had made constable of the important castles of Pembroke, Tenby, Manorbier, Haverfordwest, and of Cilgerran, the gate to Cardiganshire. Elaborate preparations were made to put Pembroke Castle in a state of defence. The woods around Narberth were cut down to supply it with fuel. The chamberlain of Carmarthen, Richard Mynors, paid Richard Newton £113.14s 6d for the expenses which he had incurred in strengthening the castle; and Henry Wogan, the treasurer of Pembroke, by an order in council, was requested to provide it with war material.[30]

Richard also relied upon William Herbert, earl of Huntingdon, whose official position in South Wales as justiciar gave him considerable power in the royal counties of Carmarthen and Cardigan. By another grant he became possessed of the castles of the late duke of Buckingham, which gave him a startling pre-eminence in Brecknock. Sir James Tyrell controlled the upper valley of the Towy from Builth and Llandovery, as well as the lordship of Glamorgan, for though Tyrell had been ordered to Guisnes the levies of the lordship were to take their instructions from him.[31] The Vaughans (Thomas, Walter, William, and Richard) were induced by various grants to continue in their loyalty and secure the valleys of the Wye and the Usk.

It will thus be seen how little, if any, foundation there is for the statement that the chief authority in South Wales was divided between Rhys ap Thomas and Walter Herbert in so far as that authority could be based on official status.[32] Neither had any official position of consequence. Walter Herbert may have represented his kinsman, the earl of Huntingdon; but Rhys ap Thomas had no such connection. The Tudor chroniclers wrote of him in the knowledge of the strong support he undoubtedly gave Henry at Bosworth. The influence of Rhys was based on the predominance of his family; and whatever forces he gathered during his journey through Wales was a tribute to his own personal ascendancy and to the strength of national sentiment.

In North Wales Richard's supposed friends were the chamberlain William Griffith, Huddleston constable of Beaumaris, and Sir William Stanley constable of Carnarvon, and lord of Bromfield, Yale, Holt, and Wrexham. The garrison at Beaumaris was strengthened; Denbigh was granted 200 marks to repair its walls.[33]

Meanwhile, Henry's preparations were advancing at the mouth of the Seine. From Paris he had moved to Rouen. There he heard that Richard intended marrying Elizabeth of York, and that the other daughter was to be married to an obscure man.

> This matter pinched Henry by the very stomach, because thereby he saw that he could not now expect the marriage of any of king Edward's daughters, wherefore he thought it was to be feared lest his friends should forsake him. Therefore it was thought to stand with their profit if by affinity they could draw into surety of that war Walter Herbert, a man of ancient authority among the Welshmen, who had with him a sister marriageable; and to procure the same, messengers were sent to Henry earl of Northumberland, who had in marriage Walter's other sister, that he would deal in that cause; but the ways were so beset that none of them could come to him.[34]

This Walter Herbert was a natural son of Lord Herbert, the first earl of Pembroke. There can be no doubt that he gave support to Henry, for he was afterwards knighted and made steward of Talgarth and Cantrecelly.[35] It will be remembered that Lord Herbert, in his will, intended that his daughter Maud, now the wife of the earl of Northumberland, should be given in marriage to Henry. Henry was of course well acquainted with the family under whose care he had been for some time before his departure for Brittany.

The marriage proposal does not seem to have reached Walter Herbert.

However, a messenger came to Henry from Morgan of Kidwely, a lawyer, who informed him that Rhys ap Thomas and Sir John Savage were wholly devoted to his cause; that Reginald Bray had gathered no small sum of money for his service; and that he should therefore set out for Wales at the earliest opportunity.[36]

This Morgan belonged to a Tredegar family. Llywelyn ap Morgan of Tredegar had two grandsons, who were cousins, Evan Morgan and Jankyn ap Philip. Evan Morgan had a son Sir John Morgan of Tredegar who, as we have seen, had already received small grants in the lordship of Usk. He was one of the receivers of petitions in the first parliament of Henry VII by whom he was knighted, made steward of Machen, sheriff of Gwenllwg and Newport, and constable of Newport 'with the making of all particular offices in those lordships during the minority of Edward duke of Buckingham'.[37] He brought Henry military assistance soon after the landing at Milford.

Jankyn ap Philip had a son Morgan ap Jankyn ap Philip of Langston who was on a few commissions with the Herberts under Edward IV. He was pardoned by that king in 1475 for some unknown offence.[38] He had two sons: Trahaiarn Morgan, 'skilled and qualified in the laws of England';[39] and John Morgan, who afterwards became bishop of St David's. Polydore appears to confuse these two brothers when he states that it was John Morgan, a lawyer, who negotiated with Henry. The lawyer was Trahaiarn. Polydore is similarly in error with regard to the Christian name of Rhys ap Thomas, whom he calls Richard. Neither Hall nor the author of the *Life of Rhys ap Thomas* falls into the same error. They call him Morgan Kidwely and Morgan of Kidwely respectively. This Trahaiarn had married a co-heiress of Henry Dwnn, and had thus become possessed of Motliscwmb, a place within a mile or so of Kidwely; and hence he is called Morgan of Kidwely. On the accession of Henry he became chancellor of Glamorgan with a fee of £20 a year, while his son, Henry Morgan, was in close attendance upon that sovereign.[40]

Remains of the monument to Sir John Morgan of Tredegar, St Woolos Cathedral, Newport. He fought for Henry VII at the battle of Bosworth, 1485.

However, the most active plotter in Henry's favour was the brother John Morgan, whom Henry afterwards presented to the parish church of Hanslap in the diocese of Lincoln, made dean of St George's chapel Windsor, and of St Mary's Leicester, and also clerk of parliament with a fee of £40 a year.

This Morgan of Kidwely has also been confounded with Morgan Kidwely the attorney general. But that official had no connection with Wales, and he is not mentioned by any authority. His connections were mainly with Dorset and the south of England.[41]

To resume. Henry, accompanied by Jasper Tudor, John Morton, and the earl of Oxford, set sail from the mouth of the Seine on 1 August with a few ships and a force of about two thousand men, whom a French authority describes as the worst rabble that one could find.[42] They were under the command of Philibert de Shaundé. The weather was very favourable and he arrived at Milford Haven on 7 August, a little before sunset. He landed at Dale on the northern shore of the entrance to the haven, though Richard was informed that the landing took place at Angle on the opposite shore. It is possible that a detachment landed at Angle so as to advance on Pembroke and Tenby Castles. Richard had kept a close watch here during the winter.[43]

On the following morning, at break of day, the invaders marched to Haverfordwest and, meeting with no opposition, proceeded five miles beyond. The association of the Tudors with Pembroke told immediately in their favour; for Arnold Butler brought intelligence that the inhabitants of the town 'were ready to support Jasper their earl'. Richard III found at least one loyal Welshman in these parts in the person of Richard Williams, the constable of Pembroke. It is noteworthy that here alone during his march to Bosworth, at least until he reached Shrewsbury, Henry met with any opposition, though it was suppressed without difficulty.[44] Williams had no force at his command which could resist an army of two thousand. He himself probably hastened to Nottingham where the king received news of the landing. This fact has never been fully appreciated, that though Nottingham is nearly 200 miles distant from Milford, Richard was informed of Henry's coming within four days of the actual event, surely a tribute to the loyalty and expeditious movements of Williams. He fought with Richard at Bosworth and was attainted in the next reign.[45]

Henry was still in the neighbourhood of Haverfordwest when he was informed that Rhys ap Thomas and Sir John Savage were hostile to him; and on the following day (9 August), when he had entered Cardigan, a similar rumour reached him that Rhys ap Thomas and Sir Walter Herbert were at Carmarthen prepared to challenge his progress. These rumours caused him some anxiety. 'He resolved to go against them, and when he had either put them to flight or received them into his obedience, to make haste against king Richard.'

He sent forward a body of cavalry, but they soon returned with the information that no danger was to be apprehended from Carmarthen. On the contrary, Richard Griffith, 'a man of high parentage', joined him with reinforcements from that very town. He is said to have 'revolted' to Henry, from which we are to infer, presumably, that the troops there with Rhys ap Thomas and Herbert were supposed to be loyal to Richard. Sir John Morgan also came in with a few followers. Was it with, or without, the connivance of Rhys ap Thomas and Herbert that these two men joined Henry? Polydore leaves the impression that it

Tomb of Sir John Savage, Macclesfield, Cheshire. Savage was commander of the left wing of Henry's army at Bosworth.

was without their connivance; and that Henry, when he left Cardigan for Shrewsbury, was uncertain of the allegiance of Rhys and Herbert.

On the other hand, there can be no doubt that Rhys intended ultimately to attach himself to Henry. The family had always supported the Tudors and the House of Lancaster. His father and uncle had fought at Mortimer's Cross. Rhys himself and his brothers had collided with Edward IV; and on one occasion Richard, then duke of Gloucester, had been called upon to suppress them. Richard III had given him a small annuity but no official status, though his family prestige in West Wales was such that he would at once have become the leader of any important enterprise among the Welsh of those parts.[46]

It is instructive to note, moreover, that Polydore couples Rhys ap Thomas with Sir John Savage. The latter was a son of Lord Stanley's sister, and drew a stipend from Holt Castle, the property of the Stanleys; and the Stanleys were deeply implicated in Henry's enterprise.[47] We may, therefore, fairly suspect that Rhys ap Thomas and Sir John Savage were agents in a common intrigue, and the suspicion is confirmed by the 'Ballad of the Lady Bessy'. The plot was deep and dark. It seems to have been arranged that when news of Henry's landing would be passing through Carmarthen on its way to Richard's headquarters at Nottingham, it would be noised abroad that Rhys ap Thomas and his confederates would oppose Henry, in order that Richard might be lulled into a sense of false security, as indeed he was; for though he heard the news on the 11th he did not move till the 15th. Further to disarm suspicion they joined Henry at intervals, Rhys two days before he reached Shrewsbury, Sir John Savage between Shrewsbury and Bosworth, and Stanley on the battlefield.

Henry had already sent messengers to inform the Stanleys, the Talbots, and his friends in North Wales that he was making for Shrewsbury along the valley of the Severn. His letter to his kinsman John ap Meredith[48] has been preserved, and is as follows:

By the King.

Right trusty and well-beloved, we greet you well. And whereas it is so that, through the help of Almighty God, the assistance of our loving and true subjects, and the great confidence that we have to the nobles and commons of this our principality of Wales, we be entered into the same, purposing, by the help above rehearsed, in all haste possible to descend into our realm of England, not only for the adoption of the crown, unto us of right appertaining, but also for the oppression of the tyrant, Richard late duke of Gloucester, usurper of our said right; and moreover to reduce as well our said realm of England into its ancient estate, honour, and property and prosperity, as this our said principality of Wales and the people of the same to their erst liberties, delivering them of such miserable servitude as they have piteously long stood in: We desire and pray you, and upon your allegiance strictly charge and command you that, immediately upon the sight hereof, with all such power as ye may make, defensibly arrayed for the war, ye address you towards us, wheresoever we shall be, to our aid, for the effect above rehearsed, wherein ye shall cause us in time to come to be your singular good lord; and that ye fail not hereof as ye will avoid our grievous displeasure, and answer it unto your peril. Given under our signet at our (   ).

To our trusty and well-beloved John ap Meredith ap Ievan ap Meredith.[49]

From Cardigan Henry proceeded northwards 'through rugged and indirect tracts'. His natural line of march would be through Strata Florida, Aberystwyth, Machynlleth, and thence to Newtown and Welshpool in the upper valley of the Severn; but, local tradition apart, there is no data which will enable us to describe his itinerary between Cardigan and Shrewsbury. But he knew enough of the temper and history of the people among whom he had landed to realize that his descent from Cadwaladr and the kings of old would win him support; and that the display of a fiery red dragon would fire enthusiasm.[50] This standard was offered at St Paul's after the victory. He was also conscious of the influence of the poets, and had utilized them to prepare the people for his reception. One of these was Robin Ddu,[51] to whose writings we have already referred in connection with Owen Tudor.

During his progress through Cardiganshire he was joined by a few local squires who were afterwards rewarded.[52] On reaching the confines of Merionethshire he probably received a North Wales contingent, several of whom were signalled out for distinction after Bosworth 'for true and faithful service done as well in this our late victorious field as otherwise'.[53] The tale runs that at Machynlleth he was sheltered by Davydd Llwyd, the poet, who was uncertain whether to prophesy failure or success, until his wife solved the difficulty by saying that he could lose nothing by predicting success; for if it proved true he might be rewarded, and if it proved false Henry would not live to reproach him. The tale is one of many fables of a later day, and is discredited by the fact that the Tudors had found no more stalwart supporter than Davydd Llwyd.

When Henry was a two days' journey from Shrewsbury he came to an understanding with Rhys ap Thomas, whom he promised the lieutenantship of Wales in return for his support. Rhys had now an effective argument for a bargain in an imposing array of followers, 'a great bande of soldiers'.[54] It was now about 12 or 13 August, and Henry might be in the neighbourhood of Newtown or Welshpool. Rhys had traversed Mid-Wales with the black raven as his standard.[55] Among the Carmarthenshire people who were rewarded by Henry after his accession were Adam ap Evan ap Jankyn 'in consideration of his true service unto our noble progenitors of long tyme passed, and to us nowe late in our victorious journey and field, to his great costs and damages'; and Philip ap Howel and his wife 'sometime our nurse', an interesting fact of Henry's childhood.[56]

Of the assistance rendered by Rhys ap Thomas there is ample evidence besides what is contained in the Patent Rolls. There is striking testimony, for example, in the English ballads of Tudor times, allowance being made of course for exaggeration. The 'Ballad of the Lady Bessy' alludes to him thus:

> Sir Rhys ap Thomas, a knight of Wales certain,
> Eight thousand spears brought he;
> ....
> Sir Rhys ap Thomas shall break the array,
> For he will fight and never flee.[57]

Again, the 'Rose of England':

> Then Sir Rice ap Thomas drawes Wales with him,
> A worthy sight it was to see
> How the Welshmen rose wholly with him,
> And stogged them to Shrewsburye.[58]

Moreover, Rhys himself was generously rewarded – the first of the family to receive conspicuous favour from the English government since the time of his grandfather, Griffith ap Nicholas, in the reign of Henry VI. Among other marks of favour Rhys was knighted on Bosworth field, and was made constable, steward, and lieutenant of Brecknock, steward of Builth, and chamberlain of Cardigan and Carmarthen counties.[59]

It is probable that Sir Walter Herbert joined Henry at the same time as Rhys, and brought with him the levies of south-east Wales, notably of Monmouth and the surrounding districts.[60]

When Henry reached Shrewsbury, about 15 August, he found the gates shut and the portcullis let down; and so he fell back to Forton for the night. The town subsequently surrendered and gave him a contingent of men at its own cost. Henry was now joined by those to whom he had sent messages soon after his landing. From Shrewsbury he marched to Newport where he encamped for the night. That evening he was joined by Gilbert Talbot and a few hundred Shropshire men. Thence he proceeded to Stafford where he had an interview with Sir William Stanley. Stanley's men were drawn largely from North Wales and the valley of the Dee. From Stafford Henry moved to Lichfield.

Richard heard now for the first time that his rival had traversed Wales

Effigies of Sir Rhys ap Thomas and his wife, in St Peter's Church, Carmarthen. Sir Rhys was one of Henry Tudor's principal supporters on his march through Wales and at the battle of Bosworth.

Seventeenth-century carved frieze of the battle of Bosworth, probably from Castle Hedingham, the seat of the earls of Oxford, now at Stowe School, Bucks. The triumphant earl of Richmond (centre) rides over the fallen figure of Richard III, who grasps his crown. Their respective supporters, identifiable by the heraldic shields, are ranged on either side.

unopposed. It threw him into a fierce rage, for he had believed 'that his men whom he had disposed for defense of that province were ready in all respectes'. He had been informed that Henry had such a small company that he 'should surely have an evell ende when he showld come to that place, where either he should be forced to fight against his will, or taken alive by Walter Herbert and Rhys ap Thomas'.[61] He immediately set out for Leicester.

Meanwhile a strange chance happened to Henry. Being still in doubt as to the disposition of Lord Stanley he lingered, accompanied by only twenty armed followers, in the rear of his army, deliberating what he should do; for he now knew that Richard was at hand. In the neighbourhood of Tamworth he lost all trace of his army at nightfall and had to pass the night in deadly fear in a village, perhaps Whittington, three miles away from them. The army was equally anxious about Henry until he returned to them early next morning, excusing himself that he had been consulting some of his friends in secret. He then had a private interview with the two Stanleys at Atherstone, and a little before evening on the same day Sir John Savage came over to his side.[62]

From Leicester Richard advanced to Bosworth where he pitched his tent for the night. A terrible dream disturbed his rest, 'for he thought in his sleep that he saw horrible images as it were of evil spirits haunting evidently about him, as it were before his eyes, and that they would not let him rest; which vision truly did not so much strike into his breast a sudden fear as replenish the same with heavy cares'.[63]

On the morning of 22 August he drew up his men with John, duke of Norfolk, on the left, the earl of Northumberland on the right, and himself in the centre. Henry, having rested his men during the night, also drew his men out for battle. The earl of Oxford was chief captain of the army. Gilbert Talbot commanded the right, Sir John Savage the left, and Henry the centre 'trusting to the aid of Lord Stanley, with one troop of horsemen, and a few footmen'. Lord Stanley was midway between the two hosts; and when Henry asked him to arrange his men for battle he sent an evasive answer that he would join him 'with his army well appointed', and that Henry should 'set his own folks in order'.[64]

Richard's troops attacked with great shouts and a flight of arrows. The battle was raging when the king was informed of Henry's vulnerable position. Giving spurs to his horse he issued from the flank and made for Henry's standard. But Henry and his men withstood him manfully until William Stanley came to their assistance. In the thick of the fight Richard was slain. Norfolk and Lord Ferrers (Walter Devereux) were slain. A few took sanctuary, but the greater part threw down their arms. The earl of Northumberland was received into favour.

Henry was crowned on the battlefield. In the evening he came to Leicester. Thither also was brought Richard's body 'naked of all clothing, and layd upon an horse back with the arms and legs hanging down on both sides', and buried at the Franciscan abbey.

Rhys ap Thomas was knighted on the battlefield, and gave considerable assistance to Henry in subsequent years. Jasper Tudor became duke of Bedford, and married the widow of the late duke of Buckingham.[65] The later history of Jasper and Rhys is beyond the pale of the present work. The new king inaugurated an era of internal peace, so that Lewis Glyn Cothi a few years later was able to say with truth, 'The boar is cold in his grave; the world is still and envenomed feuds asleep.'

A'r baedd oer i'r bedd a aeth
A'r egwyd a'i rywogaeth.
A'r byd es enyd y sydd
A'i holl wenwyn yn llonydd.

THE HERBERTS

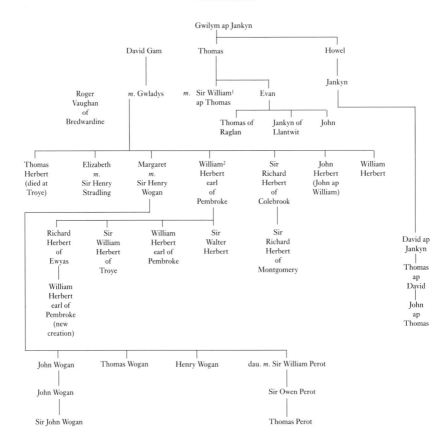

1.   Cal. Inquis. post mortem, 47: Elizabetha quae fuit uxor Gulielmi app Thomas, armigeri, – nulla tenuit in com. Hereford nec march.
2.   He had other sons: George, John, Philip, Thomas, William, Richard.

THE DWNNS

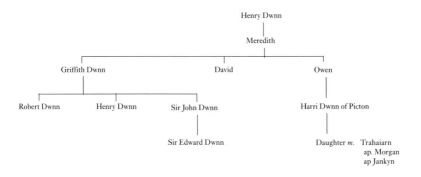

THE MANSELS

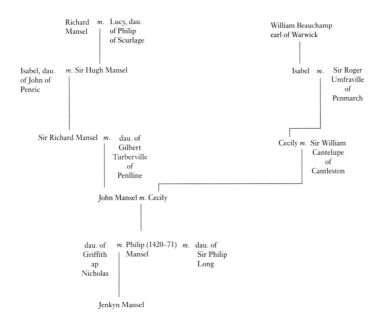

FAMILY OF GRIFFITH AP NICHOLAS

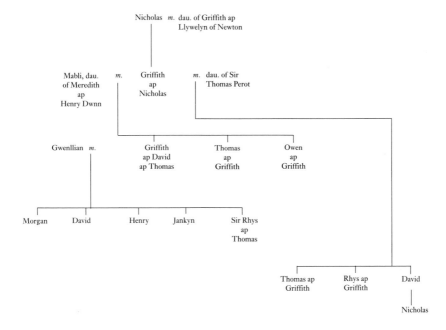

Notes

Chapter One

1. See p. 39.
2. This is a brief summary of the tale which is given in full, in the original text, in an appendix to this chapter. For authorities other than those of Wales see list of sources.
3. *Gorchestion Beirdd Cymru*, 142–4.
   Saith gastell sy i'th gostiaw,
   A saith lys y sy i'th law;
   Tri dug a brofes trwy dwng
   A dau ustus dy ostwng;
   Nes iddynt na'th ddiswyddaw
   Dramwy ar draed dri mor draw.
4. For an account of the original authorities of the period the reader is referred to *Historical Literature of the Fifteenth Century*, Kingsford; and Ramsay, *Lancaster and York*.

Chapter Two

1. 'The Libell of English Policye,' *c.* 1436, in *Political Songs and Poems*, II. 190. Rolls edition.
2. In 1411 there were 300 men-at-arms and 600 archers in these places. In 1415 Strata Florida had 40 men-at-arms and 80 archers; Cymmer and Bala 300 men-at-arms and 60 archers each. *Acts and Proceedings of the Privy Council*, II. 14–18, 37–8, III. 146.
3. Rymer's *Foedera*, IX. 300–1. *Rot. Parl.* 4 Henry V, 64–6, 102. Appendix to Nicholas, *Agincourt*, 19. David Howel was accused 'sans aucune manere de droit'. For his subsequent history see ch. 3.
4. Rymer, IX. 283, 330. 5 July 1415 and 24 February 1416.
5. Rymer, IX. 147–8. 3 July 1414.
6. *Rot. Parl.* (1413–14) I Henry V. 10. 'Plusieurs des dits rebelles étaient encore en vie, et autres de sang prochain à ceux rebelles ou leurs amis font graunde pursuite envers les loiaux lièges, surmettant en eux. Ils demandent haute amende. Les dits loiaux lièges sont grevousement vexés en plusieurs parties et seigneurs de Galles, aucuns de eux par enditements, acusements, ou empechements, et aucuns par menaces et distresses prisés, et aucuns par leurs corps prisés et emprisonnés.' See also ibid. 1427, 329.
7. *Rot. Parl.* 1413, 10. See also the complaint of William ap William ap Griffith. *Rot. Parl.* 1439–42, 16.
8. Ibid. 1427.
9. Que nulle homme Galeys desormes soit Justice, Chamberlain, Chaunceller, Seneschal, Resceivour, chief Forestier, Viscompt, eschetour, ne conestable de chastel. . ; mais, soient angloys en mesmes les offices . . ; Item que nulle homme Engloys par touz les partiez de Gales soit endité ou attaché par hatie et envie de Galoys, . . soit convict par enquest des Galoys de nulle chose a luy surmys; Item que nulle homme ne femme Engloys se marient à nulle homme ne femme Galoys; Item, que les Burges Englois de Villes ne receveint nulle homme de demy sang del partie Galois destre enfranchiez deinz leurs villes. *Ordinates Walliae.* 2 Henry IV, 18 March. *Record of Carnarvon*, 239, seq. See also 'Statute of Wastours and Rymours' 4 Henry IV.
10. In 1438 he was made steward of Cardigan, Cantrefmawr, and Glyncothi. In 1441 he and a few others received the alien priories of St Clear's and Llangenneth. In 1444 he received Gerardston, Cardiganshire. *Rot. Parl.* IV. 6; and *CPR*, *passim*.
11. *Rot. Parl.* (1413–37), 130.
12. *Letters of Margaret of Anjou*, 34. *Rot. Parl.* IV. 44–5.

13. *Rot. Parl.* IV. 45, Nicholas, *Agincourt*; 379–85. *Record Reports* (1885), 546, which state that John Montgomery was bailiff of Calais and captain of Domfront. In 1430 he was on an embassy to the duke of Burgundy. *Proceedings*, IV. 72, 324. Rymer, IX. 594–5; X. 458, and *passim*.

14. *Rot. Parl.* 1427, 325. *CPR, sub ann.*

15. *Rot. Parl.* 1430–1, 372. *Record Reports* (1887). He received protection to cross to France in the duke of Bedford's retinue on 7 February 1425–6.

16. *Record Reports* (1887). 5 January 1442–3. He was on a commission to investigate disturbances in 1456. *Proceedings of the Privy Council*, VI. 289. June 1456. Also, Morgan Meredith of Carmarthen; 1441. *CPR*, 560.

17. *Rot. Parl.* 10 Henry VI. 415. The relations between Owen and Catherine are discussed fully in ch. 4.

18. *Rot. Parl.* 1439, 16; and 1442, 45. See his pedigree in Dwnn, II. 89.

19. *CPR*, 26 September 1468, 107–8.

20. I refer to the account of him in the 'Life of Sir Rhys ap Thomas' in the *Cambrian Register*, 1795. The original MS appears to have been written in the early part of the reign of James I, as already stated, see ch. 1.

21. Lewis Glyn Cothi, II, I. See also Iolo MSS 699, a poem by Iorwerth Fynglwyd. *Gorchestion Beirdd Cymru*, 155, a poem by Gwilym ap Ieuan Hen. The historic eisteddfod at Carmarthen, 1451, was held under Griffith's protection.

22. *Minister's Accounts*, 1166–8. John Perot was associated with him.

23. *Rot. Parl.* 1439–40, 14. Lewis Glyn Cothi, I, 100. *Arch. Cambrensis*, 1864, 247.

24. *Rot. Parl.* 1436–7; July 497–8.

25. *CPR*, 29 April 1448. See a grant to Lewis ap Meredith, esquire of the household, of £20 yearly rendered by Griffith ap Nicholas for Tregaron and Pennarth. The grant to Griffith bears date 24 July 1443.

26. *Rot. Parl.* 1444, 104.

27. *CPR sub ann.* 369; Stephenson, II, 508. Other members of the above commission were Owen Dwnn, David Morys, Morgan Doe (?Dwnn) and William Burley.

28. For a fuller treatment of this question see an article by the author on 'The Welsh and the Early Municipalities', in *Celtic Review*; January 1908.

29. *Rot. Parl.* 3 Henry V, 91. Humphrey, duke of Gloucester, was their overlord. His tenants petitioned that 'l'avant dites terres ne serroient seisez en vos mains autrement que la loi Galoise demande.'

30. *Acts and Proceedings of the Privy Council*, II. 215–16. February 1417. See a writ issued to the sheriff of the seigniory, Morgan ap Evan ap Jankyn his lieutenant, and Morgan ap Roger (Rosser) his coroner. The lord of the seigniory was the earl of Stafford.

31. *CPR*, 29 March 1446. Cf. Wynne, 83.

32. See the original document printed in *Beaumaris Bay*, 25, bearing the date 20 June 1449. For this William Griffith see before. Compare this with the tendency to emancipate bondmen in England, e.g. on the lands of the monastery of St Albans. Whethamstede, II, *passim*.

33. Ni welir Sais diddirwy
    Na Saison mewn Sessiwn mwy,
    Na dyn o Sais yn dwyn swydd.
    Lewis Glyn Cothi, *Works* I. xxiv.

34. Mae bywyd trist, mae byd trwm;
    Meibion a gweision oedd gaeth
    Myned weithion maent waethwaeth.
    Ibid. I. xx.

35. A'th gledd bydd geidwad
    . . . .
    Ar gwmmin werin hyd gaer Warwig cron
    Ac ar y gwirion o'th gaer gerrig.
    Glyn Cothi, *Ode to Watcyn Vaughan.*
    'From thy stone castle come forward, sword in hand, to defend the common people and the defenceless.'

36. Gwae ni o'n geni yn gaeth
    Gan ladron; gwna lywodraeth.
    Dyred dy hun, Edwart hir,
    I ffrwyno cyrph rhai anwir.
    Guto'r Glyn, MSS, Cardiff. Hafod, 3.

37. Rhoi cyfraith berffaith i'r beilch
    Rhoi devawd i'r rhai diveilch.
    Glyn Cothi, I. 139.

38. Enyn y gyfraith unig i Gymru.
    Ibid. I. 35. Also *Cein. Llen.* II. 193.

39. Lewis Glyn Cothi. *Ode to Thomas ap Rosser.*

40. It is not our intention to digress upon the constitutional position of the lord-marcher. For a full exposition the reader may be referred to the admirable work of Morris, *Welsh Wars of Edward I.* See also Skeel, *Council of Wales*, Introduction; George Owen's *Treatise on the Government of Wales*, in the *Cymmrodor*, vols. XII and

XIII; etc. For the lawlessness of the Marches, see Wynne's *History of the Gwydir Family*, Wright's *Ludlow*, Eyton's *Shropshire. Archaeologia Cambrensis*, vols. II, III *Rot. Parl. Statutes of the Realm*, etc.

41. There are many references to the affair in *Trevelyan Papers* (Camden Society). *Powysland Collections*, I. 335–8, II. 139–168; XIV. 126–38.

42. *CPR*, 21 Henry VI, 397.

43. 'Ou le brief du roy ne court.' *Rot. Parl.* 1413–37, 52.

44. *Rot. Parl.* 1430–1. 'En grande nombre arraiez en faire de guerre.' Ibid. 1427, 332.

45. *Acts of the Privy Council*, IV. 208. 28 April 1434.

46. Lewis Glyn Cothi, VII. iii; V. vii. A dark episode called the 'Black Affray of Beaumaris' between the burgesses of that town and the Welsh of Anglesey ended in the death of the leader, David ap Ieuan of Llwydiarth. For more minute details of the lawless state of the Snowdon district, see Hengwrt MSS in *Arch. Cambrensis*, 1846–8; viz. the *Records of Inquisitions for Merionethshire* (1452–4).

47. *Ordinances of the Privy Council*, 14 February 1424; III. 138. *Rot. Parl.* 1424, 254. The names of some of the retainers may be of some interest: William ap Rees, David ap Jankyn, Thomas Walter, John Rotherwas, John Gam, John Roger, William Prees, Philip Madoc, David Miskyn, Jankyn ap Adam, Hugh ap Adam, John Gronowe, Walter ap Hugh, Griffith Kilbrest, Howel Sheplod, John ap David, Ieuan ap Gronowe, Ieuan Vaughan, Philip Iorwerth, Morys Penreth, Thomas ap Richard, Griffith Elvel.

48. *Rot. Parl.* 1425, 275 and 312. Both petitioned parliament to compel Talbot to give security that he would keep the peace.

49. *Rot. Parl.* 1422, 193; and ibid. 1414–5, 30, 87. Also, *Record Reports*, 1419, 709.

50. Wynne, *History of the Gwydir Family*, 44–7.

51. *Rot. Parl.* 1441–2, 53–4 etc.

52. *Glamorgan Charters*, 1500 (1423).

53. Lewis Glyn Cothi, *passim*.

54. *Glamorgan Charters*, 1590 (1443, 3 March). *CPR*, 95 (1442).

55. *CPR*, 1442, 42.

56. *Rot. Parl.* 1442, 42–3.

57. *Statutes of the Realm*, 1444–5; *Rot. Parl.* 1444–5, 106.

58. *Proceedings of the Privy Council*, V. 209. 29 August 1442. 'A levy to be made of various sums due to the king from South Wales. Rhys ap Thomas ap David, 10 marks; John ap Rees ap Thomas, 10 marks; David ap Thomas ap David ap Llewelyn, £71. 13s. 4d.; Meredith ap Owen, £133. 6s. 8d.; Rees Vaughan ap Rees, £90; Maredydd ap Ievan ap Rees, £22. 13s. 4d.; Llywelyn ap David ap Rees, £11 2s. 0d.' Also, ibid. III. 78, 1423. *Rot. Parl.* 1442.

59. See document in Wynne's *Gwydir Family*, 34–5, note 3.

60. *CPR*, 1444, 281. In July of that year Griffith Vaughan of Treflidyan, Kt, Ievan ap Griffith of Gildesford, Reynold ap lord Griffith of Treflidyan, and David Lloyd ap Ievan ap Griffith of Gilesford, etc. were outlawed, and their property (Breamiarth, in Pole) given to John Sutton, Lord Dudley. See above for the murder of Griffith Vaughan by Henry Grey, Lord Powys, in 1447.

61. *Acts of the Privy Council*, V. 244, 233. 5 March 1443. Griffith ap Nicholas was in London in January 1442. *CPR*, 12.

62. Lewis Glyn Cothi, II. ii.
     A mi'n nhiredd Gwynedd gynt
     Yn herwa, yno hirhynt,
     Owain i gadw fy einioes
     Ei aur a'i win i'm a roes.
'When formerly I was wandering in Gwynedd, Owen gave me his gold and his wine to save my life.' I can see no evidence to support the generally accepted view that Lewis Glyn Cothi was hunted as a Lancastrian partisan. See the editor's note on the above passage, for example.

63. *Ordinances of the Privy Council*, 23 January 1415, 339. See a petition from Gerard Strong praying that a warrant might be issued commanding the exchequer to grant him a discharge for the metal of a brass cannon called 'Messager' weighing 4,480 lbs, which was burst at the siege of Aberystwyth; of a cannon called the 'King's Daughter', burst at the siege of Harlech; of a cannon which burst in proving it; of a cannon with two chambers; of two iron guns, and three other iron guns; with gunpowder, cross-bows and arrows delivered to various captains of castles or used at the aforesaid sieges.

64. Ibid. 25 October 1417, 238–9.

65. Rymer's *Foedera*, X. 254. 3 October 1422.

John Talbot, William Talbot, and Edmund Ferrers of Chartley were on this commission.

66. *Proceedings of the Privy Council.* 9 February 1422, 320–1. *CPR*, 1446, 264.

67. *Proceedings of the Privy Council*, V. 3. 21 November 1436. Minutes on the Government of Wales.

68. *Proceedings of the Privy Council*, V. 81–2. 25 November 1437.

69. *Proceedings of the Privy Council.* 16 February 1438, vol. V. 92. Ibid. 1442, 211–13.

70. For a history of the Council of Wales see Skeel's *Court and Council of Wales and the Marches*; The *Cymmrodor*, XII–XV and XIX; and the authorities quoted. For the above conference see *Medieval Boroughs of Snowdonia*.

71. *Antiquary*, vol. XVI. *Ministers' Accounts.*

72. *Statutes of the Realm*, 1431, C. 3. *Rot. Parl. sub ann.* 377. In 1442, at the instigation of the border counties, parliament passed a number of laws against the harbouring of robbers, and called upon the sheriffs to be more alert and stringent.

73. *CPR* 1415–16, 129. Nicholas, *Agincourt*, 175. Cf. Appendix I, p. 39.

74. Vicker's *Humphrey, duke of Gloucester*, Appendix A, 437.

75. *Powysland Collections*, I. 254.

76. *Rot. Parl.* IV. 474. *CPR*, 19, 376, 452; Mathew Wogan and Thomas Perot were present at the investigation.

77. *Proceedings*, V. 138–9; Introduction, LXXXVI and III. 267. See also Doyle II. 23.

78. *CPR*, 1447, 68, 74–5. Vicker's *Humphrey, duke of Gloucester*, 273–4.

79. *English Chronicle*, edited Davies, 116.

80. *Three Fifteenth Century Chronicles*, 150.

81. Rymer, XI. 179; a pardon to Thomas Herbert 'armiger, formerly of Greenwich', which states that Gloucester proceeded from Greenwich to Bury. He appears to have passed through Wiltshire. Stow, 386.

82. Welsh MSS. British Museum, *Edward Owen*, I. 618. Sir Roger Chamberlain and one Thomas Weryot were also among those who were arrested that day.

83. This is probably an error for David ap Thomas. There is no son Howel in the list given by Ellis, although there is a David ap Thomas, and his two sons Griffith and Rees. This Thomas Herbert, according to William of Worcester, *Itinerarium*, 122, had fought in France under Richard, duke of

York, and in Portugal at the head of 300 men. He was a brother to William Herbert, and died at Trove. He appears in a plea of debt in 1442. *CPR*, 1442, 14.

84. *English Chronicle*, edit. Davies, 117–18.

85. Ibid. 62.

86. Gregory's *Chronicle*, 188.

87. Lewis Glyn Cothi, V. I. *Ode to Sir Roger Kynaston.*

Wyr y Dug, a vu wr da
O Glousedr, myn bagl Assa.

'He (Kynaston) was a grandson of the duke of Gloucester, who was an honourable man.' This Kynaston had married Elizabeth, daughter to Henry Grey, Lord Powys, who was created earl of Tankerville by Henry V, and who had married Antigone, a daughter of Humphrey, duke of Gloucester.

88. The full list of prisoners is as follows, the names in brackets showing where they were imprisoned: Sir Henry Wogan, Thomas Herbert, Griffith ap David ap Thomas, and Evan ap Jenkyn (London); Jenkyn Thawe, Jankyn Lloyd Wogan, and John Wogan (Berkhampstead); William Wogan, Evan ap Jankyn ap Rees, and William ap John ap David ap Thomas Lloyd (Reading); William Wogan, William ap Thomas ap Robert ap Rees, and Henry Wogan (Leeds Castle, Kent); Alun ap Meredith ap Philip Madoc, Rees ap David ap Thomas, and Thomas ap Jankyn ap Rees (Norwich); Owen Dwnn, and Hugh Bennoth (Wallingford); John Eynon, and Hugh ap Thomas (Guildford); John ap Rees, Richard ap Robert, and William ap John (Southampton); David ap Thomas, Hugh ap Thomas, and Griffith ap Nicholas (King's Bench); Morgan (Nottingham). *Ellis Letters*, second series, I. 108–9.

89. *Proceedings*, V. 229, 272. He appears as a pledge for Griffith ap Nicholas on the latter's appointment as farmer of Dynevor. *West Wales Hist. Society Transactions*, II. 107–11.

90. *English Chronicle*, edit. Davies, 118, Appen. *Three Fifteenth Century Chronicles*, 65. Gregory, 188. *Lords Reports*, V. 254–5. *CPR*, 174. Suffolk also got some of the lands of Herbert. Rymer, 1447, 178. *CPR*, op. cit.

91. *Statutes of the Realm*, II. 344. *Rot. Parl.* 1447, 139.

92. *Proceedings*, VI. 60. 19 March 1447.

93. *Rot. Parl.* 1447; and 1449, 154. *Statutes of the Realm*, 27 Henry VI, c. 4. The Justices

of the Peace were again given additional powers to deal with the disorder.

94. *Paston Letters*, II, 113. 16 October 1449.

Chapter Three

1. Nicholas, *Agincourt*, 334–84. The lists have been taken from Harl. MS 782, collated with a copy of the MS marked I in the College at Arms. Also the unpublished collections for Rymer's *Foedera*, Sloane MS 4600, British Museum. *Calendar of Norman Rolls*. See also *Royal Historical Society Transactions*, 3rd series, vol. V. 1911. It states that the retinue of Devereux as given in the lists is impossible.

2. Skydmore remained at Harfleur to garrison the town. *Royal Hist. Soc. Trans.* 1911, 112. Sir John Skydmore of Kenchurch had married the daughter of Owen Glyndwr.

3. John ap Henry received protection, 11 July 1415, and Thomas on 12 July. *Record Reports*, 1885.

4. *Exchequer Accounts* 46/20, 45/5.

5. Merbury's retinue came from Cardiganshire, Brecknock, and Carmarthenshire, for whose wages he received £436 at Hereford. For indentures, with seals signed at Carmarthen and Brecknock, 26 January 1415, see *Exchequer Accounts* 45/5 (10), 46/20. The following are the names of the men-at-arms. From (a) Carmarthenshire: John ap Rys, Henry ap Ievan, Gwyn Rys ap Llywelyn, Griffith Vychan, David ap Ievan ap Trahaiarn, Griffith ap Meredith ap Henry (total 5 + 102).
(b) Cardiganshire: Meredith ap Owen, Owen Mortimer, Owen ap Jankyn, Yllort Llywelyn ap Cliffort, Walter ap Ievan (= 5 + 238, 13 of whom were wounded).
(c) Brecknock: Watkin Lloyd, Andrew ap Lewis, Ievan ap Richard, Jankyn ap Meurig ap Richard, Jankyn ap John ap Rhys, Philip ap Griffith Bras, Richard ap Rys, Meurig ap Rys, Richard Prys (= 9 + 160, 14 of whom were wounded).
Of the above 5 + 54 were on the sick list at Harfleur. See *Exch. Accts.* 45/1. Hunter, 51. The West Wales men came from Gethinog, St Clear's, Llanstephan, Emlyn, Penryn (Pemb.), Tallagharn, Elvet, Wydegada, Trayne and Osterlo (Pemb.), Iskennin, Maenordeilo, Penarth (Cardigan),

Hyrcoryn, Cayo, Isayron, Mabwynion, Caerwedros, Uwchcerdyn, Iscerdyn, Iswyle, Uchayron; the men of Mid-Wales from Glyncawy, Cantrecelly, Hay, the Forest, Ystraffelte, Llywch, and Conwt. See *Trans. Roy. Hist. Soc.* 1911, 135. Penryn and Osterlo are now in Carmarthenshire.

6. Cal. French Rolls, 718

7. Sir William Stradling (temp. Richard II) had two sons, Sir Edward, and William. Edward married Jane, a daughter of Cardinal Beaufort. Their son was Sir Henry Stradling who married Elizabeth, a sister of William Herbert, earl of Pembroke. They had a son Thomas Stradling and a daughter who married Miles ap Harry. The other son of Sir William Stradling had a daughter Gwenllian, by whom Anthony Woodville, earl Rivers, had a daughter Margaret.

8. He was farmer of the lordship of Dynevor. 1433–52. *West Wales Hist. Soc. Trans.* 162–3.

9. Received protection July 1415. *Record Reports*, 1885. Cal. French Rolls.

10. Ibid. 1 June 1415. He received protection again on 2 May 1416, being then in the retinue of John, earl of Huntingdon; and again on 5 February 1416 in the retinue of Thomas Carew. Ibid. He was then designated 'armiger'. Rymer's *Foedera* IX. 249.

11. Received protection 22 May 1415. Cal. French Rolls, in *Record Reports*, 1885. 545–637, *passim*.

12. Received protection 6 August 1415; ibid. He is perhaps the John ap Rys given in Merbury's list. See before.

13. Nicholas, *Agincourt*, 369. Hardyng, note.

14. The men of note slain were the duke of York, duke of Suffolk, Sir Richard Kighley, David Gam, esquire, Thomas FitzHenry and John de Perditon. The account referred to is British Museum, Cottonian MS. Julius E IV, and Sloane MS 1776. See Nicholas, *Agincourt*, Intro. IX and 136–7. Also Harl. MS 782.

15. Nicholas; Appendix, 60; and Dwnn's *Visitations* I. 107, note. See the list of Brecknockshire squires above.

16. *Record Reports*, 1885, 545–637; William of Worcester's *Itinerarium*, 161; Stephenson, *Wars of the English in France*, II. 437.

17. *Record Reports*, 1887, February–May 1435–6; May–August 1437–8.

18. Stephenson II. 436. The poet Guto'r Glyn is more reliable. See MSS Cardiff, 2114/96.
19. Stephenson, II. 394, 543.
20. Hall, 127.
21. Quicherat, *Procès*, IV. 14, note I; 17, note 2. Wavrin, 282.
22. Guto'r Glyn MS Cardiff, op. cit.
23. See Appendix I, p. 39.
24. *Ordinances of the Privy Council*, February 1422, 320.
25. Appointed to take the muster of the Earl Marshal etc. at Dover, and of the duke of Exeter at London. 28 May 1423. *Ordinances of the Privy Council*, 100.
26. Rymer, IX. 595.
27. *Record Reports*, 1885, 715, 314.
28. On 18 November 1419, he was appointed guardian of the lands of John Wogan, deceased, of Carmarthenshire, during the minority of the heir. *Record Reports*, 1880. A John Ogan received a commission to array the men of Gournay and Neauflé, 27 March 1420. Ibid. 1881.
29. Stephenson, II. 385; Hall, 118, 121. William of Worcester, *Itinerarium*, 357.
30. *Proceedings of the Privy Council*, III. 66, 87, 101.
31. Wavrin, 47–69.
32. Hall, 121.
33. Stephenson, II. 411. Hall, 127. *Issues*, Easter, 1425.
34. Hall, 138, 143.
35. Wavrin, 287. 'Gens de bonne estaoffe.'
36. Ibid., 294. Monstrelet. Hall, 141.
37. Wavrin, 46–50. Monstrelet, I. 630. Hall, 165. Polydore Vergil, 42.
38. At St Denis Gough was taken 'by founderyng of his horse'. Hall, 175. Polydore Vergil, 79.

  Bu ar gler bryder a braw
  Ban ddaliwyd, beunydd wylaw.
Guto'r Glyn. Hafod MS 3.
'The bards were disconsolate, and there was universal sorrow when Mathew Gough was taken prisoner.'
39. Wavrin, 66, 88–93. Fabyan, 608. Hall, 185. Wavrin, 274.
40. *Paston Letters*, I. 37. 30 September 1435.
41. Blondel, *Reductio Normaniae*, 277, 287–8, 375. Wavrin, 28, 222, 276.
42. Wavrin, 278–9. This was the Griffith Dwnn of the district of Kidwelly, who, as we have seen, was denizened in 1421. The names are given in *Itinerarium*, William of Worcester,

118–19. Homines lanceati Gryffith Don armiger apud capcionem domini Gaucourt: Johannes Mabbe de Kedwellylond, Johannes Whyte, Galfridus Doore, Geffrey Harflete, Johannes Davy, Johannes ap Gryffyth, Howel ap Gryffyth, Davy frater ejus, Jevan de Vawres (i.e. Ievan Vawr), Jevan Ragland.
43. Stephenson, II. 331–2.
44. He held one knight's fee in Raglan in 1425 from Edmund, earl of March. See *Calendar Inquis. post mortem*, 96, 141. Sir John Skydmore received letters of attorney on going abroad, in February, 1440–1; and Richard Hore of Laugharne, Carmarthenshire, in February. *Record Reports*, 1887. Sir William ap Thomas was infeoffed of Bassaleg, in Gwent, by the duke of York. For the close relationship which subsisted between them, see Proceedings (1441) 136–7.
45. Lerwis Glyn Cothi, I. i. 3. Dwnn's *Visitations*, I. 292–3. *Proceedings*, V. In 1420 he served on a commission in South Wales with Maurice ap Meurig, John ap Howel ap William, and John Dansy 'to arrest Thomas Wykeham'. Also on a commission concerning the acquisition by John Havard from William ap Thomas of the royal lordship of Talgarth. Also in 1432 with Humphrey, duke of Gloucester, 'for the keeping of certain monasteries'; also with Gloucester, Sir Edward Stradling, and Griffith Dwnn 'for the custody of St John's, Carmarthen', 1432. Also with Stradling and others 'to enquire as to the malefactors who took at sea a ship called *Le George* of Sluys laden with wines and honey of certain merchants of Flanders and Picardy, and brought her to Tenby, sold the ship and distributed the wines' (1432). Also, in 1434, with Stradling and Sir James Audley 'to make inquisition concerning acts of piracy, the goods having been carried to Cornwall and Wales and disposed of'. In 1442 he and a few others investigated treasonable proceedings in West Wales. *CPR. passim*.
46. Wardrobe Account, 1426. Q.R. Misc. Wardrobe. Hall, 138. *CPR*.
47. Collins, *Peerage*, III. 25; and Dwnn's *Visitations*, I. 292, are both misleading. The list of knights in Rymer, X. 357, is incomplete.
48. Clark, *Glamorgan Charters*, V. 1539, 1635–7, refuses to identify them on the ground that it would be below Sir William's

dignity. We need only remark that a Neville was sheriff in 1450. *Cardiff Records*, V. 536.

49. Stephenson, I. 79–86, 160, 169.
50. Eschouchy, I. II; Vallet de Viriville, III. 47.
51. Stephenson, 363–8.
52. *Letters of Margaret of Anjou*, 109–10. In one of her letters to the earl of Northumberland, Margaret evinces much concern for the safety of Gough.
53. *Record Reports*, 1887, *sub ann.* 1446.
54. *Record Reports*, 1887. He received letters of protection, 5 July 1446.
55. Stephenson, II. 696–7.
56. Ibid. 693–8.
57. Ibid. 702.
58. Stephenson, II. 361–5. Rymer, XI. 204, 216.
59. *Record Reports*, 1884, 330. Mathew Gough signs his name 'Matheu'. Stephenson, II. 333.
60. Ibid. 1887, 12 June 1447–8. Stephenson, II. 702–14. A John Morgan witnessed the surrender.
61. Stephenson, I. 280.
62. Blondel, *Reductio Normaniae*, 76, 621.
63. Blondel, 88–9, 277. Wavrin, 134. Stephenson, II. 621.
64. Stephenson, I. 311–13. An Ap Madoc was among the French men-at-arms in Normandy after the conclusion of the war.
65. Blondel, 95. Hall, 214–16.
66. Stephenson, II. 625. Herbert apparently crossed the Channel about 1440. See later.
67. 'Droit bons combatans dont estoit capittaine Mathieu Gone,' Wavrin, 150. 'Ducentis enim barbaris sub Mathaeo Goth belligerantibus,' Blondel, 156. Berry, 329. Stephenson, II. 625–8.
68. Stephenson, op. cit.
69. 'The name "Matago" is to this day retained at Bellême in memory of this valiant Welshman,' Wavrin, 150; and note, 282.
70. Hugh Donne of Wales, in the retinue of the duke of Somerset, and John Hokes of Tenby, in the retinue of Henry, Lord Bourchier, received protection, October–November 1448–9. *Record Reports*, 1887.
71. Blondel, 160. Berry, 331. Wavrin, 155.
72. Blondel, 169.
73. Berry, 333. Blondel, 171–2. The text is a free translation of the original. See Appendix II, p. 40.
74. Blondel, 175. Wavrin, 153.

75. Stephenson, II. 630. *Paston Letters*, I. 67–8; II. 147.
76. Lewis Glyn Cothi, I. viii, VII.
    Y vo gedwis ei vywyd
    I Vathew Goch vyth i gyd.
    'It was he who then saved the life of Mathew Gough.' See also William of Worcester, *Itinerarium*, 120–2, where this Herbert is described as 'consanguineus domini Herbert locum tenens de Penigele'. This 'Penigele' is probably 'Pengelly' in Breconshire.
77. Stephenson, II. 630, 730.
78. Stephenson, I. 502. Hall, 216. The governor of Cherbourg in 1449 was Sir John Gough.
79. Ibid.
80. Wavrin, 154–5. Berry, 342.
81. Blondel, 212. See Appendix III, p. 40.
82. Polydore, 78.
83. Hall, 221. In Lewis Glyn Cothi's ode to Gwilym Gwent (op. cit.) there are possible references to the engagement on London Bridge.
84. *Three Fifteenth Century Chronicles*, 68, 151. Gregory, 193.
85. *Itinerarium*, 357.
    Morte Matthei Goghe
    Cambria clamitavit, Oghe!
86. *English Chronicle*, edit. Davies, 67. Stephenson, II. 768. Hall, 221–2. Polydore, 86.
87. William of Worcester, *Annales*, 768. See also the will of Sir John Fastolf for a proof of his affection for Gough. *Paston Letters*, I. 456. 3 November 1459.
88. For the above details see *Record Reports*, 1887, 387, 388, etc. Also French Rolls, 1459–61. Other Welsh ships mentioned are the *Trinity* of Newport and the *Mary White* of Tenby.

Chapter Four

1. Stow. Strickland, *Queens of England*, II. 150, *passim*.
2. See before, Chapter 2.
3. Ramsay, *Lancaster and York*, I. 496, seems to cast doubt upon it. It is suggestive of the admitted legality of the marriage that not even Richard III, in his proclamation against Henry Tudor, attempts to discredit the marriage.
4. Revenues from the following Welsh estates were assigned to Queen Catherine on the

death of Henry V: Hawarden, Montgomery, Builth, Talybolion, Lleyn, Maltraeth, Menai, Cemmaes, Newburgh, Beaumaris, Aberffraw, Flint, Coleshill, Mostyn, Englefield, Caldecot, Newton. *Rot. Parl.* I. Henry VI. 203.

5. *London Chronicle*, 123. Stow, 377.
6. Hall, 185. Miss Strickland gives the name Owen instead of Thomas.
7. Wynne, *History of the Gwydir Family*.
8. *Acts and Proceedings of the Privy Council*, V. 46.
9. *Proceedings*, V. 46–9.
10. *Proceedings*, V. 46–50. Introduction, xvii. It appears from the *Claus Rerum*, 239, that he was at one time a prisoner 'notabilis' in Windsor Castle. No date is assigned.
11. *London Chronicle*, 123. 'Fraudulenter et subtiliter.' Rymer, X. 709.
12. Rymer, X. 685–6.
13. Rymer, X. 686, 24 March, 16 Henry VI. Miss Strickland suggests that this may have been the priest who married Owen and Catherine.
14. A formal pardon was granted to the sheriffs of London for their negligence in the matter. *CPR*, 29 July 1438. Rymer X. 709–10.
15. *CPR*, 344. General pardon to Owen Meredith for all offences.
16. Robin Ddu. *Ceinion Llenyddiaeth Gymreig*. 217–18.

    > Yr un dyn o'i rieni,
    > Blodeuyn oedd blaid i ni,
    > Sy' ngharchar, gyfar gofid,
    > Yn Nghaerludd, anghywir lid.
    > Gwae fi fod ym margod mur
    > Yn eu tid, Owain Tudur.
    >
    > . . . .
    >
    > Nid am ddwyn march mewn ffrwyn ffraeth
    > Yn lledrad anllywodraeth;
    > Nid am ddyled ef am credir
    > Y mae'n y rhest, y meinwr hir;
    > Ni bu leidr pan filiwyd,
    > Na thraetur, llin Tudur Llwyd.
    > Er iddo gynt, ar ddydd gwyl,
    > Fwrw ei serch frowys archwyl
    > Ar ferch brenin y gwindir
    > Oedd yn hardd wiw addwyn hir.
    > Duw a ro rhag cyffro cur
    > Iddynt hoedl, ŵyrion Tudur;
    > Y mab y mae genym obaith
    > A ddel cynt o ddwylo caith.

17. *History of Wales*, Ellis Griffith MS in the Mostyn Library. Ellis Griffith was a soldier in Calais. The above account is a summary translation. (The original is given in the Appendix, p. 52.) It should be observed that the *History* is unreliable in many details. For example, it states that Owen Tudor was put to death for marrying Catherine, that the marriage took place in 1425, and that Edmund Tudor and Jasper Tudor were raised to the peerage in 1436.

18. Rymer, X. 828.
19. In 1440, Catherine petitions the king to pay her the £52. 12s 0d which is due to her for the upkeep of Edmund ap Meredith ap Tudor and Jasper ap Meredith ap Tudor, this amount being arrears since the last day of February, 17 Henry VI. Rymer, X. 828.
20. The will is printed by Miss Strickland, vol. II. 153.
21. Ibid.
22. Issue Rolls. *CPR*.
23. The curious may consult Dugdale's *Baronage*, II. 256. Jones, *History of Brecknockshire*, vol. II. pt ii. 449–51. *Arch. Cambrensis*, 3rd series, IV. 16–30. Hist. MSS Commission, 8th Report, *Ashburnham Collection*, vol. VIII. 35 b, and 6th Report, 454 a. The story goes that when Herbert was made earl of Pembroke and installed at Windsor, Edward IV commanded the earl and his brother Richard to take their surnames after their first progenitor Herbert Fitzroy, and to forego the Welsh method of retaining pedigrees; and that the king under his first great seal commissioned Ieuan ap Rhydderch ap Ieuan Lloyd of Gogerddan, Cardiganshire, to summon the bards to Pembroke, and to certify the lineage of Herbert and his brother. 'Thereupon the above Ieuan ap Rhydderch, Howel Swrdwal, Ieuan Deulwyn, and Ieuan Brechva, having traced the pedigree, presented to their majesty their certificate in Welsh, Latin, English, and French, which stated that Herbert was descended from Peter Fitzherbert in the reign of king John, and from Herbert, son of Godwin, son of Elfrid, who had married a sister of Earls Harold and Tostig. Dated Aug. 12, 1460.' Of course the earldom was not conferred upon Herbert till 1468. He never was named Welsh fashion even before 1460. There is no such commission upon the

Patent, Close, or Exchequer Rolls. See also Catalogue Welsh MSS, British Museum.

24. Lewis Glyn Cothi and other poets. The editor identified 'y Gwindy Gwyn' of one of Glyn Cothi's poems as the London residence of Sir William ap Thomas, but gives no authority, I. xviii. There was a house in London called le Herbert, but apparently it did not belong to the family. Rymer, 1461, 473.

25. *CPR*, 2 February 1440, 374. *Record Reports*, 1887. 26 December. John Stradling of Glamorgan was also in Kyriel's retinue at this time.

26. Pat. Rolls, 22 May 1457, 353. On 10 October 1457–8 protection was given to his brother 'Thomas Herbert of Troye, Wales' in the king's service on the high seas. William of Worcester, *Itinerarium*, identifies him with Thomas of Greenwich. *Record Reports*.
Howel Swrdwal refers to Herbert's commercial enterprise in the lines:
Dau lu aml dal o iwmynn
Dwy long yn dyfod ai lynn.
'He has two armies of tall yeomen, and two ships trading in wines.' Swrdwal's poems have been published by the Bangor Welsh MSS Society. The poem from which the above lines are taken is dated 1450. This is impossible. There are references to Edward of York, which could not apply at least before 1461. There are indications that it may have been written just before Mortimer's Cross.

27. *CPR*, 1 March 1462. Perhaps it should be stated that the name is variously spelt as Herbert, Herberd, Herbard, and even Herebard, though Herberd is more common at first. It is not easy to distinguish the many Herberts of contemporary records. A William Herbert of Gloucester kept Newport Castle in 1468–9. A Thomas Herbert of Gloucester was constable there in 1468–9, sheriff of Somerset 1468, High Bailiff of Guisnes 1468. There was another of the name in Salop and Staffordshire (1443), while Thomas, Gilbert and William Harbard of Stood supported Cade in 1450. *CPR, passim.*

28. William of Worcester, *Itinerarium*, 122, as we have seen, mentions a William Herbert ap Norman who fought under Mathew Gough in France, and describes him as 'locum tenens de Penigele'. Elsewhere, ibid. 120, he

is called 'Willelmus Norman consanguineus domini Herbert'. He fought at Banbury. Ibid.

29. He may have accompanied Gough. See ch. 3.

30. See the duke of York's letter to Henry VI, printed in *Paston Letters*, Introduction; and also in Holinshed.

31. Ibid. also William of Worcester, *Annales*, II. 769. Hall, 225.

32. Rymer's *Foedera*, XI. 276.

33. *CPR*, 497. He had eight soldiers. 21 November 1441.

34. Ibid. 129, 16 August 1448. He succeeded one Meredith ap Cynwric.

35. The garrison of Beaumaris Castle was increased to twelve in 1446, and to twenty-one in the following May. This was probably the garrison till 1460. The constable was William Beauchamp. The author of *Calendars of Gwynedd* gives no authority for making Bulkeley constable of Beaumaris in 1440. Beauchamp was followed by John Butler in 1460, who was supplanted by William Hastings on the accession of Edward IV. In 1451 an annual sum of £20 was allowed out of the issues of the borough for four years for repairs. *Minister's Accounts*, in *Medieval Boroughs of Snowdonia*. Hall, 226. *Paston Letters*, op. cit. *CPR* 1439; 301, 308.

36. William of Worcester, *Annales*, 769.

37. Hall, 226.

38. 'Festum natalis Domini rex tenuit apud Grenwych, ubi fecit duos fratres uterinos milites et comites, viz. Edmundum Richemund et Jasper Penbroch, ac Thomam et Johannem Nevyle, filios comitis Sarum, ac etiam Wyllelmum Herberd, Roger Leuconer et Wyllelmum Catysby, milites.' William of Worcester, *Annales*, II. 770. (*The Dictionary of National Biography*, Doyle's *Baronage* etc., under William Herbert, are misleading.)
It will also be noted that William of Worcester asserts that the king's half-brothers were made earls on this occasion. This piece of evidence has been discarded on the ground that Edmund's charter is dated 23 November 1452. See later.

39. See p. 150, note 35, showing how Glamorgan came into Warwick's possession.

40. It was annexed to the earldom of Lancaster by Henry IV.

41. He was summoned to parliament as Baron Bergavenny (5 September 1450) in right of

his wife, Elizabeth Beauchamp, daughter and heiress of Richard, earl of Worcester.

42. Humphrey de Bohun, earl of Hereford, left two daughters, Eleanor and Mary. Mary de Bohun married Henry IV, so that her portion of the estates, which were in Herefordshire and Monmouth, was annexed to the Crown. Eleanor de Bohun was married to Thomas of Woodstock, duke of Gloucester (d. 1397). They had a daughter, Anne, who married Edmund Stafford, killed at Shrewsbury, 1403. Anne received from Henry VI the lordship of Brecon and the patronage of Llanthony Abbey for her and her son. Their son was Humphrey Stafford, lord of Brecon, created duke of Buckingham in 1444. He was killed at Northampton in 1460. He was married to Anne Neville, daughter of Ralph, first earl of Westmorland. Their son was Humphrey Stafford, who was killed at St Albans in 1455. His wife was Margaret Beaufort, daughter of Edmund, first duke of Somerset. Their son was Henry Stafford, duke of Buckingham and lord of Brecon. He married Catherine Woodville, lived in retirement at Brecon during Edward IV's reign, and was executed in 1483.

43. He gave charters to Ceri and Cedewain from Montgomery in August, 25 Henry VI. *Collections of Powys Club*, vol. II. 388.

44. William of Worcester, *Annales*, II. 770. Chronicle of the White Rose. Bonville was besieged in Taunton.

45. Ellis, *Letters*, 1st series, I. 11–13, dated 3 February 1452.

46. Hall, 226. We seem to have no reliable means of estimating the numbers of troops raised during these wars.

47. Hall, 226; Fabyan, 626–7.

48. *Privy Seals and Wardrobe Accounts.*

49. The pardon was subsequently confirmed in the parliament which met immediately after the first battle of St Albans, 1455. *Rot. Parl.* V.

50. *CPR* (1452–1461), 17. Dated 10 October 1452.

51. *CPR*, 30 September 1452, 17. It appears that the earl of Warwick was at Cardiff on 31 October 1452. Clark, *Glamorgan Charters*, 1632.

52. 'Rex Vicecomiti London – nos nuper per considerantes quae et quanta mala gravamina Willus Herberd, miles ligeis et subgitis uris in diversis partibus fecit et perpetravit per vobis precepimus quod statim post receptam in singulis locis infra civitatem, praedictam et suburbia ejusdem publice proclamari faciatis.
Ne quis prefato Willo aliquod receptamentum aut auxilium praebit – sed ipsum Willum tanquam notabilem rebellem ab omni gratia nosta – privatum fore et exemptum habeat et reputat.' *Claus Rerum*, 300.

53. As has already been stated William of Worcester gives an earlier date. But the date of Edmund's charter is 23 November 1452, and the two may have been ennobled at the same time. Jasper's creation appears under a parliamentary ratification of both titles on 6 March 1453. See *Paston Letters*, II. 285. *Rot. Parl.* 250.

54. 'Quod Edmundus et Jasper declarentur vestri fratres uterini in legitimo matrimonio infra regnum vestrum predictum procreati et nati ac indigine regni vestri supradicti et nedum sic declarentur verum etiam sic auctoritate supradicta realiter et in facto existant.' *Rot. Parl.* 250.

55. *Rot. Parl.* 251–3.

56. 'motu proprio non ad ipsius vel alterius pro eo nobis super hoc oblate petitionis instantiam sed de nostra mera liberalitate in comitem Pembrochie prefecimus.' Ibid.

57. 'non obstante jure titulo et interesse Margarete Regine Anglie precarissime consortis vestre, si que habeat in eisdem.' Ibid.

58. Included in the lordship and members of Pembroke were, 'Pembroke, Castle Martin, St Florence, Coedraeth, Tenby, Roos, Kemmaes, Burton, Milford, Cilgerran, Emlyn, Llanstephan, Dyffryn Brian, St Clear's,' etc. *Rot. Parl.* 253.

59. Wethamstede, I. 92–3. Jasper is described as 'vir illustris frater regis ex parte matris qui *de novo* per ipsum regem in comitem Pembrochiae erectus.' The chronicler remarks on the incident 'a friend at court is often better than a fig on a plate, or a penny in a purse'. It will be observed that the quotation suggests the 'recent' creation of Jasper as earl of Pembroke.

60. *Paston Letters*, I. 253–4, and note to letter 187.

61. *CPR* (1452–1461) 124. 12 August 1453.

62. Ibid. 173. 12 September 1453.

63. Ibid. 65. 4 March 1453.

64. *CPR* (1452–1461); 49–112; *passim*.

65. Ibid. 104, 24 July 1453. Edmund Tudor was given 'a house in London called Baynard's Castle'. Ibid. 79, 30 March. Both received the keeping of the possessions of John, duke of Somerset, during the minority of Margaret. Ibid. 79; 24 March. Two Welshmen, Morgan Meredith and John Roger, were keepers of the armoury of all the king's castles in South Wales. Morgan Meredith was in the service of Humphrey, duke of Gloucester, and held this post in 1442. Ibid. (1441–1447) 65. *CPR*, 106, 5 July 1453. A certain Henry ap Griffith of Backeton, Herefordshire, late of Newcourt, received a pardon. Ibid. 26 March. He was steward of Usk and Caerleon. Welsh MSS British Museum, I. 643.

66. *Proceedings of the Privy Council*. At the PC meeting, 21 November 1453, York again protested that he had come to do all he could for the king's welfare. See *Paston Letters*, Introduction, and Appendix.

67. 'The erls of Warwyk, Richmond, and Pembroke comen with the Duke of York, as it is said, everych of them with a godely feleschip, and as Geoffrey Poole seithe, the Kynges bretherne been like to be arrested at their comyng to London, yf they come.' *Paston Letters*, I. 266. 19 January 1454.

68. *Paston Letters*, Intro. This Geoffrey Poole was perhaps the king's servant and keeper of tents. Patent Rolls, 1459, 499. A Geoffrey Pole was constable and steward of Haverfordwest, after the death of Sir Rowland Lenthal. *CPR*. 28 January 1442, 67.

69. Edmund was Lord Attendant on the king 13 November 1454. *Proceedings*, VI. 222.

70. *Proceedings*, VI. 167, *passim*.

71. Ibid. He was absent on 1 April 1454, when George Neville was recommended for the next vacant bishopric.

72. York and Jasper were present at a council at Greenwich, 4 March 1455, when Somerset was cleared. Ibid.

73. Whethamstede, II. 161. He collected his army 'in finibus Walliae et de prope infra regnum Angliae exercitum fortem et grandem'. See also Fabyan, 629.

74. *Paston Letters*, I. 327. Though his name is not on the list given on page 332, he was probably in attendance on the king.

75. *Rot. Parl.* 282. 23 July 1455.

76. *Paston Letters*, I. 392. 7 June 1456.

77. Pat. Rol. 2 June 1455, 245. These offices were re-granted to Jasper on 21 April 1457. The earl of Wiltshire, a royalist at St Albans and afterwards, was at this time sheriff of Carmarthen and Cardigan shires; see Act of Resumption. The constable of Aberystwyth since 1443 was the duke of Somerset. In that year he was ordered to appoint no man his deputy without the authority of the council. He succeeded Sir John Griffith. The castle had one man-at-arms and twelve archers. *Proceedings*, V. 134, 244.

78. *Rot. Parl.* 453.

79. *Rot. Parl.* 279, 1455.

80. *Arch. Camb.* I. i–iii; *passim*.

Chapter Five

1. *CPR* (1446–1452), 432.

2. *Paston Letters*, I. 392.

3. *CPR* (1452–1461) 326; 26 October 1456.

4. His name appears on numerous commissions in London, Kent and Sussex in 1456. *CPR* (1456–1461), 306–7. See also ibid. 359. viz. a grant to him and the kind's sergeant, Thomas Vaughan, of Garlek and Stebenhithe. See Glyn Cothi's ode to Edmund Tudor (VIII, X).

5. There are glowing panegyrics on Jasper in Lewis Glyn Cothi and other contemporary Welsh writers.

6. Political Poems, *Archaeologia*, 1842, 328.

7. The *Cambrian Register*, already alluded to.

8. Y gwr hwnnw a garwn
   A dry gwyr gyda'r goron.
   Lewis Glyn Cothi, I. 133.

9. Cywir a gwirion yw'r gwr i'r goron,
   Cynghor fydd i hon ger bron brenin.
   Lewis Glyn Cothi.
   The editor of Lewis Glyn Cothi states that the poet is here advocating the rights of Richard, duke of York, and that Griffith was preparing to assist the Yorkists at Mortimer's Cross, as if that event could have been foreseen. He takes his cue, it need hardly be said, from the biography of Griffith already criticized.

10. Mastr Owen o'r mwstr *reial*. 'Owen of the *royal* army.' Lewis Glyn Cothi, I. 139.
    The editor gives a curious interpretation to *reial* in these lines, which we cannot admit. He translates it as strong or very good.

11. Aeth dano m'Iago! egin Deheubarth,

Hebog y Queen Catrin;
Un brawd ynn a barai win,
Un fron yw hwn a'i frenin.
. . . .
Henri frenin fordd ydd êl hinon
Ev a â'r gwareu, ev a'r goron,
Edwart dywysog heb dretusion
A gieidw'r ynys a gwaywdur union.
    Lewis Glyn Cothi.

This ode contains an inspiring panegyric on Jasper.

12. Ev a wery'r sies vry â'r Saeson. Ibid.
13. Cardiff MSS.
14. *CPR* (1452–1461) 494.
15. *Arch. Cambr.*, Vol. XIII. 5th series (1457). The castle walls of Tenby even to this day bear witness to his activity.
16. *CPR* (1452–1461).
17. Ibid. 340, 21 April 1457. Rymer, XI. 388. It has been stated, without authority, that Jasper received Denbigh in this year. *Dict. Nat. Biog. sub nom.* It seems impossible, for Denbigh belonged to York. Jasper received the constableship of it after Ludford.
18. *CPR*, 280. 12 March 1456. Sir Thomas Rempston was constable. For a number of commissions to Jasper Tudor and others see ibid. April–June 1456, 306–7.
19. *Privy Seals*, 1456–7.
20. *Privy Seals*, Fabyan, 630. *Paston Letters*, I. 416–17.
21. Clark, *Glamorgan Charters*, op. cit. V. *passim*.
22. *Paston Letters.* The correspondent apparently regarded him as such.
23. Dated 1 October 1454. The grant was ratified in October 1460. *CPR*, 627. The same year he and Sir Walter Devereux, Sir Henry Wogan, Henry Stradling, and Walter Devereux were associated in another grant. Ibid. 215.
24. *Minister's Accounts*, 1168, No. 8. *West Wales Hist. Soc. Trans.*, II. 112. Lewis ap Gwilym ap Thomas was associated with him, with Henry ap Gwilym as a pledge. The Herbert referred to is designated 'William Herbert, armiger'.
25. The reference in the *Claus Rerum* to Herbert's treason, already mentioned, may be in connection with these events. In any case it cannot affect the argument in the text.
26. *Privy Seals*, 22 May 1457. *CPR*, 353.
27. *CPR*, 360. Among those pardoned were: William ap Morgan ap David Gamme,

gentleman, late of Raglan; John ap Richard, late of Weobley, clerk; John ap Robert Raglan, late of Llantwit, gentleman; John ap Gwilym, late of Chepstow, gentleman; Thomas Herbert of Little Troye, the elder, squire; Adam ap Howel, late of Cardiff, gentleman; Philip Vaughan, late of Llamekon, alias Llamelion; Roger ap Rosser Vaughan, late of Tretower; Richard Herbert of Abergavenny; Miles ap Harry of Newcourt; Thomas Trahaiarn ap Ievan ap Meurig of Usk; Thomas ap Roger Vaughan of Hergest; Hugh ap Jankyn ap Ievan ap Madoc of Usk; Thomas Herbert the younger of Little Troye; William ap Rees and Henry Griffith of Herefordshire. Ibid. 367.

28. For the Vaughans of Bredwardine see end of chapter.
29. Catalogue Welsh MSS, British Museum, I. 667.
30. *Paston Letters*, I. 416–17. Written at London, 1 May 1457.
31. Gairdner refers to Herbert as 'a steady Yorkist'. Ramsay, Oman, and others have taken the same view, which is not strictly accurate. Editors of fifteenth-century Welsh poetry have laboured under the same delusion, and have thus been compelled to distort obvious references to him as a Lancastrian.
32. O bai ar Siasper daro,
        Trwy fil y t'rawai fo.
    Again,
        I'r goron, rywiawg eryr,
        Vry i Iarll Penfro a'i wyr.
    Lewis Glyn Cothi, VIII. vii.
    This Gwilym Gwent I identify with William ap Norman who is mentioned by William of Worcester, *Itinerarium*, 122. He had fought shoulder to shoulder with Mathew Gough in France, see before.
    Again,
        Bendith canmil i Wilym,
        Barti i'r iarll Herbert rym.
    Ibid. The editor interprets 'parti' as 'opponent', an impossible translation. He wrongly supposed that 'Herbert was a Yorkist to the last and of course an opponent of Jasper'. The Welsh epithet 'iarll' was a mark of respect to a patron.
33. See before. His home was in the vale of Towy. From evidences in contemporary poetry we gather that he was a partisan of Jasper.

34.   Iesu gwyn i wisgo ei art
       A geidw y t'wysawg Edwart.
       Iarll o Went arall aeth
       Yn oes hwn i'w wasanaeth,
       Iarll William. . . .
       Lewis Glyn Cothi, VIII. viii.
       That the poet here refers to Prince Edward,
       and not to Edward IV, may be inferred
       from another ode to Jasper, written about
       the same time, in which Jasper is eulogized
       as the defender of the right of King Henry
       and Prince Edward. In the poem Edward is
       called duke of Cornwall. This can only
       refer to Henry's son, who was created duke
       of Cornwall, earl of Chester, and Prince of
       Wales in March 1454. The son of Edward
       IV was made duke of Cornwall in July
       1471. See before. Henry ap Gwilym was of
       Court Henry in Carmarthenshire and
       remained true to Lancaster.
          Jaspar wayw llachar myn bedd Llechid!
          O dir Gwynedd y darogenid,
          Henri a'i deulu'n hir au dilyd
          Ai wayw du llyfn wedi y llivid.
       Ibid. III. iv.
35.   Clark, V. 1638. See also *CPR*, 518.
       Warwick obtained Glamorgan by marriage.
       His wife was Anne Beauchamp, heiress of
       her niece of the same name who died in
       1449. This niece was the daughter of
       Henry Beauchamp, earl of Warwick and
       lord of Glamorgan (d. 1445). This Henry
       was the son of Richard Beauchamp, earl of
       Warwick and lord of Glamorgan (d.
       11439), and Isabel Despenser, heiress of
       Thomas, earl of Gloucester.
36.   *CPR*, 398.
37.   Ibid. 433, 'except those in Lincolnshire'.
38.   Ibid. 486–7.
39.   *English Chronicle*, edit. Davies, 79–80.
40.   Fabyan, 634.
41.   *English Chronicle*, edit. Davies, 80. Audley
       held the barony of Cemmaes, Pembrokeshire.
       He was the great-great-grandson of Joan,
       daughter of William, baron Martin of
       Cemmaes, and Nicholas Audley.
42.   *Gregory's Chronicle*, 204. She was at
       Eccleshall about five miles distant.
43.   Gregory, 204.
44.   It has been supposed by some writers that
       Thomas   Salesbury   of   Denbigh
       distinguished himself on that day. I can find
       no authority for it. A Roger Salesbury was
       made Chief Forester of Denbigh soon after

the accession of the Yorkists to power (May
1461). Thomas Salesbury the younger was
made constable of Denbigh in January 1466.
CPR, 24, 421. Gregory, 204. Hall, 240.
45.   *Rot. Parl.* 369–70. On 15 December 1459, a
       pardon was granted 'to William Stanley of
       Chester of £166 on his petition showing
       that as late receiver of Richard duke of
       York, of the lordship of Denbigh, he was in
       arrears of £278 of which he paid £166
       which is due to the king by the treason of
       the Duke of York, and remains in the hands
       of the tenants of the lordship and cannot be
       levied because the custom of Wales is that
       arrears due to any lord are wholly lost by
       the removal of the lord.' *CPR*, 570.
46.   Roger Kynaston was the son of Griffith
       Kynaston of Stokes and Margaret, daughter
       of Roger Hoord of Walford, Salop. He
       married Elizabeth, daughter of Lord Powys.
       Another son was Philip Kynaston of Walford,
       who married a daughter of Robert Corbet of
       Moreton, Salop. Others on the commission
       (10 July 1453) were William Kynaston, John
       Hanmer, and Nicholas Eyton. Cal. Paat.
       Rolls (1452–1461). See also an Indenture in
       Ancient and Modern Denbigh, 91. On
       12 January 1459, Richard Grey, Lord Powys,
       was licensed to grant to him and others a
       moiety of a manor in Southampton. Ibid.
       475. Lord Powys was a Yorkist at Ludford.
       See also *Montgomery Collections*, Vol. XV. 5.
47.   They were attainted at Coventry. Devereux
       and Grey of Ruthin submitted the
       morning after Ludford. It is therefore not
       strictly true that, apart from the Nevilles,
       Lord Clinton was the only nobleman with
       the duke. Richard Grey (d. 1466) was the
       son of Henry Grey, earl of Tankerville (d.
       1450) – this earldom lapsed with the loss of
       France – and Antigone, a natural daughter
       of Humphrey, duke of Gloucester. Henry
       Grey was the son of Sir John Grey, who
       was created earl of Tankerville by Henry
       VI (d. 1421) and Joan, daughter and co-
       heiress of Edward Charlton (d. 1421) the
       great-grandson of Sir John Charlton (d.
       1353) who married the sister and heiress of
       Griffith de la Pole, Lord of Powys.
       Powysland Collections, I. *passim*. *CPR*, 121.
48.   *Rot. Parl.* V. 348.
49.   *Three Fifteenth Century Chronicles*, 168;
       'cum grandi comitatu'. *Paston Letters*, II. 4.
50.   Gregory, 205.

51. *Rot. Parl.* V. 348–9. Whethamstede, I. 343.
52. *Three Fifteenth Century Chronicles*, 168. Gregory, 205. *English Chronicle*, edit. Davies, 83. *Rot. Parl.* 348. Third Croyland Continuator, 453–4. Hearne's *Fragment*, 284.
53. Gregory, op. cit. Polydore, 104.
54. Gregory, 207. *English Chronicle*, edit. Davies, 83.
55. This was Edmund Grey, afterwards earl of Kent; 'to the king's grete plesir', *Paston Letters*, I. 500. Also Gregory, 207. For the close relationship between Devereux and the young earl of March, during the latter's residence at Ludlow, see *Ellis's Letters*, First Series, I. No. 5.
56. Gregory, 207.
57. Third Croyland Continuator, 454.
58. *English Chronicle*, edit. Davies. *Three Fifteenth Century Chronicles*.
59. Polydore, 104. Gregory.
60. *Paston Letters*, I. 499, 7 December 1459. 'Yesterday in the mornyng came inne th' erle of Pembroke with a good feleschip.'
61. *Rot. Parl.* 368. Roger Kynaston, having 'rered werre ayenst youre Highnes in the Feld of Luddeford', was pardoned, but fined.
62. *Paston Letters*, I. 499. *English Chronicle*, edit. Davies, 84. William Worcester, 771. *Rot. Parl.* 349, 368. *CPR*, 536, 539. See a letter from the two sons of the duke of York to their father, written from Ludlow, complaining of Croft's 'odious rule'. *Ellis's Letters*, First Series, I. 9–10.
63. *CPR*, 531. Weobley was of course the home of Devereux. The date given is 1 April 1459. The activity of Devereux was therefore a few months before the Ludlow campaign.
64. Ibid. 548, 552.
65. Ibid. 5 February 1460.
66. *CPR*; ibid. 574. 5 March 1460. It appears from this entry that Sir William Herbert was already in possession of these offices in virtue of grants from York and Warwick. The fact only shows how skilfully he had manoeuvred during these years of crisis. Sir Thomas Neville, a younger brother of the earl of Warwick, was sheriff of Glamorgan in 1451. *Cardiff Records*, I. 51.
67. *CPR*, 532. 19 December 1459.
68. Rymer, 435. *CPR*, 547. The date, 5 February 1460, was that on which Herbert received various offices in South Wales.
69. The persons mentioned are Ievan ap Ievan

Gadarn and David ap Rees ap Llywelyn. *CPR*, 561. The entry gives additional proof of the success of Jasper in West Wales.
70. *CPR*, 585. 29 May 1460.
71. *CPR*, 530, 533.13–18 December 1459.
72. Ibid. 548–9. 12 December 1459. In the following February a general pardon was issued to a Sir John Middleton and his son John, and to Richard Middleton.
73. Ibid. 554. 22 March 1460. Cf. ibid. 51, 1453.
74. Ibid. 550. 5 February 1460. These also were forfeited by the duke of York. Thomas Cornwall became steward of Radnor.
75. Ibid. 543. 13 January 1460.
76. *CPR*, 602–6. Among those appointed on commissions in Wales and the borders were Jasper Tudor, the duke of Buckingham, Sir John Skydmore, Thomas Cornwall, Richard Croft, Thomas ap Roger, Maurice ap Griffith, Thomas FitzHarry.
77. Denbigh was given to Henry de Lacy, earl of Lincoln, by Edward I in 1284. He restored the castle or rebuilt it on a new site, for there is apparently a Norman motte three miles from Denbigh. Rhuddlan also was not on the site of the ancient motte. He parcelled the estate among vassals with the exception of a few manors. He died in 1310. According to the *Inquis. post mortem*, the lordship embraced Abergele, Rhuvoniog, Cymmerch, etc. The next lord was Thomas, earl of Lancaster, who married Alice Lacy. He was succeeded by Hugh Despenser, from whom it passed to Roger Mortimer. He was executed in 1330. On his death, Denbigh was bestowed upon William de Montacute (d. 1344), but on the reversal of the Mortimers' attainder in 1356, it was restored to that family. By the marriage of Anne Mortimer (daughter of Roger Mortimer, earl of March, d. 1398) with Richard, earl of Cambridge, Denbigh passed to the duke of York, and thence to the Crown. See *Ancient and Modern Denbigh*, *passim*. It seems to be a unique instance of Lancastrian land not restored to Lancaster.
78. *CPR*, 534. 5 January 1460.
79. Rymer, XI. 445. *CPR*, 550, 565.
80. Rymer, XI. 444–6. *CPR*, 574–8.
81. *Rot. Parl.* 366. Cf. *Glamorgan Charters*, 1618, 24 March 1450. Another petition, Robert Whitney of Hereford being one of the petitioners, appealed for more drastic

action against lawlessness. *Rot. Parl.* 368, 1459–60.

82. *Glamorgan Charters*, loc. cit.

Chapter Six

1. This lord was the murderer of Tresham in 1450.
2. William of Worcester, *Annales*, gives the name of 'John Cleger, a servant of Lord Stanley', 773.
3. See also *English Chronicle*, edit. Davies, 98–9, which states that she was robbed of ten thousand marks. Stow, 409, and *Chron. of the White Rose.*
4. 'Eight', according to *Eng. Chron.* edit. Davies.
5. Gregory, 208–9. William of Worcester, *Annales*, 773–4. *Eng. Chron.* edit. Davies, 98–9.
6. *CPR*, 607, 608. 28 July.
7. Ibid. 13 August 612.
8. *Proceedings*, VI. 303. 9 August 1460.
9. In the records the name is given incompletely as 'Edward Bou———.' Probably Edward Bourchier is intended. He was a son of Viscount Bourchier, earl of Essex, and Isabel, daughter of Richard, earl of Cambridge. He was slain at Wakefield, 1460. *Proceedings*, VI. 303.
10. *Rot. Parl.* 38 Henry VI, 349.
11. Doyle's *Baronage.* 'Before July, 1460.' Sir Walter Devereux was the first Lord Ferrers of Chartley.
12. *CPR*, 594. 26 June 1460. Thomas Herbert was associated with his brother on this occasion.
13. *Proceedings*, VI. 304–5. In *Paston Letters*, I. 538, there is reference to a 'Richard Harbard' who was evidently familiar with the Pastons and at the time (29 October 1460) in communication with Warwick. But there is nothing to show conclusively whether the brother of William Herbert or some other of the name is intended. He may have been the Richard Heberd mentioned in another letter, the date of which is not established; Ibid. I. 76. Apparently the only other person of the name Herberd or Harbard mentioned in this correspondence is Julian Herberd of Thornham (1 March 1426) and one 'of my iii adversaries'; ibid. I. 26.
14. Gregory, 208. The Paston correspondent was under the belief that York had landed at

Chester. *Paston Letters*, I. 525–6. 12 October 1460. 'My lord of York hath dyvers straunge commissions fro the kyng for to sitte in dyvers townys comyng homeward; that is for to sey, in Ludlow, Shrewsbury, Herford, Leycestre, Coventre.' See also William of Worcester, *Annales*, 774.

15. Waurin, 312, which states that York sent to many of the Welsh chieftains for help and came up to London with a large following of Welshmen.
16. He was summoned in October 1460.
17. *Paston Letters*, I. 525–6.
18. William of Worcester, 774. Gregory, 208–9. Ramsay, *Lancaster and York*, II. 236, states that Margaret moved from Harlech to Denbigh, but the authorities quoted do not warrant the statement.
19. Gregory, 209.
20. *Paston Letters*, I. 525–6. 'They seythe here he (the duke of Somerset) propose hym to go to Walys to the Queen.'
21. William of Worcester, 774–5; 'cum multis militibus et generosis de partibus occidentalibus.'
22. Gregory, 209. Stowe.
23. *Three Fifteenth Century Chronicles*, 155. Brief Notes.
24. William of Worcester, *Annales*, 775–6. *Three Fifteenth Century Chronicles*, 76. *English Chronicle*, edit. Davies 203, states that Edward received news of his father's death at Gloucester, and then moved to Shrewsbury. The *Annales* put him at Shrewsbury.
25. William of Worcester, *Itinerarium*, 328, gives him a knighthood. I can see no evidence to show when he had been knighted. In addition to those given in the text, the same authority mentions the following as being with Edward at Mortimer's Cross: 'Stafford, Dom. Audley, Reg. Gray, Sir John Skydmore, Sir Wm. Skydmore, Sir Morys Skydmore, fratres, milites in armis in Francia.' This Stafford may have been Humphrey Stafford of Southwick, son of that William Stafford who was killed during Cade's rising in 1450, and who, at the coronation of Edward IV, was raised to the peerage as Lord Stafford of Southwick. There is a good deal of confusion about the Skydmores. Sir John and Sir William are given in the list of prominent Lancastrians as well. Sir John Skydmore held Pembroke

Castle for Jasper and could not have been among the Yorkists. We may safely dismiss these three brothers from William of Worcester's list. Philip Vaughan of Hay is described as 'homo guerrae in Francia, nobilior armiger lanceatus inter omnes alios, fuit occisus apud obsidium castri de Harlaugh per librillam et nullus homo honoris occisus ibidem praeter ipsum.'

26. William of Worcester, *Itinerarium*.
27. See a letter from Jasper to Roger Pulestone, given later.
28. *Three Fifteenth Century Chronicles*, 76, describes the army as 'Frenchmen and Bretons and Irishmen' who came by sea. *Engl. Chron.* edit. Davies, 110, describes them indiscriminately as 'Walsshemen'.
29. 'Who had been dragged from a seclusion of three and twenty years to do battle for the dynasty' – an unfortunate gloss in Ramsay, *Lancaster and York*, II. 243. As we have already seen, Owen Tudor had left his seclusion before this.
30. William of Worcester, *Itinerarium*, 328, whence the list is taken, Skydmore had endeavoured to recoup himself for his losses in the French Wars by exporting tin. *Record Reports*, 30 July 1455–6. He was reckoned the most influential knight in Herefordshire. *Proceedings*, VI. 341.
31. William of Worcester, *Itinerarium*, 327–8.
32. *Three Fifteenth Century Chronicles*, 76–7. It is there stated that Wiltshire was present at Wakefield. It is difficult to reconcile these assertions. So also Hall, 250. If he was at Wakefield there was no need for him to have come by sea to join Jasper in Wales. Moreover, it is impossible that he could have transferred an army by such a circuitous route in less than five weeks (31 December–2 February). A short time previously he had been in Ireland stirring up Irish opposition to Yorkist rule. *English Chronicle*, edit. Davies, 87, seq.
33. Lewis Glyn Cothi, VIII. i. seq.
34. I have already shown in the first chapter that Lewis Glyn Cothi was aware that Jasper had gone abroad to seek reinforcements and that he would land at Milford Haven about the end of December (the Feast of St John). See ibid. VIII. i, iii, iv.
35. *CPR*, 1442.
36. *Rot. Parl.* V. 244. Carte's *Life of Ormond*, Vol. I. lxxx. He was lord-deputy of Ireland in

1451, in the absence of the duke of York. See Ellis, *Letters*, Second Series, I. 117; it refers to the activity of the Wogans in Ireland.
37. *Three Fifteenth Century Chronicles*, 76–7.
38. This is the date given by Gregory, 211. He places the portent on the same day. *Three Fifteenth Century Chronicles*, 77, also states that the portent and action occurred on the same day, though 'Sunday, Candlemas Day', which was 1 February, is self-contradictory. *English Chronicle*, edit. Davies, 110–11, gives 3 February, and places the atmospheric phenomenon on the day before the battle, Monday. William of Worcester, *Annales*, 775, gives 3 February.
39. *English Chronicle*, edit. Davies, 110. 'By the morrow appeared the sun as three suns sundry on him in the east and closed again together.' Gregory says that the Yorkists were mustered 'withoute the towne wallys in a mersche that ys callyd Wyg mersche'; i.e. Wigmore, which is a few miles to the north.
40. Whethamstede.
41. William of Worcester, *Annales*, 776.
42. *Three Fifteenth Century Chronicles*, 77. I find no contemporary authority for Ramsay's statement that they were pursued as far as Hereford. *Lancaster and York*, II. 243. On the contrary, considering the directions along which the two forces respectively were moving, the Lancastrians were pursued, if at all, towards Presteign and the Welsh border. It was reported that Pembroke was taken near Nottingham. Brief Notes, in *Three Fifteenth Century Chronicles* 155. *Itinerarium*.
43. That is, if we may identify him with the Sir Richard Vaughan of Stow, 377, quoted in *Proceedings*, V. Intro. xix.
44. Gregory, 211. Stow. The bard Robin Ddu makes a touching allusion to the death of Owen and then turns his hopes to Jasper, whom he styles Owen, and refers to as:
Draig wen ddibarch yn gwarchae,
A draig goch a dyr y cae.
Ceinion Llenyddiaith Gymreig, 219.
'The dishonourable white dragon has triumphed, But the red dragon will yet win the field.' It is interesting once more to note the play on 'red' and 'white'.
45. William of Worcester, *Annales*, 776. 'Ac Owenus Tedere et Johannes Throgmertone, armiger, cum aliis captaneis decollati sunt apud Herforde.' In

the *Itinerarium*, 327, the same chronicler gives the following list of captured: 'Owen Tudor, about fifty age years of, beheaded. Reginaldus Gwyneth, camerarius Gwynneth landes jacente prope castrum Harlegh, beheaded. Master Lewis Powes, armiger, de Powesland, beheaded. Hopkyn Davy, Carmarthenshire, arm. cum comite Pembroke, beheaded. Philip Mansell, armiger, v mark annui valoris de Gowerland, beheaded. Lewis ap Rhys, armiger of Carmarthenshire, beheaded. Thomas Fitzharry, jurisperitus. Hopkyn ap Rhys of Gowerland comitatu, de Carmarthen, beheaded. James Skydmore, occisus, son of Sir John Skydmore. Sir Harry Skydmore of Herefordshire, son of the same Sir John Skydmore, beheaded. Sir William Skydmore, brother of John Skydmore, militis, obiit in . . .' Sir John Skydmore, chevalier. Stow, 413, gives the following as having been taken and beheaded. David Lloyd, Morgan ap Rhydderch, Sir John Skydmore and two sons, Thomas Griffith (? Thomas ap Griffith ap Nicholas), John Throgmorton, Thomas Fitzharry, and another. Both lists are somewhat inaccurate. See text.

46. Hall, 252, copying Stow, says that David Lloyd and Morgan ap Rhydderch were put to death. David Lloyd was probably the same who, for his services in the French wars, was made a royal official in the Forest of Glyn Cothi, Carmarthenshire; 20 March 1444. *CPR*, 259.

47. A diwedd braint, a dydd brawd
Yn Henffordd, mawr yw'n hanffawd.
Howel Swrdwal.
'The day of judgment and the end came in Herefordshire. Great is our distress.' Ode to Watcyn Vaughan. Watcyn Vaughan was the son of Roger Vaughan and Gwladys. Swrdwal has been published by the Bangor Welsh MSS Society.

48. Life of Sir Rhys ap Thomas, in the *Cambrian Register*.

49. Lewis Glyn Cothi refers to Griffith at an earlier period as one of the 'party of the lily', an allusion to the fleur-de-lis of Margaret. Deio ap Ieuan Hen also has a reference to the lily in a poem to Sion ap Rhys of Glyn Neath:
Tri fflowr de lis gedwis gwart,
Maes hyder grymus Edwart.
This is the poem which contains the Welsh

motto: 'Y ddraig goch ddyry gychwyn.'
The poem of Gwilym ap Ieuan Hen entitled 'Cywydd i ddau Garcharor,' may possibly refer to the retreat of Owen and Henry ap Gwilym to Harlech at this time. *Gorchestion Beirdd Cymru*, 156, 170–2.

50. The Dwnns are generally known as the Dwnns of Kidwely, where they obtained an official status later.

51. A Griffith Nicholas appears as farmer of Dynevor, 1485–90, but he cannot be the same person. *Ministers' Accounts*. See *West Wales Historical Society's Transactions*.

52. Rymer, XI. 471, 12 February 1461. *Three Fifteenth Century Chronicles*, 77. 'And forthwith he made again ready in the march.'

53. William of Worcester, *Annales*, 777.

54. Ibid.

55. Gregory, 215.

56. *Proceedings*, VI. 307–10. *English Chronicle*, edit. Davies, 107.

57. Oman (*Warwick*, 108) loosely states that 'the moment that he had crushed the Welsh Lancastrians and settled the affairs of the March, Edward had set out for London. He had hoped to arrive in time to aid Warwick; he could not achieve the impossible.' There is no evidence whatever that Edward made any attempt to settle the affairs of the March. He did not even go in pursuit. If that had been his aim, Edward could have reached London in a week after Mortimer's Cross, the time he actually took after hearing the news of the second battle of St Albans. Ten years later he covered forty miles a day; on this occasion he had covered less than forty miles in three weeks.

58. Gregory, 211.

59. *Three Fifteenth Century Chronicles*, 77, 155, 173. *English Chronicle*, edit. Davies, 108, 110. Gregory, 215.

60. Rymer, XI. 473, 'dilectis et fidelibus'. The above list of those present at the council is that given by William of Worcester, 775. Rymer gives the archbishops, the bishops of Salisbury and Norwich, Grey of Ruthin, Viscount Bourchier, William Herbert, John Wenlok, and William Falconbridge.

61. Gregory, 215.

Chapter Seven

1. Hearne's *Fragment*: 'The kinges footemen (were assembled) in a grete numbre of

which the moost parte were Wallshmen and Kentishmen.' Wavrin, 340. It is generally supposed that David Mathew of Llandaff was Edward's standard-bearer at Towton. I find no authority for it. In fact, according to *Rot. Parl.* VI. 93, the king's standard-bearer on that occasion was Ralph Vestynden who got an annuity of £10 for his services.

An old political song refers to some important Yorkist personage from Wales, as follows:

> The Dolfyn cam from Walys
> Three carpis be his syde.

Political Songs, *Archaeologia*, 1842, 346.

2. *CPR* (1461–1467), 8 May 1461. Ibid. 7, 30.

3. This Herbert is also known as Thomas Herbert of Troy. A Thomas Herbert the elder was constable of Gloucester in 1461 (23 June). They are apparently the same; for on 10 July 1461 he was given an annuity of 50 marks from Gloucester, being designated as Thomas Herbert, esquire of the body; while on 12 July 1462, a grant was made to the king's servant, Thomas Herbert the elder, esquire of the body, of certain manors in Gloucestershire, and of the lands of Sir William Mulle in Herefordshire, lands which Sir William Herbert was empowered to seize. In 1462 and 1464, he was on a commission of array in Gloucestershire. 13 December 1461 he was given a messuage (Garlik) in Middlesex. 27 May 1465, he received a pardon for the escape of one William Glover from Gloucester. In August 1467 'Thomas Herbert the elder' was made chancellor of the earldom of March, receiving the profits of Usk. On 12 February 1470, the reversion of the office of constable of Gloucester was given to Richard Beauchamp. Thomas Herbert died before June 1471. On his death the lands of William Mulle were given to his son who died without male heir. *CPR, passim.*

4. He was a younger brother of Sir William, and was made king's attorney in the counties of Carmarthen and Cardigan. *CPR*, 12 August 1461, 69.

5. *CPR* (1461–1467) 30, at York. Also ibid. *sub dat.* This John Dwnn was one of the Dwnns of Carmarthenshire, who took part at Mortimer's Cross and became prominent later. On 11 March 1461 a John Dwnn, usher of the chamber, was made Sergeant of the Armoury in the Tower of London. *CPR*, 9. He was on many commissions with the Herberts, and is not to be confounded with the Dwnns of Cheshire. He is sometimes referred to as John Dwnn of Kidwely, but it does not appear that he was given official interest there till 1463–4. See later. He was constable of Kidwely in 1485. Laugharne is in Carmarthenshire, and Walwyn's Castle in Pembrokeshire.

6. In July 1461 Devereux received a grant of the king's brewhouse called 'le Walsheman', without Ludgate in the ward of Faryndon. *CPR*, 126.

7. *CPR*, 31 July 1461, 26.

8. Ibid. 1 July 1461, 17. It thus reversed the decree of a few months earlier.

9. Ibid. 25 November 1461, 62. Hastings, Audley, and William Stanley were given possession of Hope and Hopedale in the Marches, and of Manorbier and Pennaly in Pembrokeshire. Ibid. 9. 16 July .

10. In the same manner as Sir John Griffith, Edmund Beaufort, duke of Somerset, late severally held Aberystwyth. *CPR*, 9 September 1461, 40. Among other grants in Wales were the following: Rees Vaughan was made provost of Raydirgey; Richard Croft the younger, receiver of the possessions of John, earl of Shrewsbury; Roger Eyton, constable of Shrewsbury; Thomas Sandeland, cannoneer and master-plumber in the royal castles of North Wales; John Moyle of Denbigh, an annuity of 10 marks for his good services to the king's father; and also letters of denizenship. *CPR, passim.*

11. Ibid. *sub ann.* 36.

12. With the two lords on this commission were Lord Herbert's brother, Thomas Herbert; a half-brother named William Herbert, and John Dwnn. This William Herbert was made constable of Cardigan on 2 August 1461. On 27 August 1464, the king's servitor, William Herbert, esquire, one of the clerks of the signet, was appointed escheator with the county of Carnarvon. In January 1462 he was given Kilpek Castle, eight miles from Hereford, the confiscated property of the earl of Ormond. The reversion of his lands was bestowed upon Lord Herbert, should he die without male heir. A William Herbert was comptroller of Bristol in 1466. On 20 July 1461, the half-

brother and Lord Hastings were empowered to seize certain lands in Northamptonshire. *CPR, passim.*

13. Kynaston was sheriff of Merionethshire. In the meantime Lord Herbert's influence increased rapidly. On 7 September 1461, he received the custody of the Welsh estates of the duke of Buckingham during the minority of Henry, the heir. It included the lordship of Brecknock, Newport, and certain other parts of Gwent. By another grant he became steward of the royal lordships of Clifford, Glasbury, and Wynfurton in the Marches. His brothers, Thomas and Richard, and Lord Ferrers, were associated with him. *CPR*, 13, 43, 98.

14. *Paston Letters*, II. 38, 41; 23 August 1461.

15. Ellis, *Letters*, First Series, I. 15–16. 'And there he will abide till Parliament time.' He was at Gloucester on 11 September. *Privy Seals.* Stow, *Annales*, 416.

16. Ellis, Letters; op. cit. 15–16. Written at Bristol, 9 September 1461.

17. The families of Tudor and Puleston were connected.

Mallt *m.* Tudor ap Grono   *m.* Margaret, dau. of Thomas ap Llywelyn ap Owen

Gwervil *m.* Griffith Hanmer

Angharad *m.* John Puleston

Meredith ap Tudor *m.* Margaret dau. of David Vaughan

Roger Puleston   Owen Tudor

In 1456 the earl of Richmond gave Roger Puleston an annuity of 10 marks for his services. *Arch. Camb.* I. i. 146–7. Dated 10 September.

18. *Ancient and Modern Denbigh*, 86; where the original letter is given as above. It is dated now for the first time.

19. *Anc. and Mod. Denbigh*, 87. Hitherto it has been found impossible to give the correct date to this letter.

20. The commission was to receive attornments from the tenants of Chirk. Others on the commission were John, abbot of Llaneguyfall; David Kyffin, doctor of laws; John Hanmer; John Trevor; John Puleston, and Robert ap Howel. John

Hanmer and Griffith Vaughan afterwards assisted in defending Harlech. *CPR* (1461–1467), 37.

21. Th'erll of March (i.e. Edward IV, the Lancastrian writer of the letter not recognizing him as king) is into Wales by land and hath sent his navy thider by sea. *Paston Letters*, II. 46. 30 August 1461. The ship for which Philip Castle and Thomas Mansel were called upon to provide mariners was the *Trinity* of Minehead. *CPR*, 99; 5 September.

22. *CPR* (1461–1467), 81. 1 April and 25 November 1461. He was granted a yearly grant of 20 marks. See also *Glamorgan Charters*, V. 1664. *Proceedings of the Privy Council*, 1453, 138. Another of the family, apparently, was David ap John of Swansea. See a revocation of a protection lately granted to him to stay in the king's service because he delayed in the city and suburbs of London instead of victualling Calais. *CPR*, 7 February 1464.

23. *Archaeologia*, 1842; 132–3.

24. *Rot. Parl.* 483.

25. Ibid.

26. *Rot. Parl.* 483 contains his Act of Attainder. Also ibid. (1472–1503) 29, which contains his petition. A schedule annexed to the petition notifies that William Herbert by the authority given to him by letters of Privy Seal, dated 13 May 1461, received Skydmore into the king's grace on 30 September 1461, at Pembroke. The attainder was reversed in 1472 (6 October). *Rot. Parl.* See an exemplification of it; ibid. 1 July 1474.

27. He was Henry Holland who married Anne, sister of Edward, but who remained a Lancastrian and was attainted this year.

28. *Paston Letters*, II. 52; 4 October 1461.

29. The original document is given in *Records of Denbigh*; dated 23 February 1462.

30. *Rot. Parl.* 1461, 477–8. In 1455 there were 20 soldiers at Carnarvon, including men-at-arms and archers. In May 1460 there were 18, including 5 soldiers of the town, who were distinct from the castle garrison and had their own captain. *Mediaeval Boroughs*, Lewis.

31. *Paston Letters*, II. 118.

32. Harlech had a garrison of 12 soldiers in 1442. Edward Hampden, governor in 1444, increased the number to 24.

33. *Rot. Parl.* I Edward IV.

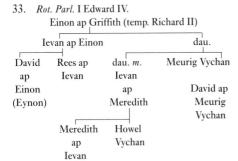

Wynne, *Gwydir Family*, 28.

34. *Three Fifteenth Century Chronicles*, 158, 175. Also *Paston Letters*, II. 45, 91, 93; February 1462.

35. Commission to William Herbert, knight, and Thomas Herbert, to take vessels and ships within the port of Bristol and other ports of the west towards Wales and ports in Wales to resist the king's enemies. *CPR*. 1 March 1462; 100, 132. A fortnight later, Thomas Herbert was given the custody of Bekford, Gloucester. Ibid. 181.

36. *Paston Letters*, II. 118.

37. *CPR*. 114; 3 February 1462. In south-west Wales Herbert was invested with the manors of Magor and Redwyk, the town and lordship of Caldecot, the castle and manor of Archenfield, late of James, earl of Wiltshire. Walwyn's Castle was also forfeited by Wiltshire.

38. *CPR*, 12 February 1462; 114, 119. On 26 August 1462, Herbert was granted the custody of the lands of one Nicolas Iwardby, during the minority of the heir. Ibid. 211. John Mowbray, third duke of Norfolk, died 6 November 1461. He was succeeded by his son John (born October 1444), the fourth duke of Norfolk, baron of Gower, Bromfield, Chirk, and Yale, on 6 November 1461. He died 17 January 1476, leaving an only child, Lady Anne Mowbray, who was betrothed to Richard, second son of Edward IV. On her death the dukedom escheated to the Crown. Doyle's *Baronage*.

39. *CPR*, 20 February 1462; 77.

40. Ibid. 11 July 1462; 192.

41. Ibid. 12 August 1461; 43.

42. Ibid. 24 February 1462; III. On 10 February the office of master of the king's armoury in the Tower was confirmed to him. One of the name was also comptroller of customs at Bristol. Ibid. 143, 188.

43. *CPR*, 20 January 1462; 76. Trahaiarn was on a commission with the Herberts in June 1463.

44. 23 January 1462. Ibid. 114, 428. In March 1465 he is stated to be possessed of Stapleton, lately the lands of Thomas Cornwall.

45. Ibid. 91, 153.

46. Ibid. 6 September 1462; 198. One Thomas Banon received Llanllwch. Carmarthenshire. Ibid. 112.

47. Dwnn's *Visitations*, I. 42, 106. Jones, *Breconshire*, III. 597. *Proceedings of the Privy Council*, V. 256. Stephenson, III. 475. In 1453 he received certain grants in Middlesex, being associated with Jasper Tudor; also 50 marks a year. *CPR, passim.* Act of Resumption, 1455. His career is not easy to follow; for he appears sometimes as Thomas Vaughan of Brecknock, and at other times as Thomas Vaughan of London. For the embassy see Rymer, XI. 504–7; and Wavrin, 412. The lands in Surrey were formerly the property of his wife's former husband, Thomas Brown, who was attainted. *Rot. Parl.* V. 534. In 1462 he received the lordship of Penkelly in Brecknock. *CPR, passim,* He was keeper of the Great Wardrobe in September 1460. On 9 November 1464, there is noted a 'Pardon to Thomas Vaughan, esquire, keeper of the Great Wardrobe of Henry VI, one of the mainpernors of Jasper, for the custody of Cantrecelly and Penkelly.' He and William Hastings were coupled in a grant of the presentation to the next vacant prebend in the college of St George's, Windsor. On 29 March 1465, certain lands in Cardiganshire were granted to Thomas Vaughan 'one of the yeomen of the king's Chamber' for his services to the king and his father. *CPR*, 438. This apparently was he of the name who was killed at Edgecote.

48. *Paston Letters*, II. 119. But Norfolk did not stay in Wales, for he was at Newcastle on 11 December 1462. Ibid. 121–3. He was at Holt again in March 1464.

49. *Paston Letters*, op. cit. *Three Fifteenth Century Chronicles*, 157. Lewis Glyn Cothi, I. xviii.

50. William of Worcester, 780. *Three Fifteenth Century Chronicles*, 158.
51. William of Worcester, *Annales*, 780. Margaret had already sailed for Brittany, 'going between Wales and Ireland with four ships'.
52. A'i wyneb yn dân ar farch anwar,
    A'i olwg mawrwych val dig marwar,
    A'i fon, a'i ddwyfron, a'i ddâr, a'i saled,
    A'i wayw yn lluched neu yn dân llachar.
    Lewis Glyn Cothi, I. xviii.
53. At the same time he became steward of Carmarthenshire and Cardiganshire, Usk, Dinas, Caerleon, Builth, Ewyas and Clifford, grants which had been previously conferred upon him by Margaret. *CPR*, 17 June 1463; 271.
54. Ibid. 23 June 1463; 280. This Trahaiarn, whom we have met with before, is addressed by Guto'r Glyn as one of the loyal supporters of Herbert, 'his lance and his shield'. Iolo MSS 705. It is worthy of notice that some of the powers conferred upon Herbert encroached upon the jurisdiction of Lord Hastings, chamberlain of North Wales.
55. This Lewis we presume to be the Lewis ap Rhys of Strata Florida, designated 'armiger of Carmarthenshire', who was reported to have been executed with Owen Tudor after the battle of Mortimer's Cross.
56. *Rot. Parl.* (1464–5), 511–12.
57. *Rot. Parl.* (1464–5), 511–12. In the records the name is given as 'Dryffryn', and is stated to be in Carmarthenshire. The spot alluded to is no doubt that mentoned in the text. Dryslwyn was a royal castle. Its constable in 1439 was Thomas Staunton, who was also master-forester of Glyn Cothi. *CPR*, 245.
    Lord Ferrers was constable of Aberystwyth in 1463. *Record Reports*, 1887, 423. *CPR*, 270, 336.
58. *Privy Seals. Paston Letters*, II. 144–5; and supplement to Introduction, 82.
59. *Rot. Parl.* 511–12. The attainder was reversed by Henry VII. Ibid. 1483, 278–9. Their confederate Lewis ap Rhydderch is not mentioned there. For details of the local history of the Mansels, see *Glamorgan Charters, passim*.
60. *CPR*, 23 March 1465; 426. A Philip ap Rhys was Governor of Strat Florida in 1443, with Lord Audley and Meredith ap Owen. *Glam. Charters*, V, 1590.

61. *Rot. Parl.* V. 534. Also Cal, Pat. Rolls, 11 March 1465.
62. *Paston Letters*, II. 151–2.
63. Gregory, 223. *Rot. Parl.* 511–12, which gives his attainder.
64. Gregory, op. cit.
65. William of Worcester, *Annales. Brief Latin Chronicle*, 178.
66. Rymer, 1464–5; 534, 539. A list of the chief men in the north after Hexham does not contain the names of either Jasper or Herbert. Ellis, *Letters*, Second Series, I. 131.
67. *CPR*, 355.
68. Cardiff MSS Tudur Penllyn.
69. Hall, 261.
70. 'Yn yr amser y ffoes Jasbar . . . y neb megis ac i klywais i vy hennaviaid yn dywedied a gymerth ysgraf i wr boneddic a oedd yn trigo yn Mostyn o vewn plwyf Chwitford yn sir y fflint ynny man a elwir pwll pictun yn yr amser y gorvu ar yr iarll ddwyn baich o welld pyse ar i gefyn wrth vyned ir ysgraf hrag ovon i neb i gannvod ef kannis nid oedd eissiau pobyl ynni esbio ef ar hyd y gwledydd ynno neithyr y vo a ddiengis ir mor ynnyr sgraf hon ai harweddodd ef oddiynno i vryttain vechan yn vwy drwy gowreindeb yr iarll nog o gowreindeb llongwyr picktun.' Ellis Griffith, *History of Wales*, in the Mostyn MSS.
71. *CPR*, 268; 12 June 1463. Also ibid. 286; 16 June 1463.
72. *Rot. Parl.* 512.
73. See Lewis, *Mediaeval Boroughs*. Henry Bolde was governor of Conway in 1461.

Chapter Eight

1. Hist. MSS Commission. Fifth Report, 590–1 (1463).
2. *CPR*, 23 March 1465; 427. All wrecks of sea were the property of the king.
3. William of Worcester, *Annales*, 786. It has already been stated that Warwick had endeavoured to influence Elizabeth Woodville to marry Sir Hugh John of Swansea. See a letter from Warwick to her in *Archaeologia*, 1842, 132–3. The partiality of Edward for new men is reflected as early as the winter of 1461. *Paston Letters*.
4. William of Worcester, *Annales*, 786. [ ] Septembris factum est maritagium apud Wyndesore inter filium et heredem domini Herberd et Mariam sororem

reginae Elizabethae, ac inter juvenem dominum de Lisle et filiam ejusdem domini Herberd. Fecitque dominus rex haeredem Herberd militem ac creavit eum dominum de Dunstarre, ad secretam displicentiam comitis Warrwici ac magnatum terrae.

Lord Lisle was the son of John Talbot, Viscount Lisle, who was killed at Chatillon in 1453. He was ten years of age when he succeeded to the viscountcy in July 1453.

5. William of Worcester, *Annales*, 786.

6. Warkworth, 25. 5 January 1467–8, Thomas Vaughan was Treasurer of the Chamber, and treated for peace with Burgundy. On 4 February 1470 the duke of Burgundy acknowledges the receipt of the order of the Garter from him at Ghent. Rymer, XI. 651. He was appointed on the council of the Prince of Wales, 8 July 1471. *CPR*. See also Grants of Edward V, xvi; and *Archaeologia*, XXVI. 277.

7. Wavrin, 1447–71, 545.

8. William of Worcester, *Annales*, 788–9. Quidam fuit captus in Wallia (portans) litteras a regina Margareta ad castrum Hardlaughe, missusque Londinium per dominum Herberd ad regem, qui accusavit . . . inter alios comitem Warrwici quod audivit suspiciosa verba ultra mare quod idem comes faveret parti reginae Margaretae.

9. Hall, 273–4. Cecille Bonville, the only child of William Bonville, Lord Haryngton, was the heiress of the Bonville and Haryngton estates. William Bonville was married to Catherine Neville, Warwick's sister. Worcester, 790–1.

10. *CPR*, 9 March 425. The patent gives a minute description of the boundary. 'And whereas Herbert holds in chief the lordship of Raglan and the manors of Penclauth, Metheny, as of the lordship of Usk, and the manor of Dyngestowe as of the lordship of Monmouth, the king releases him of all rents and services,' etc.

11. *CPR*, 533. Annabill, Pyll, Steynton, Copped Bush, Thywode, Lamburston. The manor of Haverfordwest, and a third of St Briavel's. His offices of chamberlain and chief justice of South Wales, and steward of royal lordships, were confirmed at the same time.

12. *CPR*, 41, 136; Thomas Salesbury, younger, was made constable of Denbigh on 23 January 1466.

13. *CPR*, 1467; 41, 49. Viscount Lisle was Talbot's heir.

14. Ibid. 54, 57. 27 October and 14 August 1467. For confirmation of grants to Richard Herbert, see ibid. 5 February 1465, e.g. Grove, Monnington, etc. Henry ap Griffith was on a commission, 28 March 1465, to ascertain what castles and manors had belonged to Wiltshire. Ibid. 451. Thomas Morgan, and Herbert's half-brother, John ap Gwilym (or William), were on another commission touching felonies in Chepstow on 11 May 1467. Ibid. 29.

15. *CPR*, 529. William Griffith and Middleton took a muster of 700 archers of the earl of Worcester's retinue at Beaumaris, 18 August 1467, ibid.; and on 3 August 1475, inquired into all shipments of wool, hides, etc. from North Wales. Ibid. 490.

16. William of Worcester, *Annales*, 791.
    Yno i daw'n arglwydd llawen.
    Tudor Penllyn, MSS.
    i.e. 'There (Harlech) our chief will land.'

17. William of Worcester; subtili modo.

18. William of Worcester, *Annales*, prope Hardlaughe. Tudur Penllyn MSS. Ramsay, *Lancaster and York*, II. 333, is misleading.

19. William of Worcester estimated them at 2,000, which is probably an exaggeration, though he is roughly in agreement with contemporary poets as to the number of Herbert's force which took Harlech soon afterwards.

20. Gregory, 237. 'He rode ovyr the contraye and helde many cessyons and cysys in King Harry's name.'

21. Dafydd Llwyd, Cardiff MSS.
    A daw herwr dewr, hirwallt,
    A'i dai ar hyd y dwr hallt.
    Wedi'r wyl i daw'r eleirch
    I dir Kent cyn medi'r ceirch
    O flaen y byd aflonydd
    Coedcrai ar Fenai a fydd

22. William of Worcester, *Annales*; cito post festum nativitatis Sancti Johannis Baptistae.

23. *CPR* (1467–72), 103, 127. The date of Herbert's commission again falsifies Ramsay's statement already alluded to.

24. For example, Dafydd Llwyd:
    Ni bu erioed a barr on
    Wr gowirach i'r goron.
    Cardiff MSS.

25. Pennant, II. 121–2. *Autobiography* of Lord

Herbert of Cherbury (Lee), 6–8. I see no evidence that David ap Eynon ever held a castle in France.

26. His name appears in records of Inquisition for Merionethshire, 1453–6. *Arch. Camb.* 1848, 69.

27. William of Worcester, *Annales*, 791, gives 10,000: ad custos domini regis, cum numero decem millium armatorum. Guto'r Glyn says '9,000 yeomen'. See poem in *Records of Denbigh*, 202–3. Another bard of the time, Hywel Dafydd ap Ieuan ap Rhys, estimates the force at 7,000.

Tynu â gwyr tonau gwin.

Also:

Saethu 'mhob parth saith mil pen.

'Men draw from men waves of wine, arrows fly in every quarter from 7000 men.' The above poem is quoted in Warkworth, 33, 35, notes; but is attributed wrongly to Lewis Glyn Cothi. The sum paid to Herbert for the siege of Harlech, £7,177, also suggests a large force. Issues, 9 Edward IV. On 6 December 1468 Lord Herbert was given the reversion of certain manors because the king owed him £3,168. *CPR*, 132.

28. William of Worcester, *Annales*, 791. Guto'r Glyn suggests three divisions of the army.

Tair cad aeth o'r teir gwlad tau
Trwy Wynedd fel taranau.

There is much tradition in Wynne's *Gwydir Family*, and in Lord Herbert of Cherbury's *Autobiography*, 6–8.

29. Wynne's *Gwydir Family*, 49–50, 66. Guto'r Glyn:

Tros greigiau mae d'olau di;
Tir âr i gwnaent Eryri.
Od ennynaist dân ennyd
Drwy ladd ac ymladd i gyd,
Dyrnod anufudd-dod fu,
Darnio Gwynedd a'i dyrnu.
Harlech a Dinbech pob dôr yn cynneu,
Nanconwy yn farwor.

Also, Hywel Dafydd ap Ieuan ap Rhys:

Dareni daiar Wynedd.

30. Guto'r Glyn, in *Records of Denbigh*, 202–3. William of Worcester, *Itinerarium*, 328.

31. Gregory, 237, and William of Worcester, *Annales*.

32. Gregory, 237. *Brief Latin Chronicle*, 182, states that Tunstall was pardoned by the king; William of Worcester 791, says that he was executed.

33. In 14 Edward IV Prince Edward gave him

licence to hold lands in Kynnowys. Hist. MSS Commission; Puleston MSS, in *Arch. Camb.* 1880, 150. *Autobiography* of Lord Herbert of Cherbury, 6–8.

34. His son Reginald received an annuity of marks from the issues of Chirk, from Richard, duke of Gloucester, 26 March 1471. *Arch. Camb.*, 1863, 55; and 1875.

35. Original document in Wynne, 50.

36. William of Worcester, 791.

37. Gregory, 237.

38. Herbert's will; *Powys Club Collections*, II. Appendix, xviii. Another daughter was to be married to Lord Powys.

39. Na fwrw dreth ar Fôn draw
Ni ellir ei chynnulliaw.
N'ad trwy Wynedd blant Rhonwen
Na phlant Hors yn y Fflint hên.
N'ad, f'arglwydd, swydd, i un Sais,
Na'i bardwn i un bwrdais.
Kymmer o wŷr Kymru 'rowron
Bob cwnstabl o Fenstabl i Fôn.
Dwc Forgannwc a Gwynedd,
Gwna'n un o Gonwy i Nedd.
O digia Lloegr a'i dugiaid,
Kymry a dry yn dy raid.

Guto'r Glyn in *Cein. Llen. Gymreig.* 192.

40. *Rot. Parl. sub ann.* Sir Roger Vaughan, of the lands of Philip Mansel and Hopkyn ap Rhys; Cantrelly, Llangoid, Alexander's Town, reversion of Penkelly. Morris Arnold, of 40 marks from Monmouth town. Thomas Herbert of the lands of Mulle in Gloucester. Thomas Vaughan, son of Sir Roger Vaughan. He, together with Lord Dunster, and John Herbert, were on a commission on 6 December 1468, to hold the reversion of certain manors for Lord Herbert, on the death of the wife of Sir William Beaumont. *CPR*, 132. John Dwnn of Laugharne (Talaugharne), Cleygyn, Pybour, 'for his services to the duke of York, and against Jasper'. See also *CPR*, 9 November 1467; and 11 March 1465; 430–1. On 9 August 1463, a John Donne was on a commission to investigate complaints of Spanish merchants. Ibid. 301. Thomas Vaughan, yeoman of the Crown, of Gerardstown, in Cardiganshire (granted, 1465–6). Richard ap Rhys, of 10 marks a year (granted, 1465–6). Hugh Lloyd and John Lloyd, of grants in the counties of Carnarvon and Merioneth. Howel Davy and John Howel his son, and

John Davy, of grants in Montgomery. Morris Gethin, of the amobrship of North Wales counties. Richard Herbert. John ap Ieuan ap Llywelyn, of an annuity of 10 marks from Radnor.

41. *CPR*, 12 September 1468.
42. Ibid. 12 October 1468; 111.
43. Ibid. 113, with payment for 24 soldiers. On 3 May 1469, he was confirmed in the possession of Chepstow, Gower, Swansea, Kilvey, and Lougher, which places he acquired by a writ 'precipe in capite'. Ibid. 154, 163; and *passim*, for grants to Devereux.
44. Ibid. 98, 518. A commission was given to Herbert and Shrewsbury to arrest Kynaston and bring him before the council, 28 August 1467. Eyton was constable of Shrewsbury in June 1467. Distinguish this Kynaston from one of the same name, of Walford.
45. Ibid. 515.
46. Ibid. 152, 28 March 1469.
47. Third Croyland Continuator, 457–8. *Paston Letters*, II. 326. From the latter it appears that Herbert was at court on 28 October 1468, and about to depart, probably for his Welsh seat. 'Sende me worde if my lorde of Pembrok be go.'
48. See the letter of Clarence and Warwick, 12 July 1469; Warkworth, 46.
49. Third Croyland Continuator, 457–8.
50. Warkworth, 6–7, says Sir William Conyers adopted this name. See also Introduction to *Paston Letters*. Hearne's *Fragment*, 24, mentions Lord Latimer as the captain of the band. He was Warwick's uncle.
51. See before. Hall, 273–4.
52. Third Croyland Continuator, 445–6.
53. Hearne's *Fragment*, 24.
54. Warkworth. Hearne's *Fragment*.
55. Guto'r Glyn, 'I Wledd.' Cardiff MSS.
    Wrth ofn Iarll yr aeth fy nêr
    I Gaeloyw â'r gwyr lawer.
    Ofni Lloegr, ein un llygad,
    Ai bribwyr oll yn bwrw brâd.
    Blino y maent o'm blaenawr
    Blant Ronwen, genfigen fawr.
    'My lord with many troops advanced to Gloucester on account of the Earl. I fear lest he be the victim of treachery. The people of England have harassed our leader, and he is the object of deep malice.'
56. Hall, 273.
57. William of Worcester, *Itinerarium*, 118. Sir Henry Ogan chevalier fuit in Francia, de Pembrokeshyre, et maritavit filiam William Thomas, chevalier; qui Sir John Ogan, chevalier, obiit apud Banbery felde.
58. Ibid. Griffith Dwnn habuit 3 filios in Francia: Robertus Dwnn non maritavit; Henricus Don in Francia maritavit filiam Sir Roger Vaughan, chevalier, et mortuus (est) apud Banbery felde; tercius filius minor Johannes Don, qui maritavit filiam domini de Hastynges, chamberlayn regis.
59. William of Worcester, *Itinerarium*; fuit occisus Bristolliae in crastino Sancti Jacobi. This may be an error for the Thomas Herbert slain there according to Warkworth, 7.
60. William of Worcester, who also mentions a Thomas Glys.
61. Hall, 273–4.
62. Guto'r Glyn, in *Ceinion Llenyddiaith Gymreig*, I. 193.
    Dyw llun y bu waed a lladd.
    'On Monday there was blood and carnage.'
    Ieuan Deulwyn, Bangor Welsh MSS Society.
    Dyw llun rwi'n deall as
    Yno yternwyd yn tyrnas.
    'On Monday, I understand, our nation was repulsed.'
    Guto'r Glyn is our authority for the death of this Thomas ap Roger on the Monday.
    Dyw Mawrth gwae ni am Domas;
    Dyw Llun, gyda'i frawd, y llas.
    'On Tuesday we mourn for Thomas, on Monday he was slain while fighting at his brother's side.'
63. Hall, 273. Warkworth, 7.
64. Croyland Continuator, 445–6. Wavrin, 580.
65. Hearne's *Fragment*, 24. Hall, 273–4. Warkworth, 7.
66. Guto'r Glyn, *Ceinion Llenyddiaith Gymreig*, I. 192, 200.
    Ni aned twyll ond ti,
    Ni bu unbrad ond Banbri.
    Arglwydd difwynswydd Defnsir
    A ffoes; ni chaffas oes hir.
    'There never was deceit or treachery like that of Banbury. The earl of Devon fled; he did not live long afterwards.'
67. Croyland Continuator, 446–7.
68. Hall, 273–4. Hearne's *Fragment*, 24. Guto'r Glyn refers, presumably, to the death of Sir Henry Neville in the line:
    Marchog a las ddyw Mercher.
    'A knight was slain on Wednesday' (25 July).

Ieuan Deulwyn also alludes to this fight:
　Ag yn nos Iago nesaf.
'On the evening of St James's day.'

69. Ramway's suggestion (vol. II. 432, note 4) that the action must have taken place within an area of half a mile, or three-quarters of a mile at most, in depth, by a quarter of a mile in width, therefore seems wide of the mark. There were two actions even on this day, the one between Thorpe and Wardington, and the other between Wardington and Culworth.

70. Hall, 274. Guto'r Glyn states that the action took place on a Thursday:
　Duw a ddug y dydd ddyw Iau.
'The field was lost on Thursday.'
So, too, Ieuan Deulwyn. There is no reliable authority for the statement of Oman that Clapham was at the head of the vanguard of the royal reinforcements, and treacherously fell upon the flank and rear of the Welsh whom he had come to assist. Oman's *Warwick*.

71. William of Worcester, *Itinerarium*, 120–1; per exercitum comitis Warici.

72. Ibid. 119. Quam plures alii de valoribus gentibus Walliae ad minimum 168 vel circa. He estimates the slain at 1,500; Warkworth at 2,000.

73. Corland Continuator, 446.

74. Hall, 275. Cf. Polydore, 122. Wavrin, 584, states that the Herberts were stoned to death by the people. 'Le comte de Warwic commanda que on les emmenast morir, et ainsi furent les deux bons chevalliers livrez au peuple, qui piteusement les lapiderent.'

75. Wavrin, 581–2. He does not give the name of the stream, but he obviously refers to the Cherwell. According to this account Devon retreated on the day of battle when he saw that the northerners had been reinforced.

76. The above is a free translation of the lines:
　Yno clywid yn unawr
　Griaw maes rhwng gwewyr mawr:
　Rhai Herbert, rhai 'n Edwart ni,
　Iarll Warwic, eraill Harri.
Lewis Glyn Cothi, I. 17.
The poet ends his poem by calling upon the three sons of Thomas ap Roger who, as we have seen, was slain, to take vengeance for their father's death. The poet was present at this hero's public funeral.

77. A charter to Neath Abbey by the earl of Warwick, 24 June 1468, is witnessed by Sir Roger Vaughan, chancellor, and Thomas ap Roger, coroner. Thomas, as we have seen, was slain in battle. Clark, op. cit.

78. See before for grants to him in South Wales.

79. William of Worcester, *Itinerarium*, 119, says that he was slain at Bristol on the following day. Warkworth says that it was Thomas Herbert that was slain there, and that this William was of Brecknock. Hall says that ten others were executed, but does not give their names.

80. Probably John Gwilym of Ytton. He and Thomas Lewis and Thomas ap Morgan were on a commission touching felonies in the lordship of Chepstow, 11 May 1467. *CPR*, 29.

81. I am inclined to the opinion that Warkworth means the son and heir of Henry Wogan, i.e. the John Wogan mentioned by William of Worcester. He was the son of Sir Henry Wogan and Margaret, daughter of Sir William ap Thomas.

82. He cannot be the son of Thomas ap Roger, for this Watcyn was addressed by Lewis Glyn Cothi (I. vi) together with his two brothers, after Banbury. Watcyn, son of Roger Vaughan, was slain in Herefordshire, perhaps at Mortimer's Cross. He is not specifically mentioned as having been at Banbury by either Glyn Cothi or Guto'r Glyn, though both mention Thomas.

83. Lewis Glyn Cothi, I. viii. He is not mentioned by Wiliam of Worcester.

84. 　Awn oll i ddial yn iaith
　　Ar ddannedd y nordd uniaith.
　. . . . .
　　Ef am llas i a'm nassiwn
　　Yn awr y llas yr iarll hwn.
Guto'r Glyn; *Cein. Llen. Gymreig*, 192–3.

85. 　Y maes grymusa o gred,
　　Ac o wall ef a golled.
　　Yn Manbri y bu'r dial
　　Ar Gymmru deg, a mawr dâl.
Lewis Glyn Cothi, I. 17.

86. *Brief Latin Chronicle*, 183. Hic W. Harberde, gravissimus et oppressor et spoliator ecclesiasticorum et aliorum multorum per annos multos, hanc tandem, justi Dei judicio pro suis sceleribus et nequiciis recepti mercedem.

Chapter Nine

1. *CPR*, 165; 12 August 1469.

2. Ibid. 17 August 1469. Rymer, XI. 647.

3. Welsh MSS Brit. Museum; part 1. 1900, 26–7. Edward Owen.

4. *CPR*, 179. In the previous year he had received the wardship of the lands of Sir Roger Corbet. Ibid.

5. Ibid. October–November 1469.

6. *CPR*, 175, 204. Margaret, the wife of Sir Richard Herbert, was given custody of her son. She afterwards married John Herle. Lord Herbert, in a codicil which he added to his will on 27 July, had given charge of his son, then nine years of age, to his brother Thomas Herbert, with a present of 'two gilt pots that came last from London, and his great courser'. Collins, *Peerage*, III. 113; Warkworth, 44; see also his will. John Herbert was one of his executors.

7. *CPR*, 175, 180, 181. *Hist. MSS Commission Report*, I. 407.

8. *CPR*, December to February 1469.

9. Dwnn married a daughter of Hastings. For the prominence of Dwnn in court functions see Record of 'Bluemantle Pursuivant', in *English Historical Literature of the Fifteenth Century*, Kingsford. Young Pembroke was knighted in 1466. In 1470 he was invested with a number of his father's offices. Ferrers was made sheriff of Carnarvon and master-forester of Snowdon in 1470. *CPR, passim.* Wethamstede, II. 103. Rymer, XI. 656. Lewis Glyn Cothi, I. viii.

10. Rebellion in Lincolnshire, *Camden Miscellany*, I. 10–12, No. 39.

11. Warkworth, 12. Polydore Vergil, 131–2.

12. The original letter is printed in *Arch. Cambrensis*, I. i. 146–7.

13. Rymer, XI. 680–1. *CPR*, 233, 236, 252.

14. Hall, 285–7. Polydore, 134–5. According to a petition of Sir Richard Corbet to Henry VII, Corbet brought Richmond to Hereford after the death of Lord Herbert at Banbury, and there handed him over to Jasper. But Jasper was out of England during the campaign. If it refers to 1471, the petition is very vague and loose. Owen and Blakeway, *Shrewsbury*, I. 248.

15. *Political Songs and Poems*, II. 280.

16. *Ode to Roger Kynaston*:

Llyma faes llawen fu ynn

. . . .

Ar ddyw Pasc arwydd paham
I dialedd Duw William.

'This was a happy victory. On Easter day

God avenged William.' The poem adds that Roger went to meet Edward on his return from abroad.

17. *CPR*, March–April. Rymer, XI. 681.

18. *Arrival of King Edward IV*, 22–7, Hall, 297. Croyland Continuator.

19. *Paston Letters*, III. 8–9.

20. Kynaston was made sheriff of Merionethshire for life in 1473, a former grant to him of that office having been annulled by a grant made in the same parliament to the Prince of Wales. He also became constable of Harlech. *Paston Letters*, III. 8–9. *CPR, passim.*

21. *Restoration of Edward IV*, 27. Polydore, 154–5. Hall, 302–3. As we have seen, he was commissioned to array South Wales for Edward on 25 April. See a poem on Roger Vaughan by Huw Cae Llwyd.

22. Rymer. *Proceedings of the Privy Council. CPR*, 1471. *Cardiff Records*, IV. 46. Jasper gave the bells to Llandaff Cathedral, and to numerous churches in Glamorgan: Cardiff, Cowbridge, Aberdare, Llantwit, St Fagans, Gelligaer, Llancarvan, etc.

23. Polydore, 155–6. Hall, 302–3.

24. *Restoration of Edward IV*. Warkworth seems to suggest that Henry of Richmond had come over from France with Jasper and Warwick. Stowe states that Jasper found him at Raglan. See also Polydore, 158–9, and note above.

25. *Paston Letters*, 28 September 1471, and 4 November 1472, III. 59. Issues, II Edward IV. Hall, 302–3. Polydore, 158–9.

26. *Rot. Parl.* 12–13 Edward IV, 46–76, and *passim. CPR*, June–August 1471.

27. He shared with the duke of Gloucester the offices of chief justice and chamberlain of South Wales. *CPR*, 275 etc.

28. In July 1471 John Devereux and John Herbert were ordered to find out what lands belonged to the late Richard Herbert in Herefordshire. They both, with Thomas Perot, John Wynne, Thomas Vaughan (son of Sir Roger Vaughan), and Thomas Morgan, were on various commissions of array in Wales and the borders in 1472.

29. Rymer, XI. 719.

30. 17 July 1471. The council was ordained on 8 July. *CPR*, 283.

31. Other members were Robert Stillington, bishop of Bath and Wells, the abbot of Westminster, Lord Dacres, Sir John Fogge,

Sir John Scotte, John Alcock, and Richard Forster. The appointment of Thomas Vaughan as chamberlain to the prince 'who is so young and tender of age that he cannot guide himself' is noted again in January 1474. In July of that year record is made of a house built by him at great cost within Westminster Abbey, for him and the prince. *CPR*, 414, 455. *Grants of Edward V, VIII.* For other ordinances see Halliwell, *Letters of the Kings of England*, I.

32. *Paston Letters*, III. 11.

33. *Rot. Parl.* VI. 159–60. *CPR*, 366. *Paston Letters*, III. 83. Their names were Miles ap Harry, Robert ap Rosser, John Vawr, Morgan Vaughan, Henry ap Roger, and about eighteen others, mostly yeomen and labourers.

34. Ramsay seems to associate the two. It will be recollected that the duke of Clarence, in spite of his previous desertion and subsequent reconciliation with Edward, quarrelled again with his brother, and was put to death.

35. *CPR*, 360, 388.

36. *Paston Letters*, III. 83, 2 April 1473.

37. *CPR*, February 1474. The rebels were William Herbert, John Herbert, and Thomas Herbert, two natural sons; and John and Roger, two sons of Roger Vaughan. *Paston Letters*, III. 107.
For the Welshmen who took part in Edward's expedition to France in 1475 see Rymer, 846.

38. Letter of Prince Edward to the Shrewsbury bailiffs from Ludlow, 8 June 1475. Owen and Blakeway's *Shrewsbury*, 252.

39. *CPR*, 574.

40. *Rot. Parl.* 203. *Lords Report*, Appendix, V. 417, 419. Ramsay, II. 431. See also *CPR*, 566.
In the ordinances for the prince's council in 1473 a more special charge was given to Rivers and John Alcock than in 1471. In November of that year Rivers was made the prince's governor and Alcock the president of the council. In January 1476, the prince was made justiciar of Wales; and in December he was given power to appoint justices in the Principality and the Marches. In 1478 the council drew up certain regulations for the better government of Shrewsbury. See the *Cymmrodor*, XII–XV. Welsh MSS, British Museum, Part I. 1900.

Chapter Ten

1. Croyland Continuator, 486; miles senilis aetatis.

2. Polydore, 174.

3. Rymer, XII. 180. *Grants of Edward V*, 7–10, 15 May. Ibid. 13.

4. *Grants of Edward V*, May. *Excerpta Historica*, 17. Richard Williams was constable of St Briavel in the Forest of Dean. In Pembroke the king relied upon Richard Newton, Richard Mynors, Hugh Huntley, and the Perot family.

5. Polydore, 182. A monument was erected to Vaughan in the chapel of St Paul's, Westminster Abbey.

6. *CPR*, 15 July. Hall, 382.

7. Polydore, 164–6; Hall, 322–3; Rymer, XII. 22–4.

8. *Letters*, etc., Richard III, I. 22–3. Polydore, 191.

9. *Letters*, etc., 39–43; 54.

10. Humphrey Bohun, earl of Hereford, left two daughters, Mary and Eleanor. Mary married Henry IV, and so her part of the inheritance had become vested in the Crown. Eleanor married Thomas of Woodstock, earl of Buckingham, and her portion had descended to Henry, the present duke of Buckingham.

11. Polydore, 195–8. Croyland, 491–2. For Hugh Conway see before. He was treasurer at Calais under Henry VII. He was previously keeper of the wardrobe, and in 1486 commissioner of mines. *Letters of Richard III*, etc. I. 231; Campbell, I. 26, 317. *Rot. Parl.* 250, 361. Reginald Bray was afterwards knighted. *Rot. Parl.* 342.

12. Polydore, 199. Croyland. *Rot. Parl.* VI. 245.

13. Croyland, 491–2. Ferrers does not seem to have participated.

14. Hall. Rymer, XII. 240. Owen and Blakeway's *Shrewsbury*, 236–7.

15. Document in Owen and Blakeway, 241.

16. *Grants of Edward V*, I. 18.

17. This Morgan was afterwards made constable of Hay. Welsh MSS, Brit. Museum.

18. Stafford MSS II. 24. The three brothers Vaughan were pardoned by Henry VII. Campbell, *Materials*, etc. I. 408.

19. Lewis Glyn Cothi, I. xv:
    Cryv oedd ar gadoedd, deunaw gwart gadarn,
       Gyda'r brenin Edwart;
       A chwedi ev o awch dart,
       I gadw rhos gyda Rhisiart.

The editor misinterprets the poem on account of his failure to distinguish between this Vaughan and the Thomas Vaughan executed at Pontefract.

20. *Glamorgan Charters*, V. 1713. Gower was part of the confiscated estates of Philip Mansel, which had been given to Sir Roger Vaughan. Polydore Vergil, as we have seen, suggests that Buckingham had been oppressive.

21. Welsh MSS, British Museum, 350 seq. *CPR*.

22. The following were also rewarded by Richard: John Huddleston, offices in Monmouthshire; Thomas ap Morgan, £40; Philip ap Rhys, parcel of Knighton; Morris ap Rhys, portreeve of Presteign; John Edwards, constable of Usk. Annuities varying from 40 marks to £100, receivable from the lordship of Usk were granted to Sir Thomas Bowles, John ap Jankyn, William Lewis, Morgan Gamage, William Herbert of Raglan, Robert ap Jankyn, Phillip ap Morgan, Philip Kemys of Shirehampton, Morgan Rhydderch, Edward ap Jankyn, John Morgan, Philip Kemys of Caerwent, and Morris Lewis. Annuities from Abergavenny to John Vaughan, John Thomas, Rice Llywelyn ap Morgan, and David Philip. Annuities from Monmouth to Hopkyn ap Howel, Philip Herbert, William Herbert esquire of the body, John Hewes, and William Serjeaunt. Others in South Wales were Walter Endreby of Kidwely, William Kemys of Newport, and Walter Wynston of Ewyas.
The following found favour in North Wales: Richard Vaughan received Aber in Carnarvonshire and Kemes in Anglesey, David Vaughan several offices in those two counties, Hugh Lloyd offices in Carnarvon and Merionethshire, William Hanmer the wardship of Robert Puleston, Thomas Tunstall constable of Conway, Sir Richard Huddleston constable of Beaumaris, Sir Roger Kynaston constable of Harlech and sheriff of Merionethshire with payment for sixty soldiers at Harlech, Thomas Salesbury constable of Denbigh with twelve soldiers, Lord Powys an annuity of £100, Sir William Stanley chamberlain of Cheshire and constable of Carnarvon, William Griffith an annuity. William Griffith was one of the ushers of the chamber. Edward IV had given him the fee farm of Monmouth. Ievan ap Tudor ap Owen received protection.

Welsh MSS, British Museum. Cf. Gairdner, *Richard III*, Appendix, 342. *Rot. Parl.* 22 Edward IV, 203, for grant to Herbert.

23. *Richard III*, 133. Gairdner quotes the introductory sketch to the Works of Lewis Glyn Cothi. But the editor, as has been pointed out, relied on the *Cambrian Register*.

24. Polydore, 201–3. Croyland, 495.

25. Rymer, XII. 226.

26. Polydore, 206–8. Richard had endeavoured to get the mediation of Austria between him and Britanny with regard to Henry. *Letters of Richard III*, II. 4.

27. Croyland, 501; Stow, 467; Polydore, 214.

28. *Paston Letters*, III. 316. Ellis, *Letters*, I. 162.

29. Polydore, 213–14.

30. For this he was paid £100 and 20 marks. Richard Owen was receiver of Kidwely. Richard Williams was to hold Manorbier and Penally by knight's service. Another recipient of favours was Howel ap John of Llanllwch in Carmarthenshire. A Hugh ap John was denizened. Richard also gave grants for the rebuilding of churches at Llandovery and Hirwaun in Carmarthenshire. Welsh MSS, British Museum.

31. Welsh MSS, British Museum. Roger Bikley was constable of Llandovery.

32. Gairdner takes this view on the authority of Polydore.

33. The following were Richard's grants in Wales this year: Walter Vaughan, steward of Elvel; William Vaughan, a brother of the Thomas Vaughan who had opposed Buckingham, an annuity; so also did Walter, the son of that Thomas ap Roger who was slain at Banbury, and Richard Vaughan; John ap Morgan of Usk; Robert ap Howel, constable of Skenfrith; David Goch of Radnor; Richard and Roger Baker of Brecknock; Sir Richard Croft was told to repair Radnor and Elvel Castles; Nicholas Spicer, receiver of South Wales, was to give the burgesses of Brecon £60 towards repairing their town walls; David Vaughan received denizenship and the ferm of Caerwys and Conway ferry. Welsh MSS, British Museum. Pat. Rolls.

34. Polydore, 215.

35. Campbell's *Materials*, etc. I. 108; II. 443. *Rot. Parl.* VI. 379.

36. Polydore, 215–16. Croyland.

37. Campbell, I. 94, 584. *Rot. Parl.* 336–84.

38. *CPR*, 561.

39. Dwnn. II. 218; 'yn ddysgedig ac yn raddol ynghyfraith Lloegr.' There is no John Morgan of Kidwely among those who received favours from Henry VII. Gairdner's *Richard III*, following Polydore, gives the Christian name of Morgan of Kidwely as 'John'. Ramsay confuses Morgan Kidwely the attorney general with (Trahaiarn) Morgan of Kidwely, the Welsh lawyer.

40. Campbell. I. 77–91, 230, 555, 597. October–December 1485. *Cardiff Records. Letters of Richard III*, etc. II. 90. Henry Morgan, Sir David Owen, and Hugh Vaughan held household appointments.

41. In May 1480 he was on a commission to investigate the concealing from the king of lands belonging to the manor of Dorset. In July he was on another commission to find out what lands belonged to Henry, duke of Somerset, in Herts and to the earl of Wiltshire in Dorset. He was on commissions of array in Wilts and Dorset in 1484. He helped Richard against Buckingham, and was rewarded with a grant of certain manors in those two counties. In February 1485 he was on a commission in Yorkshire. He was attorney general after the accession of Henry. There were others of the family: Geoffrey Kidwely was comptroller of the port of Southampton. Maurice Kidwely was another. *Grants of Edward V*, 30–1; xxxi. *CPR, passim.*

42. Comines Dupont, II. 246. Molinet, II. 406.

43. Polydore, 216. Hall, 409–10. Bernard André, *Memorials of Henry VII*, 24–5. Croyland, 500–1. See also a letter of Richard to Henry Vernon on 11 August 1485; *Hist. MSS Commission Reports*, MSS of the duke of Rutland, I. 7, 'departyd out of the waters of the Seine the first day of this present month and landed at Nangle beside Milford Haven on Sunday last passed, entending our destruction'. Sunday would be 7 August. Soon after the landing Sir David Owen was knighted.

44. It is significant, too, that in the list of those who were rewarded by Henry VII there appears to be only one Pembrokeshire man. The Arnold Butler of the text was of Dunraven in Glamorgan.

45. *Rot. Parl.*

46. One of the inaccuracies of his 'Life' in the *Cambrian Register* is to make him at this period constable of Carmarthen Castle. That office was held by Sir John Dwnn who was also sheriff of the two counties. We hear nothing of Dwnn during these great events. He was probably away, as he was an officer at Calais and deputy of Risbank. He retained his positions under Henry VII. *Rot. Parl.* 341. *Letters of Richard III*, etc. I. 15.

47. Polydore, 216 seq. *CPR*. 'Ballad of the Lady Bessy.' When Lord Strange unsuccessfully tried to escape from court he confessed that his father was implicated and threw himself on the king's mercy.

48. Wynne's *History of the Gwydir Family*, 55–6.

49. It will be observed that the date and place are left blank. I do not find John ap Meredith's name among those who were rewarded by Henry, which is curious if he assisted him.

50. Hall, 410. Bernard André, 9. Croyland, 501.

51. Y mae hiraeth am Harri,
    Y mae gobaith i'n hiaith ni.
    'We look forward to the coming of Henry; our nation puts its trust in him.' Robin Ddu, in *Ceinion Llenyddiaith*, 221. See also the unpublished poems of Bedo Brwynllys (Cardiff MSS), and other contemporary poets.

52. The chief of these were Rhys ap Philip, who became rhaglaw of the county; Owen Lloyd, who was made constable of Cardigan, where he was followed by Rhydderch ap Rhys next year; David Glyn; Phillip ap Rhys ap Thomas Vaughan of Mabwynion, who became steward of that district and bailiff of Isaeron. *Rot. Parl.* VI. 363. *CPR, passim.*

53. The following came from North Wales: Edward ap Ednyfed, who received the woodwardship of Merioneth; Howel ap Griffith ap Howel who received the fee-farm of Penmaenllwyd; Richard Pole, who became sheriff of that county; Rheinallt Davy, who got an annuity of 100s from Pennal; Robert Gethin of Snowdon; Edward Margan of Aberffraw; William Eynon; William Griffith ap Robin, and Rhys ap Llywelyn, who became sheriff of Carnarvon and Anglesey respectively, and both of whom received denizenship early in 1486. Also Piers Stanley and Piers Egerton. Campbell, 295, etc., *Rot. Parl.* 353, seq.; Rymer XII. 89; *CPR, passim.*

54. Polydore, 217.

55. 'Ballad of the Lady Bessy.'

56. The Carmarthenshire grants are as follows: John ap Thomas, who became steward of the Welsh courts of Carmarthenshire and

Cardiganshire; Morris Lloyd of Wydegada, for service in our late triumph; Owen ap Griffith, who was made steward and constable of Laugharne; Geoffrey Rede, receiver of Kidwely with an annuity of £20, and with Rhys ap Thomas and Morris ap Owen supervisor in the duchy of Lancaster; Adam ap Evan ap Jankyn, attorney in the two counties; his brother David, rhingyll of Kidwely and Carnwallon, escheator in South Wales, and the amobrship of Iscennin; Richard Owen, receiver of Kidwely; Morris ap Owen, a similar office in Carnwallon and Iscennin, for his services; Hugh Vaughan forester in Kidwely lordship; John Aubrey, rhaglaw in Carmarthenshire for his services at Bosworth; Walter ap Lewis, bailiff and attorney in Kidwely and the district; Philip ap Howel and his wife an annuity of £20 'for true service done unto us'. *Rot. Parl.* VI. 350. *CPR. passim*; September–December 1485. Campbell, *passim*.

57. *Early English Poetry*, XX (1847).
58. *Child's Popular Ballads*, III. 331–3. The Lady Bessy also tells Lord Stanley:

> Your brother dwelleth in Holt castle
>
> . . . .
>
> All the Welshmen love him well;
> He may make a great company.

59. Campbell, I. 105–9, II. 91. He was also a commissioner of mines.
60. Evan Lloyd Vaughan, constable of Neath and Aberavon, for service etc. Hugh ap Howel, £20 out of the fee-farm of Monmouth for service at Bosworth 'where it happened him to be sore hurt and maimed'; John ap Howel, steward and receiver of Monmouth; Walter ap David ap John, coroner of Gower; William Llywelyn of Newport and Thomas ap Morgan; Hugh Richard of Cantrecelly; Nicolas Williams of Monmouth; Mathew Cradock, constable of Caerphilly; William Herbert, receiver of Monmouth, Whitecastle, Skenfrith; others in Glamorgan and Abergavenny. The affairs of the earldom of March were to be managed by nine commissioners including Jasper, Morgan John Philip, and Thomas Morgan of Gloucester. *CPR, passim*. Campbell, 253, 298. Jasper became lord of Glamorgan.

61. We have already shown that Richard had no real grounds for this reliance on Rhys ap Thomas at least.
62. Polydore. Hall. Croyland.
63. Polydore, 222.
64. Bernard André, 29. Polydore, 222–6.
65. The following Welshmen found favour with Henry in the first year of his reign in addition to those already mentioned: Morris ap David ap Griffith of Knighton; David ap Madoc Gough of Ceri and Cedewain; William Lloyd, constable of Denbigh; John Thomas, constable of Hay; Hugh Lloyd, escheator of Denbigh; John ap Evan ap Llywelyn of Radnor; Thomas Havard of Caerleon; Hugh Lewis of Denbigh; David Middleton, escheator of Denbigh; John ap Meredith ap Ieuan Lloyd of Denbigh; David Lloyd, one of the keepers of the Tower of London; David Owen, chief carver of the king. *Rot. Parl.* 344–66. Campbell, 208–30. Robert ap Gwilym ap Thomas of Hereford, Walter ap Gwilym of Archenfield, and the Vaughans who opposed Buckingham, were pardoned.

List of Sources

Acts and Proceedings of the Privy Council. H. Nicolas. (Record Commission, 1834)

Ancient and Modern Denbigh. John Williams. Denbigh, 1856

André, Bernard. *Vita Regis Henrici Septimi,* Memorials of Henry VII. J. Gairdner. (Rolls Series, No. 10)

Antiquary. Vol. xvi. etc

Archaeologia. Vol. xxix. etc

Archaeologia Cambrensis

Basin, *Thomas. Histoire de Charles VII et Louis XI.* J. Quicherat. (Société de l'Histoire de Paris, 1855)

Beaucourt, G. du Fresne de. *Histoire de Charles VII.* (Paris, 1885)

Bekyngton, T. *Letters of.* G. Williams. (Rolls Series, No. 56)

Berry, *see* Blondel

Blakman, J. *Liber de vita et miraculis Henrici VI.* Printed by Hearne (1734)

Blondel, R. *De Reductione Normanniae.* J. Stevenson. (Rolls Series, No. 32)

Brief Latin Chronicle, see Three Fifteenth Century Chronicles

Calendars of Gwynedd. Breece

Cambrian Register, 1795. Life of Sir Rhys ap Thomas

Campbell, *Materials for the History of the Reign of Henry VII.* 2 vols (Rolls Series)

Capgrave, John. *De Illustribus Henricis.* (Rolls Series, No. 7)

Cardiff Records

Ceinion Llenyddiaith Gymreig

Chartier, Jean. *Chronique de Charles VII.* (Edit. Vallet de Viriville, 1858)

Chronicle, Davies. English Chronicle, printed for the Camden Society, by Sylvester Davies. No. 64

Chronicle, Giles. A Chronicle (Henry IV–Henry VI) printed by Dr Giles from MSS. Sloane 1776, and Reg. 13. C. 1.

Chronicle, London. English Chronicle of London, printed by Sir H. Nicolas, 1827

Chronicle of the Rebellion in Lincolnshire. J.G. Nichols. (Camden Miscellany, vol. 1). An official account by someone in the royal service

Chronicles of the White Rose of York. (Bohn, 1845). A collection of documents relating to the reign of Edward IV

Clark. *Carta et Munimenta Glamorganiae. Glamorgan Charters*

Claus Rerum. Record Office, Fetter Lane

Collections, Historical and Archaeological, relating to Montgomeryshire. Powys-Land Club

Comines, Philippe de, *Mémoires de*; edit. Dupont. (Paris, 1840. Société de l'Histoire de France)

Croyland Abbey; Ingulph's Chronicle of, with Continuations; edit. Riley. (Bohn, 1854)

Cymmrodor. Cymmrodorion Society

Davydd Llwyd, *Poems by.* Cardiff MSS

Deputy Keeper of the Public Records, *Reports of*

Devon Issues. Issues of the Exchequer, Henry III–Henry VI, from the Pell Records, by F. Devon. (Record Commission, 1837)

Doyle, J.E. *The Official Baronage of England,* 1886. 3 vols

Dugdale, Sir William. *The Baronage of England.* 2 vols (1675)

Dwnn's *Heraldic Visitations of Wales.* 2 vols. Welsh MSS Society. 1846

Ellis, Sir Henry. *Original Letters Illustrative of English History.* (Three Series, 1825–46)

Escouchy, Mathieu D'; *Chronique de.* (Société de l'Histoire de Paris)

Excerpta Historica. Sir H. Nicolas. (London, 1831)

Fabyan, Robert. *The New Chronicle of England.* H. Ellis. (1811)

Foedera, Conventiones et Litterae. T. Rymer. (London, 1709)

Fortescue, Sir John. *The Governance of England.* Edit. Plummer. (Oxford, Clarendon Press, 1885)

Gairdner, James. *Life and Reign of Richard III.* (London, 1879)

Gorchestion Beirdd Cymru. Edit. Rhys Jones. Shrewsbury, 1773

—— Edit. Cynddelw (revised). Carnarvon

Grafton, Richard. *Chronicle of England.* (London, 1809)

Grants etc. of Edward V. J.G. Nichols. (Camden Society, No. 60)

Gregory, William. *Historical Collections of a London Citizen*; 1189–1469. J. Gairdner. (Camden Society, New Series, No. 18)

Guto'r Glyn, *Poems of.* Hafod MSS. Cardiff Library

Hall, E. *Chronicle containing the History of England from Henry IV to Henry VIII.* H. Ellis. (London, 1809)

Hardyng, John. Metrical *Chronicle*, with continuation of R. Grafton. H. Ellis. (1812)

Historical Literature of the Fifteenth Century. Kingsford

Historical MSS Commission Reports

Historie of the Arrivall of King Edward IV. J. Bruce. (Camden Society, 1838)

Holinshed, Raphael. *Chronicles of England*, etc. H. Ellis. (London, 1807)

Howel Swrdwal. *Gwaith Barddonol.* Bangor Welsh MSS Society. J.C. Morrice, 1908

Huw Cae Llwyd. *Poems of.* Cardiff MSS

Ieuan Deulwyn, *Casgliad o Waith.* Bangor Welsh MSS Society. Ifor Williams, 1909

Inquisitiones post mortem, Calendar of

Iolo MSS

Issues. Issue Rolls; Pell Issue Rolls. MSS. Record Office, Fetter Lane

Letters and Papers Illustrative of the Reigns of Richard III and Henry VII. 2 vols. James Gairdner. (Rolls Series, No. 24)

Letters of Margaret of Anjou. C. Munro. (Camden Society, No. 80)

Lewis Glyn Cothi. *Poetical Works of.* 2 vols. (Oxford, 1837) Cymmrodorion Society Publications

Liber Niger Scaccarii. T. Hearne. (Oxford, 1728)

Life of Sir Rhys ap Thomas. See *Cambrian Register*

Lords' Reports. Reports of the Lords' Committee on Matters appertaining to the Dignity of a Peer. (1829)

Mediaeval Boroughs of Snowdonia. Lewis. University of Wales Guild of Graduates

Ministers' Accounts

Monstrelet, Enguerrand de. *Chroniques.* Buchon. (Panthéon Littéraire, 1836)

More, Sir Thomas. *Life of Richard III.* Lumby. (Pitt Press) *Opera Omnia.* (London, 1689)

Mostyn MSS. History of Wales by Ellis Griffith

Paston Letters. J. Gairdner. 3 vols. 1872

Patent Rolls, Calendar of. Prepared by the Deputy Keeper of the Records

Pecock, Reginald. *Life of*, by John Lewis. (Oxford, Clarendon Press, 1820)

Plumpton Correspondence. T. Stapleton. (Camden Society, No. 4)

Political Songs and Poems. T. Wright. (Rolls Series, No. 14)

Polydore Vergil. (Camden Society, No. 29)

Popular Ballads, Child

Privy Seals. MSS, Record Office. Fetter Lane

Queen's Remembrancer's Miscellanea, etc. MSS, Record Office, Fetter Lane

Receipt Rolls. MSS, Record Office, Fetter Lane

Record of Carnarvon

Records of Denbigh and its Lordship. Williams. Wrexham, 1860

Repressor of Over Moche Wijtyng the Clergie. C. Babington. (Rolls Series, No. 19)

Rotuli Parliamentorum. (Record Commission)

Royal Historical Society's Transactions. 1911

Rutland Papers. (Camden Society, No. 21)

Rymer. *Collections.* etc

Stafford MSS. See Historical MSS Commission Reports

Statutes of the Realm. (Record Commission, 1810)

Stevenson, J. *Letters and Papers Illustrative of the Wars of the English in France.* (Rolls Series, No. 22)

Stow, John. *Annales or Generall Chronicle of England, with Continuation by Howes.* (London, 1615)

Three Fifteenth Century Chronicles. J. Gairdner. (Camden Society, 1880)

Transactions of the Cymmrodorion Society

Trevelyan Papers. (Camden Society)

Tudur Penllyn. Cardiff MSS

Warkworth, J. Halliwell. (Camden Society, 1839)

Wavrin, Jehan de. *Recueil des Chroniques*, etc. (Rolls Series)

Welsh MSS. British Museum. Edward Owen. Cymmrodorion Series

West Wales Historical Society's Transactions

Whethamstede, Johannes. *Registrum*, etc. Riley. (Rolls Series, No. 28)

Worcester, William of. *Annales Rerum Anglicarum.* Printed by Stevenson. (Rolls Series)

—— *Itinerarium.* 1777. Printed by Simeon

Wynne. *History of the Gwydir Family.* Oswestry. 1878

Index